Rape, Incest, Murder! The Marquis de Sade on Stage

Volume Two
Later Prison Plays

John Franceschina

Rape, Incest, Murder! The Marquis de Sade on Stage
Volume Two
Later Prison Plays

Published in the USA by:
BearManor Media
P O Box 71426
Albany, Georgia 31708
www.bearmanormedia.com

ISBN: 978-1-59393-735-5
Printed in the United States of America
Book design by Robbie Adkins

Contents

Love Makes the Misanthrope

Introduction

While the title page of the manuscript indicates that *Love Makes the Misanthrope* was accepted unanimously by the Comédie-Française on 16 September 1790, Sade's biographers agree that the comedy must have been written at least a decade before. Lély argues that the play was one of eight written between 1780 and 1788 while Sade was in prison. Narrowing the date down even further, Maurice Heine has demonstrated in *Le Minotaure* 1 (February 1933) that the first draft of the play was completed by 12 July 1782 while the Marquis de Sade was an inmate of Vincennes Prison. In his biography, *Donatien Alphone Francois, Marquis de Sade*, Maurice Lever cites yet another reference to the play in a letter from Madame de Sade, date 6 July 1782 which refers pejoratively to *Love Makes the Misanthrope, or Sophie and Desfrancs* as the play his old tutor, Abbé Amblet, did not like at all:

> After reading it, he did not want to put his opinion down on paper, because he said frankly that there was nothing good to say. If you enjoy this work, then you can carry on with it for enjoyment, but as for appearing in public, he said that cannot be. You wanted him to give an honest opinion, and that's honestly what he told me.

Clearly then, this play belongs to the same period that produced Sade's other play about incestuous love, *Henrietta and St. Clair*, the comedies, *The Twins, or Difficult Choices* and *The Freak, or The Man Who Can't Make Up His Mind*. Lély adds that the *Dialogue between a Priest and a Dying Man* was likewise completed on 12 July 1782, and Lever suggests that the first sketches for the *120 Days of Sodom* were produced at the same time. Sade's early years at Vincennes were certainly prolific. Maurice Lever notes that Sade was treated better at Vincennes than he was perhaps willing to admit. His wife saw to it that his regular tailor continued to make him his clothes and that his demands for material items were always fulfilled. Among these were candles, sponges, head bands, cologne, a "calico cap," a cushion to enable him to sit without aggravating his hemorrhoids, a thirty-minute sand timer, paper and quills. While critics such as Annetta Foster tend to emphasize the dark side of Sade's incarceration, it is clear that he was not without his creature comforts.

While it may be difficult today to understand the abbé's violent reaction against the play, an examination of Sade's notes for an earlier draft might shed some light on the controversy, since Lély considers the draft much more provocative and filled with Sade's "natural genius" than the finished product.

Entitled *Zelonide*, (Maurice Heine reports that Sade added the note: "This comedy is played under the title of *Sophie and Desfrancs*"), the early draft involved the illicit love affairs between Isabelle de St. Elme and a young man named Sérigny; and Julie Nelmours and her lover, Melville. Because they are under the age of consent, both pairs of lovers set out for Spain to escape their parents' persecution. Before they can reach their destination, each of the women gives birth to a child: Isabelle has a daughter named Zelonide, and Julie, a son named Candeuil. No sooner have the babies been born than Isabelle's father abducts her and returns her to Paris. Melville, who kills Isabelle's cousin during the abduction, flees to avoid a charge of murder after leaving a note telling Sérigny, who was conveniently off on business during the abduction, all that had happened.

On his return, Sérigny witnesses the death of Melville's wife, Julie, and decides to switch the children, thinking he would have a better chance at recapturing his Isabelle's affection by presenting her with a male child. Here, Sade is emphatic about Isabelle's never having seen the sex of her child (her father evidently arrived simultaneously with the child's birth). To put his plan into action, Sérigny bribes the midwife who was present at the birth and writes to Melville saying that his wife, now dead, gave birth to a girl.

Back in Paris, Sérigny finds Isabelle, who has finally reached legal age, still very much in love with him, and they agree to get married. But because of her parents' conservative attitude, they decide to keep the marriage a secret and to keep the child in the dark regarding his true parentage (which, in fact is not his true parentage, but Isabelle is unaware of this). To this end, the trio of husband, wife, and son travel to the Poitou district where husband and wife live as neighbors and the son as Isabelle's ward. Sérigny suddenly dies and Isabelle is forced to raise her "ward" alone. Candeuil begins to develop a strong romantic attachment for his guardian. This puts Isabelle in a bind: she can't reveal her marriage to Sérigny or her assumed relationship to the boy without risking her reputation, not to mention her fortune.

Sade is emphatic about the logical possibility of such a romantic attraction. He argues that the boy must be 16 or 17 years of age and Madame Sérigny 30 or 31, and he sees no reason why such a disparity between ages should cause a problem. (The chronology Sade provides is especially interesting: Isabelle would have been 14 at the time of her giving birth. She was 25 when she was reunited with Sérigny and the eleven-year-old child she had never seen. Five more years passed before Sérigny's death.)

Prior to his death, Sérigny had invited Melville to join his family at Poitou. Because of his wife's demise, and fearing the reaction of her living relatives, Melville had likewise raised his "daughter" as his ward. When Melville arrives at Poitou, he is 32 and Zelonide is 15.

Having dispensed with background information, Sade proceeds to introduce the characters who actively participate in the action of the play:

Madame Sérigny: a young widow, 31 years old, who believes that she is the mother of Candeuil but is not;

Candeuil: a young man of 17, in love with Madame Sérigny, who has no reason to think she is his mother, and who only considers her his guardian;

Mr. Melville: Madame Sérigny's friend, around 33 years old, who believes he is Zelonide's father, but is not;

Zelonide: a young woman of 16, madly in love with Mr. Melville, whom she in no way views as a father, but considers him her guardian;

Despontis: the husband of the nurse in Bayonne whom Sérigny had bribed to switch the babies; he was Sérigny's valet and remained in the household as steward for the estate. He is the only character who knows the secret; he should be naturally attached to Zelonide since he knows she is his mistress's daughter;

Madame Hébert: Zelonide's confidante, to whom she had been given by Melville. She is Zelonide's friend, and honestly believes her to be Melville's ward.

Having provided the necessary on-stage relationships, Sade allows the dark imagination characteristic of his prison creations to thicken the plot until Despontis reveals the secret and everyone pairs off and gets married.

What the abbé found so objectionable is a matter of conjecture. Perhaps he found the double incest plot too immoral, or too unbelievable, or both. What is certain, however, is that the Marquis de Sade did rework the plot using basically the same characters, and adding a highly innovative pantomime device to link the acts together. While it was not unusual for opéra-ballets to include interludes of song and dance between the acts, Sade's pantomimes were highly unusual and original additions to French verse comedy. To emphasize this point, in her dissertation, "The Place of Theatre and Drama in the Life of the Marquis de Sade, *Homme de Lettres Extraordinaire*," Annetta Foster cites Quinault and Lully's opera *Psyche* as an example and goes on to describe the link with classical theatre achieved by means of Sade's pantomimes.

It is difficult to understand why the play, though accepted by the Comédie Française, was never produced. Having heard nothing from the theatre three months after the parts had been copied, Sade began to voice his undisguised dissatisfaction. He received the following undated and unsigned reply:

> This work was accepted by the previous Comédie-Française only to provide its author with free access to the theatre and in the hopes that he would substitute another play. The administration of the Théâtre-Français cannot permit the production of any doubtful work.

While Foster suggests that everything in the 1790s in France was doubtful, "so such a veto in such tumultuous times seems reasonable," Maurice Lever offers a more telling explanation from recently discovered documents from the Sade family archives.

An active member of the Society for Authors, Sade found himself the subject of controversy over the issue of daily compensation to be paid performers at the Comédie-Française. When the minutes of the meeting on 28 June 1791 (when a vote was taken on the matter) were published, Sade appeared to have supported the lesser salary. The actors were furious and Sade began to fear that his works would be boycotted at the theatre. He looked to Sedaine, the pillar of society for support but only received the following response in an unpublished letter dated 20 September 1791:

> I assure you, sir, that I don't have the slightest recollection whether you voted to give eight hundred or seven hundred livres to a company that wants neither agreement. It is true that I've always attached so little importance to the matter, and that's part of the reason for my distraction regarding these differences of opinion. It's not that I don't believe that any author who needs the talents of actors shouldn't be terribly afraid of making them angry. Mr. Beaumarchais signed all of these papers, and I know nothing more about it.

Sade replied with an official denial in the *Petites-Affiches* on Saturday, 24 September 1791:

> To the Editor: 20 September 1791. I beg you, sir, to insert in your newspaper, the formal disavowal of my signature at the bottom of a document entitled Report to Dramatic Authors on the Salary Proposed by the Comédie-Française. It is true that I was present at the meeting of dramatic authors when this subject was discussed, but it is absolutely untrue that I placed my name with those authors who voted to give the actors of the Comédie-Française only seven hundred livres a day. I certify that I signed only the article under discussion that, for special considerations, awarded eight hundred livres a day to the Comédie. Having verified my signature on the document, and having seen it among the names of those who voted for eight hundred livres, I can't imagine by what error it found itself among those of the opposite opinion. I couldn't give too much publicity to the disavowal of a way of thinking that I've never had, and that would make my public opinion contradict my private feelings for a spectacle which I will not cease to support and defend.

From all of this, Lever concludes that the actors, not believing a word of Sade's denials, decided to teach him a lesson and boycotted his *Love Makes the Misanthrope*. Sade still had the five years' free admission to the theatre which had been granted him when the play was accepted in 1790. Instead of seeing his own innovative work produced, he would have to satisfy himself by hissing the dramas of his rivals.

Love Makes the Misanthrope

With dramatic interludes

Unanimously accepted by the Comédie-Française 16 September 1790 and having provided the author with free access for five years.

> So, love, what do you want and what do you intend to do?
> ....
> What does your imperfect whisper say to his heart ...
> Tell it nothing at all or tell it everything.
> *Heraclius*, Act II, scene 4.[1]

---

[1] Sade paraphrases a speech from Pierre Corneille's 1647 tragedy *Heraclius*, misidentifying the actual source. The actual quotation, found in Act IV, scene 4, of Corneille's play reads: So, nature, what do you want and what do you intend to do? / If I no longer had a son, could I still be a father? / What does your imperfect whisper say to my heart? / Tell me nothing at all, or tell me everything.

Foreword

Here is a dramatic work in which the attempt has been made to complete the action to such a degree that the spectator cannot ignore for a moment any movement of the various characters presented to him during the two hours he watches them in performance.

Not only will he know them onstage, but he will be able to discern everything they do regarding the action of the play during the moments of silence in the dialogue; so that by linking the acts with the pantomimes that follow them, the spectator will have the clearest possible enhancement to the action.

It is believed that such an intimate connection will result in a unity, if not perfect, at least of such a completeness that the mind of the spectator will find nothing more to be desired. Here, no distraction can cool the interest in the drama; everything connects. It all ties up, everything rushes to achieve the goal without interruption. It seems that pleasure should be gained in that way. Certainly Aristotle intended these intimate connections when he complained bitterly about the bad example Agathon had introduced in tragedy by cooling down the action with choruses that were foreign to it. "The chorus must be part of the whole," he says. What difference is there in assigning words that are foreign to a play or inserting in that play pieces of another work.[2] Who doubts that it was not the intention of Horace as well when he wrote:

> Actoris partis chorus officiumque virile defendat, neu quid medios intercinat actus
> quod non proposito conducat et haereat apte. (*Poetics*, 193, 544.)[3]

The most perfect unity of action has then been recommended at all times by the great men who wrote about dramatic art, and the desire to adhere to their advice is the motive for the framework of this play.

---

[2] At this point in the manuscript, Sade added the note: "Aristotle's *Poetics*, chapter 17."

[3] "Let the chorus sustain the role of an actor and the function of a man, and let it not sing anything between the acts that does not purposefully and aptly serve and unite with the action." Again Sade mislabels the source: the quotation is derived from lines 193-195 of Horace's *Ars Poetica* (*The Art of Poetry*.)

"Now that choruses are abolished," says Mr. le Batteux[4] in his learned remarks on Aristotle, "there is such a large void to fill that the strict unity of the poem must necessarily suffer."

Doesn't filling these voids with pantomimes that stem from the action and continue it offer a solution to this disadvantage? Besides, it is only through trials that the arts enrich themselves. What would our tragedy be today if no one had dared to add anything to the dialogue of Thespis?[5] And our comedy if we were still performing Atellan farces?[6] If this audacity is displeasing, one should be aware that it is easier quite simply to put the action of this play back into a room in Desfrancs's house. Nothing absolutely requires it to leave; and if the opposite undertaking is blameworthy, at least the reason would not be since it comes from a desire to increase the public's enjoyment by giving it a spectacle with as much unity, passion, interest, and splendor as it can take, without violating the rule of verisimilitude, the most important of all the rules in our art.

What I have set out to do here has necessitated two things which are good for the reader and actor to know: first, the most precise indications of entrances and exits, from which one must not depart for any reason. They will be found carefully established at the beginning and ending of every scene. Second, the acts must only begin when the characters in the pantomime are out of sight.

The orchestra conductors must pay the greatest attention not to be misled by the actions of the pantomime actors and take them for characters entering onstage who ought to interrupt their music. Following the usual practice, they must stop the music only when the speaking character happens to appear, but not when it is simply the actor in the pantomime.

There is something deadly in plays of this kind; the more romantic its plot, the more the impatient mind of the spectator tries to anticipate the poet's work. From the first act, he's trying to think of every possible way to the resolution; and since the brief length of a comedy does not allow the catastrophe to be veiled as densely

---

[4] Charles Batteux (1713-1780), arguably the founder of aesthetics in France, commented on early poetics in his *Les quatres poétiques d'Aristot, d'Horace, de Vida, et de Boileau.*

[5] According to Aristotle, the first person to appear as actor on the Greek stage impersonating a character rather than appearing as himself.

[6] Vulgar comedies named after the town in Campania where they were created. Very popular in ancient Rome, the farces employed stock characters that were the antecedents of the commedia dell'arte.

as it might be in a novel, and since one is almost always forced to lift a slight corner of those gauzes, the spectator attentively seizes the opening and cries out *that he's guessed it immediately*, that one hasn't used enough skill to hide the *peripeteia* from him. While the opening itself is only one of the art's most polished efforts, a little more patience perhaps, a little less arrogance (for it is incredible what branches one finds on this main trunk of human vices) would increase the public's enjoyment. But in the theatre like everywhere else, the public wants to have it without paying for it.

If the disproportion in age necessarily established between the two lovers in this play is found to be a little excessive, to get over the unfavorable feeling that this hasty thought could cause, one is asked to recall the tears one has shed over the loves of Heloise and Abelard, the difference in whose ages was greater than twenty-two years, the lover being over forty when his mistress had hardly reached the age of eighteen. The difference here is seventeen to thirty-six, and certainly only natural, unless one adopts the life-style of that indefatigable author (Restif de la Bretonne)[7] who, for thirty years, every month, ruthlessly caused the groaning of a press whose fruits passed with the same speed into the anterooms and grocery stores; a lifestyle undoubtedly consoling for humanity since he tends to demonstrate in Welsh, often even in low Breton, that at forty, both sexes must give up the joys of love forever. Some mono-graph, some anagraph, some mimeograph will have undoubtedly informed the public of how wrong we are for not adopting that way of thinking, and we refer them to the reader certainly already scandalized to see us pressing so long on nonsense of this nature.

Since there are a lot of people in the world for whom a similar-ity of names immediately determines an idea, it is to those I am speaking to warn them that the name of Desfrancs, used in *Famous Frenchwomen*, and in a short one-act drama entitled *Sylvie*, based on that novel, is used here only because it was more suitable than any other.[8] But there is no sort of connection between the novel, the drama based on the novel and this comedy, the subject of which absolutely comes only from the author's imagination.

---

[7] Nicolas-Edme Restif (23 October 1734 – 3 February 1806), a prolific author who maintained a mutual hate relationship with the Marquis de Sade.

[8] The drama, *Silvie*, was written by Paul Landois; the novel, *Histoire de M. Des Francs et de Silvie*, was written by Robert Challe.

A word about the police scene: the duty of the dramatic poet is to correct vices by unmasking them and to cause abuses to be despised by revealing them. These axioms have been met. Therefore, it is necessary to show, speak, and prove to arrive at either of these objectives. What is depicted in this scene used to happen every day. It is, nevertheless, entirely certain that the government did not know about it, and morally reliable that it would not have tolerated it, if it had known about it. However, is it not necessary to reveal abuses of this order and the scandalous, indecent, and inhuman way they were carried out? That they no longer exist, well and good, but such abuses did exist, and it is good for those who use to claim that we did not have any restraints to know about the horrible weight that had to be borne by those who indulged in the abuse of power.

Now will someone want to quibble about the title? We're not frightened a bit. Desfrancs isn't as misanthropic as Alceste,[9] but the painful situation in which Desfrancs finds himself, the extreme violence of a love ever excessive and constantly repressed, the painful state of a man always crushed between nature and his duties—the combination of all these things, you will agree, should have cast upon his character some hints of an estrangement from humanity strong enough to cause him to be called misanthropic. In the same way, there is undoubtedly no comparison between Alceste's faults and those of Desfrancs. The first is misanthropic by nature, the other is that way because of his situation, but let us venture to say that both of them are misanthropic constantly. Each licentious character presented formerly on stage can, without fear of reproach or criticism, be repainted either under the faces given it by a different set of circumstances, or according to the different flashes of inspiration, having escaped the first artist, that the second artist is allowed to repaint and recapture.

---

[9] Alceste is the protagonist of *The Misanthrope* by Molière, produced 4 June 1666 at the Théâtre du Palais-Royal.

Love Makes the Misanthrope

Free verse comedy

in

Five Acts

CHARACTERS

Desfrancs, *a landowner*
Sophie, *a young lady raised by Desfrancs*
Anselm, *neighbor and friend of Desfrancs*
Madame Armance, *Sophie's governess and her former wet-nurse;
36-40 years old*
Germon, *Desfrancs's old valet, enamoured of Madame Armance*
William, *the village magistrate and managing agent*
Julie, *young peasant girl affianced to Alan and Sophie's best friend*
Alan, *William's son*
A Policeman
Bailiff's men
A crowd of Basque peasants

*The action occurs in the vicinity of Desfrancs's home, located at the
entrance to a forest at the foot of the Pyrenees Mountains between Pau
and Bayonne.*[10]

---

[10] Pau is a winter resort and the capital of Basses-Pyrenees, in southwest France. Bayonne is a
seaport in southwest France close to the Bay of Biscay.

The Nature of the Roles and Costumes

Desfrancs and Anselm are the two main roles, with Desfrancs being the more important of the two. But it wouldn't be advisable to have Anselm played as a father, or a *raisonneur*.[11] He should be markedly dissimilar to them.

The character of Sophie, passionate though it may be, absolutely should be an ingenue.

It is anticipated that the role of Desfrancs presents some difficulties which are not always explicable in the notes. The actor's intelligence alone can grasp the nuances. He should feel that the character he's playing is almost always in the violent state that creates, in his soul, the perpetual struggle between love and virtue, between the most extreme passion and the most rigorous duty, the superior voice of which curbs his sinful feelings. But these passionate feelings often manifest themselves against his will. If he shows too much, the play is immoral. He must therefore maintain this difficult middle ground. Though constantly troubled by a deep and terrible feeling which he dare not admit to himself, which he restrains and subdues, but which escapes him continually, nevertheless, we see only a wise and virtuous man. And if by this skillful behavior he could steer clear of some of the pitfalls with which this character is filled, perhaps, then he could humbly expect to have successfully performed a role that is somewhat more difficult than what is found in the typical high comedy.

Desfrancs and Anselm are dressed simply, like people are dressed in the country, far from Paris. There is something a little more serious in Desfrancs's attire than in that of his friend.

Sophie is dressed similarly with the utmost simplicity. She is nothing like a coquette, one of those artificial girls, carefully raised in the convent and having the personality of those people who make a point of replacing all the feelings that the heart inspires with insincerity. Sophie is a simple, artless girl, a kind of uncivilized person. She is the child of nature; she knows only its voice and that of her own heart. She dresses herself, but she doesn't primp. She likes to be pleasing, but she has no intention of either deceiving or

[11] The voice of reason in the play.

seducing anyone. The climate in which she was born makes her passions terribly active and she finds this perfectly natural . . . because it is, and because, except for frankness, filial devotion, charity, and human nature, she knows no other virtues. She should blend something of the Béarn[12] district into her clothing.

Madame Armance is dressed a bit above the position of a governess; she was born a lady and is only thirty-six years old.

Germon is dressed as an old country manservant. All the peasants are dressed in the Basque style, with hair nets and Spanish laced boots.

Regarding the young people of either sex who have to take part in the action, they will be in white with narrow ribbon trim, in pink, green, or blue.

Julie is dressed like the other village girls but with a little more ornamentation. The same thing goes for Alan. After all, it is their wedding day.

Certainly it would have been better to make the peasants speak the language of the region where the action takes place, but since the first law of the theatre is to be understood, and since very few people would have understood the ungrammatical idiom of the highlanders from Béarn, I had to make them speak in the jargon from the provinces close to the capitol. That compromise will clash a bit with the costumes. It will destroy the illusion, perhaps, but it was necessary. Molière sets the example for us and makes all the peasants he uses, from every possible district, speak in this way.

The policeman: a blue overcoat with gold trim.

The bailiff's men: blue, without trim.

They all wear round hats.

---

[12] A province of France located in the Pyrenees mountains, bordering on Spain to the south.

ACT ONE

The setting depicts a picturesque view of the Pyrenees mountains. The back of the stage is occupied by a mountain, inaccessible in its appearance, and top of which is lost in the clouds. It declines gradually on either end: to the spectators' left, it leads to a thick forest which completely fills that side of the stage; on the same side, at the foot of the mountain upstage, is a road so long that it disappears in the expanse of woods. It is called Bayonne Road. Next to one of the trees that cover the left side of the stage, 10 or 12 feet from the slope of the mountain, is a grassy bank. Toward the middle of the mountain, a little to the right, is a small thatched village, resting on a kind of plateau.

On the spectators' right, where the mountain leads to the plain, is Desfrancs' house whose simple façade is unadorned, ornamented solely with a flight of steps, forming a diagonal line with the slope of the mountain. The Bayonne Road leads up to the house. Extending from the right corner of the building to the right corner of the stage are a few hedges, a little less wild than the rest of the foliage. This area as well as the pathway where the action takes place are adjoining the walls of the house. A rope footpath encircles the entire mountain on the same level as the village, which it crosses. On the right, it goes from the village to the house; on the left, to the edge of the mountain that sinks into the forest. There it disappears without joining the Bayonne Road. It is the middle of summer. The action of the play takes place around 1780.

MADAME ARMANCE (*Alone, and working at a few flimsy pieces of crochet; seated on the bed of grass.*) The overbearing tendency that captivates my heart,
You, who oppress me and cause my unhappiness
By yoking me to your power,
By dazzling me with your delusions,
At least don't keep me in this state of dependency
That hides from us the horror of our crimes.
Ah! Am I committing a crime because I love Desfrancs?
What? When everyone respects and esteems him,
When everything around him constantly proves

The goodness of that loveable and fascinating man.
Should I alone resist the love that he inspires?
Should I tremble to be called his lover,
And blush, admitting it?
No! But an evil deed is allied with this passion. (*She gets up.*)
There's no longer time for turning back,
No! Let me finish hatching the plot.
Desfrancs, Desfrancs, in the depths of your soul,
You scorned my heart, you slighted my passion.
I can too clearly recall it.
Who? Him? What am I saying?
I never had the courage to speak of it.
It doesn't matter. More than once,
He could read my fondness on my face.
He's slighting me, that's for sure!
Let me dare to punish this outrageous behavior.
Don't let me hesitate for a moment.
The time is right . . . no more weakness.
Let's see the letter I received. (*She takes it out of her bag. Reading.*)
All will be ready for Wednesday night, the twenty-sixth of
August. Engage in the amusement you've planned. We'll be on
time for the meeting. Come look for us with Sophie. You must
reap the fruit of your labors; it's waiting for you! You can count
on the gratitude of an entire family, for whom you are doing the
greatest favor, by freeing her from a creature she is being made to
accept against her will. She's going to be permanently cloistered
in a convent, and that very day, you'll get your money. Paris, 13
August.
Oh, vile self-interest,
How one believes that, in disgrace,
No heart can cling to your deadly charm!
But I need someone, or clearly whatever I do,
I won't succeed in this scheme.
Old Germon alone can share in the brazen deed.
Let me take advantage of the eagerness he'll venture to show me;
Let's give him the opportunity to yield
To the feelings he so willingly expresses
Against his master,

And he is of use to me against my mistress.
Today, chance sends him my way, at exactly the right moment.
Ah! Unable to attend to my love,
I'm going to nurture my hate!
(*To* GERMON, *coming out of the house.*)
Well, Germon, I notice that they're getting ready
For a celebration.
Kindhearted Desfrancs is constantly
Trying to make people happy.
He's going to give Julie in marriage to young Alan,
And he's loading the two of them down with presents.
GERMON. Eh! It's just to please Sophie.
You know she likes those young workers;
Their marriage is the delight of her life.
So, it's kept Desfrancs busy.
He's such a nice man!
ARMANCE. (*A little forced.*) Oh! he's such a good master.
How happy he is when he excites
The gratifying feeling of an innocent pleasure.
GERMON. By being kind he relieves his suffering,
Since he is unhappy, that's for sure.
His eyes . . . the things he says . . . disclose a sorrow,
An extraordinary grief he tries to hide.
In providing for the happiness of those around him…
In sweetening their situation,
He can soothe somewhat the bitterness
Of the secret anxieties to which his heart is addicted.
But, seeing that chance brings us together, unobserved,
Tell me what you think
About the torment that pursues him.
ARMANCE. (*Acting indifferent.*) I don't know anything about it;
I've told you that already!
GERMON. (*More insistent.*) You're lying to me, Madame
Armance,
And perhaps you're questioning the silence
That I would impose upon myself if you were to tell me.
Look, I'll throw myself at your feet
And beg you to tell me

The cruel cause that can make a master,
Whom I adore, so sad and unpleasant.
I won't hide it: honestly, I'd rather
That heaven made me miserable in his place.
I'm a poor devil,
Condemned to every hardship since birth.
If I have a little more, or a little less suffering
Will I be any worse for it? (*He wipes a few tears.*)
But him?
ARMANCE. Your sentiments are a credit to your soul,
And I applaud them.
GERMON. (*Begging.*) In that case, madame,
You who know all the secrets?
ARMANCE. People of your station are often indiscreet.
GERMON. (*Still more insistent.*) No, don't worry about it;
I swear I'll keep my mouth shut.
ARMANCE. All right, Germon, I'll have to consent, then.
But see if we're alone here.
(*GERMON goes to take a look at the entrance to the roads, and
behind several tall trees. During this time MADAME ARMANCE
speaks to herself.*)
ARMANCE. Telling him everything wouldn't suit my purpose.
Love won't extinguish what he feels for his master.
Let me hide my weakness from him, and only let him know
What can make him a slave to me.
GERMON. We're alone.
ARMANCE. I'll risk explaining
These dangerous secrets to you
But you have to promise me
That you'll never go and accidently
Reveal what I've told you.
GERMON. (*Taking her hand, affectionately.*)
Ah! Trust me that never ...
ARMANCE. All right! Very well. I'm counting on it.
And I'll take the risks to have the pleasure
Of fulfilling your desires.
(*GERMON listens with the greatest attention. MADAME
ARMANCE continues after a pause, stressing the details.*)

Oh! Good Germon, Sophie,
Young, pretty, and sensitive, and whom everyone desires,
Whom Desfrancs introduces every day
As his beloved ward,
Who believes she is, and who, without any obstacles
Has known Desfrancs throughout her life
Only as a guardian with whom she is delighted . . .
Sophie, all the same, is just a love child.
GERMON. (*Astonished.*) Oh! Heavens, you amaze me.
Would Desfrancs be her father?
Why hide it? What good is this mystery?
ARMANCE. Hear me out.
In his tender youth,
At the age when everything's alluring,
When simple attraction is assumed to be love,
Desfrancs dared to seduce his mistress,
And carried her away.
GERMON. God! I see it all.
ARMANCE. She was followed and captured at Bayonne.
For close to this village, (*Indicating the place.*)
In this wilderness,
Was the place where Desfrancs took her.
No longer was there any cure for the misery that was feared:
Her father, furious, let vengeance overcome him.
He beat his daughter, and the young lady,
Taken to Paris, at the height of her agony,
Passing through Bordeaux one day, sent this child
Whom you know by the name of Sophie,
And whom she was not allowed to see again
For the rest of her life, even for a single moment.
GERMON. She was put in your care.
ARMANCE. Reduced to the depths of extreme misery,
By parents who were much too strict,
Alas! To stay alive, I had to agree
To the sad employment
That you see me still pursuing.
I took that child. A most happy fate
Was promised me as my reward

By a lawyer at the house where Hortense lived—
That was her mother's name.
As for Desfrancs, that tender fruit
Of his indiscretion was restored to him.
I wrote to him. Desfrancs appeared
And immediately became aware
That his only goal should be
To overcome my dislike,
And to hire me quickly
To bind me to the destiny of his child.
(*She sighs.*)
I agreed to it. That memory is painful to me.
It was my destiny. I was wrong, no doubt,
But heaven that foresees our ends,
Has sealed our fate in its mysteries.
GERMON. (*Still highly interested.*) What happened to
Hortense?
ARMANCE. She completed her journey,
Went to Paris and died of grief.
At that time, Desfrancs had no other intention
Than to separate himself from the world
In this somber retreat,
Originally designed for pleasure.
And although still young to give up his leisure hours,
His only desire was to give his beloved Sophie
A rank which, for life at any rate,
Would wash away the blemish of her situation.
And he worked very hard to earn her gratitude.
He claimed she was born of a marriage.
GERMON. A forbidden marriage!
ARMANCE. That's what he said. That's what he meant;
He does everything he can to justify it.
He constantly keeps working on Hortense's parents.
An overbearing pride is crushing them:
Not accepting Sophie, they still persist
In calling her the love child
Of a sinful daughter who, in her madness,
Has ended her deplorable life.

Germon, that's the reason for the mystery,
Why Desfrancs wants to say nothing
About his work and who he is.
"What if I expected too much out of my plans?" says he.
"People think she's my ward.
Is it absolutely necessary
To make her play another role
In this situation?
Let me conceal everything until my death."
See how he thinks! And this policy,
The worthy result of the virtues he lives by
Is certainly not to be criticized,
But hard to get used to. (*Somewhat distressed.*)
I'm even more afraid that Sophie won't be able
To spend her life here, living with Desfrancs,
Without falling in love with him.
Under an impressive veil, the abyss is hidden from her,
And her young heart will be swallowed up
In the crime without her being aware of it.
Desfrancs doesn't see the danger:
He mistakes her vigorous caresses for friendship,
For gratitude he mistakes her very passionate behavior
Which, in Sophie's mind, and in her naïve heart,
Are only the expressions of love.
GERMON. Oh, heavens! How to save her from the pit
In which this mysterious intrigue will bury her?
ARMANCE. Either tell her about this scheme,
Or speak to Desfrancs.
GERMON. That's satisfactory.
ARMANCE. Well, often I don't like it
When I have time to think about it.
I find it unreliable. It's a bad idea.
Let's look into something else:
To begin with, let's establish one principal fact:
Sophie's in love with Desfrancs.
GERMON. Everything we see confirms it.
ARMANCE. (*Insistant.*) But with an illegitimate love.
GERMON. That seems certain.

ARMANCE. (*Passionately.*) Then, let's prevent the crime . . .
Nature and its laws make it our duty.
Let's separate them so they'll stop seeing one another;
That's the only course that's suitable . . .
And we can manage it as early as tonight.
It's only a matter of coming to an agreement.
GERMON. What about Anselm who's supposed to come today
To visit Desfrancs, his closest friend?
Doesn't he intend to marry into the family?
ARMANCE. Him! No! Desfrancs could perhaps
Sound him out about a wedding
But you'll never see Sophie's heart
Give rise to the feelings Germon would need
To consider this arrangment.
So that doesn't solve our problem.
GERMON. But the other way is excessive.
ARMANCE. Isn't evil just as excessive?
Ah! My friend, we ought to do anything
To destroy a desire like that.
Consider it without trembling!
I believe that Desfrancs is sincere.
Entirely convinced that he's her father,
His virtuous heart certainly
Does not conceive any feeling
That might be offensive to heaven;
But he's weak, and it's easy to see
That he yields too much to nature
Without fine-tuning its impulses.
Now, from this weakness, and from the strategy he's pursuing,
You can see a misbegotten feeling beginning to grow,
And its danger is clear.
We have to guard against it.
GERMON. That's true, but how?
ARMANCE. Today's celebration is clearing the way for us.
GERMON. Very well. I happily accept your plan
And put both my life and my fate in your hands.
ARMANCE. There are a lot of methods we can use,
But to be most successful,

Let's suggest a stroll into the depths of the forest;
In our part of the world, such pastimes are very pleasant.
You know the oak tree that's bathed by the spring
Where the village feast took place the other day?
GERMON. Yes.
ARMANCE. I'll be there. Try to get her to come there.
From that spot until Bayonne, there's not much of a road.
That's where I'll take Sophie. It'll be easy.
I'll have some people to do my bidding. Tomorrow,
I'll seclude myself with her in a convent,
Convince her of the reasons for my behavior;
Someone will send word to Desfrancs
Who will consent to everything,
And he, immediately, will decide for us
What plan to follow in this situation.
At the moment, can I count on the assistance
Which you see I need, Germon?
GERMON. Oh! I promise it to you. It serves good sense,
Offended nature, and my master himself!
That's what I'll do, but my grief is excessive
Since in reaching your goal, you'll be leaving the house.
(*Tenderly.*) And what will become of my only hope?
For a long time you've known how I feel about you.
You see, Madame Armance,
To serve you, I'm giving up my happiness.
ARMANCE. I'll reward your zealousness and confidence.
But let's think about our duty. Marriage will have its turn.
Here, before our eyes, everything exposes the offense:
Let's banish it from this place.
By accepting my justifiable plan,
You're becoming much dearer to me, today,
Since the feelings of faultless esteem
Are reliable roads leading to love.
GERMON. (*Enraptured.*) Such a charming hope encourages
and inspires me.
You can count on me. I'll take care of everything.
Someone's coming. I'll slip away to give us a better disguise.
(*He exits toward the forest.*)

(*SOPHIE enters from the house. MADAME ARMANCE goes to her immediately.*)

ARMANCE. Well, Sophie, are you happy?
Will those tender bonds they're preparing
Fulfill all of your desires?
SOPHIE. Yes, dear Armance, and this celebration
Should give me much more pleasure by far,
Since Desfrancs wanted so eagerly to add
The element of surprise to this endeavor.
How talented he is at making people happy.
ARMANCE. (*Somewhat stiff and restrained throughout the scene.*)
Don't you recognize that sensitivity
Which singles out your guardian?
Haven't you, a hundred times,
Experienced all the warmth of his tenderness?
He likes to conceal the good deeds that he squanders on people;
Very often he plots to hide them
With the same effort that everyone else would use
To reveal them.
SOPHIE. (*Blushing.*) Oh! I confess, my dear guardian
Deserves to be adored!
ARMANCE. How you like it when I praise him!
SOPHIE. (*As soulfully as possible.*) It definitely pleases my heart.
Oh! Am I not right?
ARMANCE. Who's saying anything to the contrary?
SOPHIE. (*Spiritedly.*) You know, he was a father to me,
He acquired me from the hands of my parents
Whom death led to the grave a long time ago.
Ah! Since then, what has he not done
To mold my character? To develop my talents?
Yes, before thanking him for whatever I'm worth,
It's right that he should, at least, have my heart as a pledge
Of my more tender feelings!
ARMANCE. (*To herself.*) Unfortunate girl!
SOPHIE. Oh! What? Are you criticizing me?
Can I escape his tender virtues?
ARMANCE. But haven't I also taken good care of you?
SOPHIE. (*Quickly, with complete honesty.*)

Do you think that I love you less?
My heart summons you at the same time:
It delights in loving you together,
And its greatest joy lies in cherishing both of you.
ARMANCE. (*Squeezing her hand with a feigned tenderness.*)
I hope so. By the way, I heard that Anselm is coming.
With his honest and simple good-humor,
Maybe he'll be able to calm
Desfrancs's uneasiness, which enslaves
His mind and his manners.
SOPHIE. (*Spiritedly, and highly astonished.*)
Anselm is coming! And what in the world for, my good woman?
Desfrancs said he wasn't expecting anyone.
ARMANCE. Obviously another surprise.
SOPHIE. (*Appearing to press the issue.*)
But really, what is the point of it?
ARMANCE. (*Staring at her, to explain to her.*)
Perhaps someone is giving you a husband?
SOPHIE. (*Impatient and spirited.*) Me? No, no, certainly not!
ARMANCE. That idea . . .
SOPHIE. (*As above.*) Frightens me terribly . . .
If someone intends to link me to him,
He'll very quickly become
The surest object of my hatred.
ARMANCE. (*Her wickedness disguised.*) Oh! Not generally,
And I imagine that, without too much trouble,
Desfrancs could sweeten in a moment
That disgusting bond, against which your mind now rebels.
SOPHIE. (*Blushing and lowering her eyes.*) But he isn't thinking
about it.
ARMANCE. Who told you that?
SOPHIE. (*Sadly.*) My heart.
Could I expect to make him happy?
I'm a poor orphan,
In all things, fated for misfortune:
Without possessions, without a name,
And without parents,
What would Desfrancs see in me?

For a marriage he needs
Someone richer than me,
And besides . . . look! I see it.
I look too much like him to expect
To charm his heart and win his trust.
In such a case, he'd have under his rule,
Only his own imperfect appearance.
Perhaps, for a brief moment, he might enjoy in himself
Some of the pleasures of pride,
But soon . . . Oh! No, no, my good woman,
No, no, I tell you, as I have suspected,
He should not have created me
In his own image.
ARMANCE. (*With well-hidden irony, since SOPHIE must not be aware of it.*)
Ah! I bet you're wrong.
Forget that foolish mistake . . .
It would be very easy to love his work:
For myself, I say it without being tasteless.
Why, the only thing I see getting in your way is age.
SOPHIE. Is it so improper? After all,
I'm sixteen years old. He was twenty
When he acquired me from my father;
Often the ages among spouses differ a great deal.
But let me leave these expectations behind.
My heart never surrenders
To such sweet impressions.
I only want Desfrancs to let me live
Close to him until I die.
ARMANCE. May your heart be elated with that hope.
Today, I see no reason at all for anyone
To stand in the way of that desire.
I hate to go. Duty calls . . .
You're always the reason behind it.
(*Her wickedness cleverly veiled.*)
I want to help out at the celebration
And to make it even more exciting,
I want to add a new diversion to those you're prepared for.

SOPHIE. Accept my fondness and my gratitude.
(*Uneasy.*) I'm going with you. I want to see why
Desfrancs didn't tell me about Anselm.
Oh! That deception is giving me chills.
ARMANCE. Calm down, calm down, Sophie.
(*They both go upstage, but as one reaches the woods, and the other the house, they part company. They stop, and SOPHIE seems to complete her thought.*)
SOPHIE. Now I realize completely
To what extent fate can unsettle our lives. (*She goes into the house.*)
ARMANCE. (*Alone, since SOPHIE can no longer hear her.*)
Soon, you'll know even more . . . absolutely.

END OF ACT ONE

PANTOMIME

MADAME ARMANCE who has gone into the woods, comes out of them, and climbs up to the village by means of the footpath which leads there from the edge of the forest. After a few moments, she returns with WILLIAM, ALAN, and JULIE. She comes down the same footpath with them and all four go deep into the forest. A little later, we see SOPHIE come out of the house with a gloomy and melancholy expression on her face. We see her arrive, likewise, at the cloisters of trees. Coming from the forest, GERMON crosses the stage next, on his way to the house which he enters.

ACT TWO

(DESFRANCS and GERMON enter from the house)
DESFRANCS. (*With the expression and tone of impatience, and
sadness without harshness. Here the actor must remember that kind-
ness is one of Desfrancs' characteristics and that the virtue of kindness
can join forces with misanthropy but not with the harshness of
ill-humor.*)
What's Sophie doing? Well! Will your laziness
Finally allow you to answer me?
GERMON. Oh! Good God, what impatience!
Sir, thinking that you'd be going
Into the forest to reflect further in silence,
Her tenderness is arriving ahead of you:
She should be there right now.
DESFRANCS. I won't go. Anselm is coming,
I owe him my prompt attention.
Tell one of my men to follow her
And bring her back right away.
(*He goes back to contemplation and stands aloof.*)
GERMON. Sir, I'm going there myself. Should I dare?
DESFRANCS. To do what?
GERMON. (*To himself.*) Oh, no, I don't dare any more. He looks
angry.
DESFRANCS. (*Overhearing GERMON.*)
 You're wrong. I'm never angry.
What do you want? Speak.
(*Impatiently.*) Speak up! (*He stands aside to return to his thoughts.*)
GERMON. (*To himself.*) I'll keep quiet.
I have to respect this mood.
(*Beginning again.*) Sir, William with his two children,
Whom your heart, always sensitive to the misfortunes of others,
Has just made so happy through the bonds of matrimony—
William and the two children want to see you.
DESFRANCS. All right, but no expressions of gratitude!
GERMON. (*Going out.*) How eternally grateful they're all going
to be

For your patronage. (*He goes into the woods.*)
DESFRANCS. (*Alone.*) Eternally grateful.
He doesn't know the pleasure I take in it.
When I do a favor for somebody,
I'm doing it for myself alone.
Besides, Sophie is the patroness
Of these good people.
What more do I need? Wait. I hear them.
No, it's Anselm.
Let me give his more immediate problems
My complete attention. It's time I do something;
At last I must unite those two objects of my sweetest desires,
In the sacred bonds of matrimony.
(*ANSELM enters, coming by way of the Bayonne Road.*)
ANSELM. (*His arms extended toward his friend who, on his part,
takes several steps toward him. His tone is cheerful and open.*)
If I didn't come here, my dear Desfrancs,
To entertain you in your seclusion,
You'd be done for!
For sure, we'd have to bury you in two years.
What the devil's wrong with you to pine away like this?
Is that the way we behave
When everyone's smiling around us?
DESFRANCS. (*Still gloomy and abrupt, without harshness.*)
Yes, I'm very happy when I'm with you.
ANSELM. Oh, my dear fellow, get rid of that tone—it annoys
me.
And what can be the cause of these sighs?
Favorably endowed with wealth
A good mind, talent, friends . . .
Why, of course, whatever people may say,
Heaven has given you a place among its favorites.
DESFRANCS. In place of all those gifts, may it grant me one
favor:
That by a sudden death, it might shorten my life.
That's what I'm hoping for, Anselm, short and simple.
ANSELM. But, in spite of everything, your misanthropy
Ought to have some basis.

People don't just hate life
Without a very important reason.
Store it, confidentially,
In the bosom of a friend who loves you,
And whose supreme happiness
Lies in somehow relieving your pain.
DESFRANCS. (*The first word spoken listlessly; the rest in a tone
clearly refusing to answer his friend's question.*) No! It's a dissatis-
faction with life:
A need to see it end;
Whose power is so terrible
That often, I have to admit,
Even I, without reluctance,
Have wanted to break the bonds
Where I see life taking hold.
ANSELM. Give up this foolishness.
Come on, trust in my experience.
People get an obvious pleasure out of life
As long as there are still responsibilities to fulfill.
DESFRANCS. Then change the system and perhaps
I would wish to be reborn in that new world.
Don't let me forever see absurdity,
Baseness, flattery,
Pride or frivolity,
Affluence and deceit
As the offerings assembled for mankind's happiness,
Which heaven's justice should only owe to virtue.
ANSELM. Ah! Forget injustice. It's in nature.
In spite of all his faults, man is interesting,
Let's take him as he is, and let that sweet murmur
Which makes us love him, be enough in us
To excuse the evil which a person endures within him.
Do you believe that people would improve
If everything were so beautiful?
The absurdity is entertaining . . . it makes a shadow on the wall;
If we suffer from it, pride makes it up to us:
It's delightful to have been wiser
And people enjoy the comparison.

DESFRANCS. But often wisdom doesn't do people any good,
They're taken in by logical thought.
To accept it constantly, without exception, is a blunder
Which every day continues to make us martyrs among fools.
ANSELM. Oh! Isn't a person's heart free from regret?
On our own, we enjoy some of the sweet things it allows us,
And even in misfortune, in the midst of sighs,
Peaceful innocence still affords some pleasures.
DESFRANCS. Men, in a word, without venturing to complain about them,
Whatever duties we see them violate,
According to you, to fit in with them,
We have to agree to dupe or be duped.
ANSELM. No. But if we can't keep from being one of them,
Without hesitation, let us dare to become
The sad individuals to be duped, my friend.
If self-respect is lost there, virtue triumphant
Will secretly console it for its rights taken away.
In short, vanity sacrifices itself in the service of a virtuous man:
Without hesitation, he makes the most extraordinary efforts
When the price of the struggle is to have no regrets.
Look. I can read your preoccupied heart better than you.
There, I secretly discover . . .
(*Putting his hand on his heart.*) Some symptoms of love you're hiding.
DESFRANCS. Me?
ANSELM. You!
DESFRANCS. Heavens, what an outrageous mistake!
I lost what I loved a long time ago
And nothing will ever replace it.
ANSELM. What if you were mistaken . . . what if Sophie . . .
Yes, there's the source of your misanthropy.
DESFRANCS. Since you suspect me of this behavior,
I must immediately acquaint you
With the sad fate of that child.
For your information, she's my daughter.
Keep it quiet.
You know how often I used to speak to you about Hortense,

How I adored her! But you are unaware
That I have a token of her feelings.
It exists in Sophie.
ANSELM. And what motive forces you
To shut her eyes about her birth?
DESFRANCS. At first, the principal motive concerned my
marriage:
I wanted more than anything for the bonds to be recognized.
But when Hortense's death
Destroyed that cherished hope,
From the bottom of my heart,
I didn't nourish less the enchanting idea
Of proving, for her daughter's sake,
The undeniable purity of those bonds,
Of one day lessening the hatred,
And the unforgiveable aversion
That Sophie's grandparents had for me.
In short, to insure her happiness,
By reconciling her with her grandparents.
I've been working at this for a long time.
If I can't restore her to her family,
What good does it do to teach the child
What will make her life miserable?
If my wishes are crowned with success,
It is sweeter, I think,
Not to reveal her secret origin to her
Than dressing it in all its splendor:
That's having happiness in store for her
Without changing the root of it . . .
That's giving her a flower
With the thorns carefully removed.
Now, you decide.
Will you find fault with this feeling?
ANSELM. I'm eager to approve of what is certainly
The result of your kindness. But what in all of this
Can be causing you distress?
DESFRANCS. Oh! Really, my friend, I'm afraid
Of not being successful, during my lifetime,

In providing for Sophie's future.
As long as they don't want to accept her as one of the family,
You predict what kind of sad and miserable place
She'll have in society.
That's the real reason . . . the only reason
For my deep distress.
ANSELM. You seem to me to get alarmed too quickly!
You have to wait for their replies.
DESFRANCS. Well, in the meantime, I want you to make a decision
On an important matter that entirely depends on you.
ANSELM. For a long time, you've known your influence over me:
I would consider myself lucky if I could relieve
The cruelty of your misfortunes in this situation.
DESFRANCS. (*Very troubled.*) If I manage to be successful . . .
If I get Sophie a comfortable living,
Will you agree to join my family?
ANSELM. (*Smiling.*) Marry her! How silly!
DESFRANCS. (*A great deal of passion mixed with a little uneasiness.*)
My dear Anselm, alas! I want her to be happy.
Who could I find more worthy of her heart?
ANSELM. (*More serious, and gracious.*)
Your proposition touches my soul and flatters me;
In any case, I would take her as a wife
And you can be sure that the helpful clause
You're adding to the bond
Would have nothing to do with it.
On that subject, I have in no way
Predetermined it to be common,
Ridiculous, or, in any way, trite.
What happens by chance is always
Nothing but a dream.
The most beautiful titles are the virtuous ones.
Be that as it may. Aren't you her father?
She's virtuous and your daughter. Ah!
For me, her name is already endowed

With a sacred personality.
But Desfrancs, at least allow me to respond
To your confidence in me. At this moment,
I cannot accept such an alliance
Without knowing beforehand
What sort of feeling now exists
In her, whom your benevolence
So earnestly wants to offer to me.
I have little desire for the bonds of matrimony,
And I only want to harness to my destiny,
Someone who's in love with me.
DESFRANCS. Ah, my friend, I think like you,
And if you did not possess my Sophie's heart,
In all my life, I wouldn't force her
To be so bold as to give you her hand in marriage.
But I have nothing to fear. She's too sensible
Not to accept such a suitable marriage.
ANSELM. Forget about sense. It's her heart that I want.
DESFRANCS. (*Uneasiness, passion, inexplicable confusion in his
feelings which should be felt deeply in the delivery.*)
You'll win her. But you haven't any aversion to the marriage?
You've known her since she was a little girl.
Haven't you ever felt your heart
Speak to you on her behalf?
You can speak in confidence.
People tell me she's lovely but I'm prejudiced.
A person is always a bad judge of his children.
ANSELM. No doubt about it, Sophie is charming.
She's honest, attractive,
Sensitive, and very talented.
DESFRANCS. (*Inadvertently.*) She's very grateful for all I do
for her ...
She's artless ... hers is a very simple nature ...
And her guileless heart is painted all over her face.
(*Recovering himself, stuttering.*)
But a father is blind. Well, will you love her?
ANSELM. Certainly. She's made to be loved ...
But until now, my heart has not made me experience anything ...

And it hasn't been attacked by love.

DESFRANCS. Today, be alone with her for just a moment,
And if you find, in her, some enthusiasm for these bonds,
That she might appear, in a word, responsive to my wishes,
Oh, my friend, we'll all be happy!

ANSELM. Demand nothing. Above all, let her be free.
I want to find her heart evenly balanced.
After all, I would only include myself in your plans
In the event that she loved me.

DESFRANCS. Here she is. Let's not look like we were talking confidentially.

(SOPHIE, ALAN, JULIE, and WILLIAM enter, followed by GERMON and MADAME ARMANCE.)

SOPHIE. (*Leading ALAN and JULIE by the hand, presenting them to DESFRANCS; everyone entering from the forest side of the stage.*)
Come, show him your gratitude,
The prize of it is due to him alone!

(*ANSELM and SOPHIE greet one another.*)

WILLIAM. (*To DESFRANCS, in a country accent.*)
M'lord, we're comin' from the village right quick
To bring ya my daughter-in-law and my son.

(*He introduces them as he names them.*)
My dear m'lord, whew!
Hush my mouth, I'm much obliged!

JULIE. (*To DESFRANCS.*) Alas! I's been mighty hungry,
And you gave us some bread . . .

(*Letting her hand fall heavily into ALAN's.*)
For, with this fine lad, oh, golly! m'lord,
I expect I'll never die of thirst.

(*Bowing.*) Thanks again for giving me this nice present.

DESFRANCS. My dear children, I myself am delighted
That your happiness is complete.

ALAN. (*Energetically.*) Oh, yes, m'lord, you made it so.

(*Indicating JULIE.*) Golly, to tell ya how much I love her . . .
There ain't a smart fella that'd even try.

WILLIAM. God bless ya, m'lord,
You gotta do us a favor...

For cryin' out loud, m'lord Desfrancs,
You gotta take their kids ...
There'll be lots of them, really ... she's so young!
The evidence of your goodwill!
DESFRANCS. I'll do better than that, William. I'll marry them off.
JULIE. (*Indicating SOPHIE.*) But m'lady has to be at the wedding.
SOPHIE. Yes, my child. Yes, I'll be there.
(*She kisses JULIE on the forehead; JULIE bows two or three times in return.*)
ARMANCE. (*Prudishly.*) It seems to me that concern is very premature.
Let's bother ourselves only with those of the moment ...
I think that's more sensible!
WILLIAM. Gracious, you see, Madame Armance, ma'am,
This here nice fella sees into the future ...
Gosh darn it! It pleasures us
When we keep ourselves going, in the belief
That one day our ship will come in!
Oh! Really, it isn't like at your house,
Where there's never a cloudy day;
But for us in our servitude ...
Instead of what I don't have, I think
Of lots of kids and a good harvest.
That's what makes the work worthwhile.
DESFRANCS. But, my dear William,
Because of all this stormy weather,
Haven't you, perhaps, been unlucky
In your harvests?
WILLIAM. No, thank God. The thatch was able to be
Fastened down jus' like we been hankerin' for ...
Now, if we only get a few more sunny days,
And the tax paid, I'll be in fat city ...
When I'm like that there, I'll be real happy!
ALAN. The year that's comin' won't be very prosperous ...
My wife and I are gonna plow and plant
That big hill ... but it's a complete wasteland.

SOPHIE. (*Touched.*) Alan, I'll see you there.
Don't put Julie to all that trouble.
I want that work to be divided between us:
I intend to help you in everything.
ALAN. Oh, no, no, no, miss Sophie,
The work's too hard for the likes of you.
SOPHIE. (*Extremely tender, and with the utmost sensitivity.*)
Ah! I'd find it quite fascinating...
And if the furrows resisted my efforts,
I'd soften them, my friend, with my tears.
Being close to you, they'd be tears of joy!
ANSELM. (*To SOPHIE.*) Yours is quite a heart!
SOPHIE. Oh! Could it be hardened
At this account of their pitiful labors?
Helping them in the troubles which they courageously endure,
Assisting them in their immediate needs,
Of nature's pleasures,
Those are the greatest and the most precious.
How I like living with these good people ...
It's where virtue is seen to the greatest degree,
Where it triumphs, where it is sublime;
And when our cold desires, our vices, our idiosyncrasies
Drive its observance away from our cities,
It's in the poor man's refuge, and under his earthy roof
Where the temples of virtue remain open ...
That's where you hear virtue's most heavenly whisper.
WILLIAM. (*Having seen and heard SOPHIE with interest and affability.*)
Lookee here! That's the heart of m'lord Desfrancs talkin'...
She should be his own little girl,
She has his personality.
To that, I say, my good people,
I've just put a little somethin' in the purse ...
And so that we'll be entertained,
Let's take a little trip.
Will you do us the honor of coming along?
It's just to celebrate their wedding ...
That's why we're here, yes indeed!

SOPHIE. (*With joy and tenderness, to DESFRANCS.*)
A trip? Ah, my dear! That's your doing too
For you know how much I like these amusements!
DESFRANCS. I don't deserve all this charming gratitude.
Don't perceive this as a token of my tender affection,
It was their idea.
They were eager to entertain you.
You must occupy their minds
When you master their hearts so well!
ALAN. Let's go back home, pop,
And arrange everything for the trip . . .
It'll be for after dinner.
Come on. Maybe they have things to do . . .
We shouldn't put them out so much.
SOPHIE. Farewell then, my precious Julie.
JULIE. (*With silly curtsies.*) Your servant, miss Sophie.
SOPHIE. Alan, take care of her, and love her dearly.
ALAN. Ah! I'll never stop tryin' . . . she'll never lack for nuthin'.
(*They leave by the back of DESFRANCS's house. They are on the foot-path climbing up the side of the mountain to the village.*)
ANSELM. (*To DESFRANCS.*) What joys, my friend!
Ah! When you can taste their sweetness,
When they have such wonderful effects on you,
How can you not believe in happiness?
You see, my dear Desfrancs, even in our own day,
You can still love the human race
And find some virtues in everyone.
DESFRANCS. (*To SOPHIE, indifferent to what ANSELM has just said.*)
Let's go, let's go, let's hurry.
You don't have to look indifferent
When you're following your inclinations.
And those we see arise in you
Are always certain to have preference in my house.
ANSELM. (*To SOPHIE.*) That's what people call a benevolent guardian!
SOPHIE. (*Rushing to leave in DESFRANCS's arms.*)
Ah! How certain he is of possessing my heart!

(*They all go into the house, but MADAME ARMANCE, preventing GERMON from also going out, brings him back onstage.*)

ARMANCE. You see! Will you say that Sophie's feelings
For Desfrancs are merely commonplace?

GERMON. Oh! That love jumps out at everybody!
The more I see her, and the more I study her,
The more I tremble at the danger she's courting.
But in any case, everything's being prepared today
To destroy . . . to conquer . . .
This unlawful passion within her.
Through your efforts, and without knowing it,
William and his son have spread the net.
Tell me what still has to be done.

ARMANCE. Take her to the meeting place without her father
If, by chance, I don't bring her there myself.
If I don't take her there, it will necessary, in that case,
For you to go there and tell the messenger
I put there a short while ago
To get his men prepared . . . and that now,
No matter what people say or do,
Nothing can ever again get her out of our clutches.
Go, get everything ready, I'll be right behind you.
Hurry the trip along . . . and above all, secrecy!
That's the important thing. It's the soul of adventure! (*She goes into the house.*)

GERMON. (*Going out.*) Oh, yes, yes, yes, you're right.
Especially when it's a little matter of foul play!

END OF ACT TWO

PANTOMIME

Going behind the house, GERMON climbs up to the village. Once he's there, we hear the sound of pipes and drums. A short time after, young girls and boys, who should be running, file out of the village with the instruments and WILLIAM and GERMON at their head. They run along the footpath, climb down the mountain and disappear into the forest. Gradually the sound of the instruments can only be heard in the distance. There is no need for any other orchestra during this intermission.

ACT THREE

(SOPHIE and MADAME ARMANCE enter, coming out of the house.)
ARMANCE. Yes, here's where he intends to talk to you,
Wait a moment more.
In front of Anselm, he couldn't tell you
What he apparently wants from you.
You're going to hear about it right over here.
SOPHIE. Oh, what he wants! Ah! How I hesitate to hear
The distressing news.
ARMANCE. Oh! really,
The way I see it,
Anselm is only coming here
To draw up the agreement ...
SOPHIE. *(Rapidly.)* Whose dictates, I swear
I'll never follow.
ARMANCE. *(Pretending to be sincere.)*
Whatever happens, you can count on me.
I'll do all I can to help you
Through the perils that might be
Hovering over your head today.
You can be sure of that!
Most of all, don't miss the celebration
We're preparing for you.
SOPHIE. *(More occupied in thought than in her response.)* No, no.
ARMANCE. By the way, my pride was hurt
Seeing you give thanks in such a fun-loving way
To the only one who never thought of it.
You adore him, and the moment that pleasure
Is offered to you, your heart inspires you
To find both the cause and effect in Desfrancs.
SOPHIE. *(Dispassionately, still deep in thought.)*
How unfair you are! Yes, I try to thank you;
I'm aware of it, unfortunately.
ARMANCE. My feelings, always full of tenderness for you,
Certainly want to forgive these moments of weakness.

Farewell. I'll return when everything's ready. (*She goes into the woods.*)

SOPHIE. (*Alone.*) Ah! Since my love has not had the power
To make its ways into your heart,
Desfrancs, at least don't make me miserable
By forcing me into a loveless marriage.
Heavens! There he is. Let me pretend in this situation,
Let me conceal my deadly passion,
And disguise myself with care.
(*DESFRANCS enters from the house.*)
DESFRANCS. (*Somewhat uneasy.*)
The weather is so uncertain that,
Without bothering you,
I took it upon myself to change
The time for those pleasures your heart desires.
In a moment, someone will take you to them.
SOPHIE. Ah! You can be sure my sweetest moments
Are always the ones I spend with you.
DESFRANCS. All alone out here in the woods . . .
Were you going over our English lesson?
SOPHIE. Yes, indeed, my beloved teacher,
And altogether just as easily as in French
I was conjugating the verb "to love"
And the verb "to be" without making a single mistake.
And to convince you valiantly
How much these memorized verses electrify my heart:
"To love is to dream of happiness . . .
To be loved is happiness itself."
See if I repeat them the same way
And if I've clearly understood the author's meaning.
DESFRANCS. (*Giving her back the paper, after looking at it.*)
Wonderfully done! One would truly believe
That you experienced the words in translating them.
You like your abilities . . . you'll need them in the world . . .
Through them you'll get ahead . . . through them you'll be successful,
But so much charm and so much spirit
Cannot be hidden indefinitely

In this unknown and gloomy refuge.
SOPHIE. (*Pretending not to understand him.*)
Are you beginning to dislike it here?
DESFRANCS. Me? No. And I confess to you,
I intend to live here forever.
After being away from the world for so long,
A person doesn't think about
Trying to make new friends.
Besides, you see, my anguish, my cares,
This sullen and unsociable personality,
The results of secret disputes and deadly anxieties,
Would hardly give me an advantage over
Those splendid creatures whom I used to equal
In the past. No. I want this hideaway
To bury me forever.
(*Looking at her with uneasiness, but with the utmost tenderness.*)
But you, Sophie, old enough to be charming . . .
Cupid's blessed handiwork . . .
You must go forward into that enchanting world;
It's waiting for you to make your life more beautiful.
SOPHIE. (*Her eyes wet with tears; hardly able to speak.*)
You're leaving me?
DESFRANCS. Why these sudden fears?
You've often heard me tell you, with distress,
That in the end we'd clearly have to part.
(*SOPHIE cries.*) Ah! Good heavens, I see your tears flowing.
(*Holding her in his arms.*)
Your heart is opening up; I have to get inside it.
Let us forsake the pleasures of being together;
Let us think only about parting.
SOPHIE. (*Weeping, but forcing herself to be optimistic so that she can control herself.*)
No, no, I can't believe this dreadful decision.
Such a misfortune couldn't happen to me.
You are incapable of this cruel behavior;
You're only testing me.
DESFRANCS. Testing you? Who? Me? It's useless to pretend.
That heart, virtue's most sacred sanctuary,

Is not put to the test in error ...
Do you think I'm calm about this eventuality?
But, my child, your happiness
Is the only thing I care about,
And what would be the result of my affection for you
If its only objective were to destine you
For this retreat where my somber self-denial
Forces me to confine myself?
No, Sophie, there are some practical duties
Prescribed by reason and common sense
That absolutely must be realized.

SOPHIE. (*In a violent state, emphasizing her words, exploding with terror.*)
Oh! I can clearly see where you're going with this,
But in vain; don't expect to win me over.

DESFRANCS. (*In as violent a state as Sophie, but contained, and with the utmost sympathy.*)
I will do more. I intend to convince you.
Should a sixteen-year-old refuse the bonds
That I'm coming here to offer you?
Were you intending, then, to pass your prime
Without using it in the way nature intended?
You were preparing yourself for some very definite unpleasant-
ness ...
Those innocent pleasures which your heart prefers
In the moments slipping away between us,
Their faint illusion soon disappearing ...
Slipping away, those innocent pleasures
Would scatter over your entire life
The horrible poison of regret.
Set your sights on the future;
Following the natural order of things,
You ought to outlive me.

SOPHIE. (*Even more breathless, rejecting this idea out of horror.*)
Oh, no!

DESFRANCS. (*Poignantly.*) You must. Would it benefit you to
live
Prone to bitter sorrows?

Alone, isolated, in the depths of this wilderness?
My friendship is delivering you to the sweetest of destinies.
I'm giving you a husband whose diligent attentions
Will recognize and appreciate your virtues.
They all will reappear on that wonderful day
When, by your side, your love will see come into the world
The fruit of this delightful marriage!
Sophie, in such touching concerns,
Citizen and mother at the same time . . .[13]
Beside her children, Sophie
Looks like a goddess on earth, to me!
(*His tears are flowing, in spite of himself.*)
Then your heart, softened
In relishing its delight,
Will force you to turn your attention here:
"I owe him," you'll say, "some gratitude . . .
In fighting against my opposition,
He proved to me he was my friend."
SOPHIE. (*No longer able to control herself, and yielding to all the turmoil of despair.*)
You, my friend! If you were, barbarian,
Your hand wouldn't have plunged a knife into my heart.
Let the vicious tiger who wants us to be separated
Come, if it wants to rip me out of your arms.
(*She runs into his arms.*)
No, nothing will tear Desfrancs away from his Sophie.
I want to spend my life with him, forever.
(*Pulling back from him, with resentment.*)
Where does this come from? Tell me.
Did you invest in my welfare so that I
Would earn your respect and your love?
Cruelly betraying the sad fate of my childhood,
Did you have to teach me to love you,
If you were going to leave me?
Since I was a little child, did you have to bind me
By the sacred ties of gratitude
If you only intended to break them?
<u>At least consent</u> not to rob me of everything

[13] The line indicates a post-revolutionary revision by Citizen Sade.

And let me live, ashamed, in the cellar of the house,
Trying to erase, if I can, the memory of your goodness
From my feeble mind.
At least I'll be close to you in my misery;
I'll be able to drench you in the flood of my tears.
Perhaps pity will return your kindness to me . . .
Accustomed to tenderness, your heart
Perhaps will speak to you in my favor.
(*Trembling, looking at him, and in the most violent state.*)
Do you grant the wishes I'm asking of you?
Will you answer me? But above all,
Listen only to your heart,
For you know mine, Desfrancs.
You know all its passionate reactions
When someone wounds it.
Take fright. Be afraid that a refusal,
Insulting your Sophie,
Might force her to tear away her life
Before your eyes.
DESFRANCS. (*Very tenderly, but nevertheless forcefully.*)
Ah! I was expecting a kinder reaction . . .
I was hoping to find you more sensible.
One day, when she knows more about this,
Sophie will determine if I'm wrong now
When I urge her to throw herself into the arms of a husband.
Calm these woes, they're driving me to despair.
Force your feelings to be led by the mind
Which is supposed to lead them.
And those recommendations
Which used to come from your heart . . .
Allow yourself to govern them
According to what I say.
SOPHIE. (*Forceful, and still very emotional.*)
Well, to whom is Desfrancs going to condemn me?
DESFRANCS. (*Without the least hardness.*)
I want your hand to be given to my friend.
SOPHIE. Anselm!
DESFRANCS. (*Quickly.*) He's worthy of it.

SOPHIE. (*Very quickly.*) Oh, no, you're mistaken.
It's not possible.
DESFRANCS. Then who do you want to marry?...
SOPHIE. (*As above.*) You're going through all this trouble for
nothing.
What good would my promise do anyone
When the gift of my heart would not follow my hand?
DESFRANCS. He'll earn it and finally obtain it.
SOPHIE. If it were free ...
DESFRANCS. What?
SOPHIE. (*A kind of resentment, from which she takes her energy;
interrupting quickly.*)
Since I was a child, I tell you, Desfrancs,
I have no longer been mistress of my heart.
I don't have to hide it from you.
DESFRANCS. (*A little more than simple interest or curiosity and a
great deal of uneasiness. This line is one of the stumbling blocks of the
role. If you introduce jealousy here, it is not believable; if there is none,
it is false.*)
Who, then, could have become attached to her?
Both of us have been living very much alone
In this hideaway for some time now.
Ah! Tell me the name ... of your lover.
I suppose he has wonderful qualifications
To have made such a conquest!
Neither your head nor your heart
Is conquered easily, I know,
And their undoing is a shining triumph
For the lucky winner.
Give me his name, my dead child.
SOPHIE. (*Ashamed, uneasy, trembling, but nevertheless, with a
strength and vigor, taking advantage of the very slight nuance of jeal-
ousy which she thought she perceived in DESFRANCS.*)
Name him? Oh, no, no. I might describe him,
And then you'll be able to recognize him easily.
But ... if I had to sketch his features,
I'd trace them on your own, Desfrancs.
And, if by chance, I wanted

A faithful portrait of his virtues,
Your heart, in that case, would act as a model.
DESFRANCS. (*Much more serious; he is far from wanting to hear a reprehensible sentiment, and the more he tries to get it out of SOPHIE, the more his strictness increases.*)
I stand aghast at this admission;
You've seen next to no one
In this tedious asylum.
If you had loved me, then wouldn't you
Have had to let me see through that biased heart?
SOPHIE. (*She is offended by this new tone. The remainder of her courage is based on resentment. Meanwhile, she's trembling.*)
Ah! Don't blame me for it. I thought
I could deliver to that exhileration
A heart shaped by you and which would adore you.
(*Even more ashamed.*)
I thought I could be in love with what resembled you
Without offense, and without a thousand indiscretions.
DESFRANCS. (*He thinks he's understood her. He's emotional and violently distressed. He takes her by the hand with the most frightening motion.*)
Oh, Sophie, alas. It's getting late . . .
Sophie, we have to part.
SOPHIE. (*Aside, and in the greatest despair.*)
Ah, God! I've said too much.
DESFRANCS. (*Aside, and almost simultaneous with SOPHIE's line.*)
What day has come to enlighten me . . .
(*To SOPHIE, with everything that the most terrible emotion can allow him regarding these truths.*) Yes, whoever may be the object
of this foolish madness
Which has been able to take possession of you,
Seeing that you're afraid to make him known,
I demand it. It's necessary. Stop yielding
To that hope you allow to arise here.
Such a husband cannot suit you. (*He pulls away.*)
SOPHIE. (*Flying to him and throwing herself into his arms. She tries to speak but her guardian's reaction freezes her.*) Oh, Desfrancs!

DESFRANCS. (*Resisting the movement without rejecting her. He is in tears.*) Leave me!

SOPHIE. (*In despair.*) There's nothing left for me but death!

DESFRANCS. (*He holds her again; he looks at her feverishly, with the most misguided passion. His tears flow gradually, his expression changes. On his face is seen only terror, remorse, and sternness. He repels her; pulling away.*)

Good heavens! (*He leaves and goes into the house.*)

SOPHIE. (*Alone.*) He's dying. He has understood me only too well . . .

I should have controlled myself better.
I had promised myself to him. I'm amazed;
He repels me with horror.
What did I do to deserve his hatred?
Of what am I guilty? And in what other bond
Will he find so much passion?
I see Anselm. Ah, what to say to him?
Let me try to get him to refuse
This dismal marriage
Which is being used to subdue me.

(*ANSELM enters from the house.*)

ANSELM. Why is it, lovely Sophie, while everyone is eager
To provide you with pleasures,
That one might say you're acting troubled
And oppressed by regret?
So, why those sighs?
Tell your friend about your sorrow
And have no doubt that he'll use
All the means at his command, today,
To relieve your anguish.

SOPHIE. With a word you're able to relieve
This despair to which my soul surrenders.

ANSELM. Me?

SOPHIE. You.

ANSELM. (*Honesty, without the least suggestion of love; he is very far from it.*)

Then how might I succeed in this affair?
Ah! You know that I only want to live

To please you and to serve you.
SOPHIE. Has Desfrancs told you his plans for the marriage?
ANSELM. I don't intend to lie to you about it:
He took me into his confidence.
SOPHIE. And do these bonds appear favorable to you?
ANSELM. It's up to Sophie to dictate my reply.
Speak to me honestly: do they make you happy?
Let your mouth decide without digression:
(*Very nonchalantly.*) If you approve of them, I'll admit they're charming.
(*More passionate.*) But if they don't have your support,
That very moment, I'll break free of them.
I don't know how to trample on a heart.
SOPHIE. Ah, very generous man, how you answer me!
So much nobility by rights should surprise me.
Have you been in love before?
ANSELM. To soothe Desfrancs's uneasiness,
To amuse him in his solitude,
I put on the appearance of scorning the voice
Of the god to whose authority I had submitted.
But I would venture to tell you
That for a long time I have lived under his laws.
Like your guardian, I was guilty;
Like his experience, in Bordeaux, a lovely woman
Presented me with the fruit of her love
Which death destroyed.
SOPHIE. But doesn't the mother exist
In your memory, Anselm?
ANSELM. Ah! You have to believe it.
Alas, my vows are united with her spirit:
She'll have my love for the rest of my life.
SOPHIE. How, according to that, were you considering Sophie?
ANSELM. (*Quickly.*) I never made any plans about this wedding
. . .
It was entirely Desfrancs's idea.
SOPHIE. So my refusal doesn't bother you at all then?
ANSELM. I have to confess to you, it pleases and gratifies me.
I've known you for a long time

And since your childhood, you've excited in my heart
Such a tender reaction, a sweet inclination
I'm unable to return ...
But passion doesn't burn there for nothing.
I don't know if you're completely conscious of
That divine fire ... what I mean to say ...
Only the eternal being can teach you about it
For it's the one by which he's worshiped
Or by which he dearly loves his creation.
And this purified sensation,
Very different from that frivolous homage
That people pay to beauty, one day
Would lose all the benefits of its holiest titles
If I were to change it into love.
SOPHIE. Well, this feeling filled with tenderness,
Which has just been appraised by you
Right here, with so much skill ...
We'll call it friendship.
(*Offering him her hand. ANSELM kisses it with the emotion from the feeling he has just described.*)
I give you my friendship, Anselm, and implore you
To take it upon yourself to break the marriage bonds
Which have recently been expressed by Desfrancs;
For my guardian, who is in favor of them,
Would not forgive me for having dared to tell you
That I'm counting on your refusal.
ANSELM. (*With cheerfulness and tenderness.*)
Ah! calm yourself. I'll be able to do away with them.
Don't be at all concerned about it.
SOPHIE. (*Enraptured, throwing herself on ANSELM's chest.*)
Oh! yes, sir, you are my friend;
You're giving me a real sign of it,
And you will soon see that my heart is sensitive
To the incorruptible feeling
Which we have just now pledged to one another.
ANSELM. (*With the greatest affection.*)
At least, Sophie, let there be a little trust between us;
It's the principal bond of our agreement ...

It alone creates strength, and kindness, and goodwill.
Tell me truthfully, do you have a lover?
SOPHIE. (*Extremely embarrassed and blushing.*)
Well, look then into my soul,
See there the deadly flame
Which has devoured it for a long time . . .
But don't tell Desfrancs
So that he'll never know that I'm the one who's refusing.
ANSELM. Can you tell me his name?
SOPHIE. No, no, I can't.
ANSELM. Are you afraid that I'll abuse it?
SOPHIE. (*Very nervous, scarcely controlling herself, and going to the house.*)
Oh! no, no! That confession would make me too ashamed.
Let's go back inside. Have pity on the state I'm in.
ANSELM. (*To himself, also going out, but on the side of the forest from which he entered.*)
Oh, good heavens! Either I'm mistaken,
Or the most horrifying nightmares
Are ready, alas! to swoop down upon that unfortunate heart.

END OF ACT THREE

PANTOMIME

DESFRANCS comes out of the house alone; a hat covers his eyes. He looks sad and dejected. He crosses the stage and disappears into the forest.

ACT FOUR

SOPHIE. (*Alone and coming out of the house; she is in the greatest despair.*)
On every side people are going away . . . people are leaving me . . .
Even Anselm is carefully avoiding me;
Nevertheless, his kindness makes my situation less unbearable.
Ah! In my repulsive state,
Only Desfrancs humiliates me . . .
Me, who wanted to spend my life
Strewing flowers over his restless days!
What? Is my hope, then, lost?
Couldn't he have misunderstood me?
I prefer this idea to the anguish I fear.
Must I dread scorn and contempt?
I should have admitted this justifiable love;
There's nothing at all wrong in loving him.
(*All of a sudden, she becomes confused; she becomes alarmed; she trembles.*)
Almighty God, I think I see an abyss
Ready to take shape beneath my feet!
I've become confused, and the melancholy,
Consuming my mind and all of my emotions,
Doesn't even allow my senses
The ability of experiencing my distress.
In this overwhelming weakness,
Ah! In the turmoil which I feel,
I see, with terror, nothing but misfortune,
Crimes, and horrors all around me.
(*She falls on the grass and takes a picture out of her pocket.*)
Come, calm me, charming image,
Yes, come relieve my misery.
Your enchanting presence eases it for a moment . . .
It calms its harshness;
If, like I expect, alas! I yield to my misfortune
Shortly, on these premises,
Before burying you with me in the grave,

Recognizing in this picture,
The one who stirred my passions without end,
They'll see the sad and wretched object
Of my foolish ecstasy! (*She lowers her voice.*)
I feel numbed by the excessiveness of my hardships:
Never will the same exhaustion
Overwhelm poor, wretched, Sophie.
May I, with this sweet sleep,
Cross the boundaries of life.
(*In a kind of drowsiness, she falls on the grass in such a way that
her head is leaning on the hand that is holding the picture, and her
lips, without touching the miniature, are nevertheless very close to it.
DESFRANCS enters along one of the roads coming from the forest;
Sophie is sleeping.*)
DESFRANCS. (*Still not noticing her.*)
Anselm is getting away. He saw her and there's no doubt about it:
She's the one who's dampening the enthusiasm
He seemed to have for carrying out my wishes.
(*Noticing SOPHIE.*) God! Look at her! How beautiful she is!
(*He lowers his voice, afraid of waking her.*)
How much this serenity adds to her features.
She submits to it with conviction.
It's the sleep of innocence;
It's the tranquility of virtue!
If, however, I am the object she prefers,
As I have been led to believe,
How I will regret the secret
That could have plunged her into this infatuation.
No, of course! I'm interpreting this delicate
Outpouring of emotions
Too quickly in my favor.
Ah! Who, then, does she love?
Oh! What distress disturbs me!
God, what devastating madness!
What! Is nature trying to seduce me?
Then, where does this urge come from?
Is it imprinted in me so vaguely
That I can neither read nor comprehend

What it's sketching inside of me at this moment?
What's that I see? A picture no doubt.
It's going to tell me
The name of that lover.
Her mouth rests on those cherished features:
Even while she's sleeping, she longs for them.
(*He goes to take it and hesitates; he approaches, he steps back.*)
Oh! No. That's taking, too dishonestly,
The secret carried in her heart.
I can't resist it. Let me go forward quickly
And discover the cause
Of that fatal attraction.
(*He gently removes the picture without waking SOPHIE, and steps
back immediately as if to look at it in a more favorable light. The reac-
tion when he has recognized himself is mixed with terror, sadness, a
kind of suffocated joy, and the deepest regret.*)
Well, am I miserable enough?!
Are there no other thunderbolts to strike me down?
(*Heeding nothing but despair, the result of his regret, and yielding to
it with his heart-wrenching cries of sadness.*)
Am I sufficiently cruel and reprehensible?
At last, am I sufficiently worthy of the horrible destiny
That hell, in its rage, owes our blackest sins?
Her offense is my doing. I alone have disrupted
The good nature of her innocence.
I'm the one. I'm the one. Without pity, without foresight,
My foolish blunder has simply overwhelmed her
With the depths of misfortune!
(*He leans against a tree in a pose depicting the utmost melancholy.*)
SOPHIE. (*She awakens. She sees DESFRANCS. She is disturbed
realizing that she no longer has the picture, and that, as a result, her
secret is out in the open. Afterwards, flying to DESFRANCS with the
ecstasy of the most burning passion.*)
Heavens! It's all over and you know my offense.
Yes. Here is your lover and here is your victim.
Destroy this heart that allowed itself to fall in love;
Wound it! Rip it to pieces because it was able to love you.
DESFRANCS. (*The cry of despair.*) Oh, misery!

SOPHIE. (*Quickly.*) Let your hand destroy your handiwork.
(*Striking her heart.*) Your dangerous image is still here . . .
You'll see it again in there. Come, come, rip it out!
Your eyes look like they're avoiding me . . .
You don't dare come near me . . .
Oh, Desfrancs, am I then a very sinful person?
Oh, why did you teach me, you proud, unapproachable man,
All of the feelings which sooner or later
Would thrust this deadly dagger into my heart?
But your disdain enlightens me, and I forgive you for it.
After all, you have to break my hateful ties to you.
Go on, it's all over. I'm leaving you.
(*Distraught.*) I'll look for the animals
Of this dark forest in their grisly lairs . . .
I'll confront them. Yes, I tell you,
Facing them without fear, I'll be happy
If I can find them as harsh and ferocious as you.
(*She is about to throw herself into the thick of the forest.
DESFRANCS stops her and holds her in his arms.*)
DESFRANCS. (*With the most controlled passion.*)
Stop . . . and in the misery which is driving you mad,
Do not judge my heart
Without having been better acquainted with it:
Less feeble than yours, it remains virtuous.
With a supreme effort,
Try to prove to me your real passion
By overcoming our sinful mistake in the same way as I do.
Isn't it pleasant to imitate the one we love?
Isn't it sweet to be guided by him?
Come on! The horrifying victory that I'm demanding today,
The total sacrifice that I want from your passion,
May be as painful to my heart as it is to yours.
But in the despair that overwhelms me,
I still have my integrity, and I find consolation.
Ah! For that emotion to be more moderate,
It will be less gentle, or less tender, and less precious.
A sensitive admirer of so many qualities,
A lover of noble souls, not of beauty,

I'll still burn for you with a legitimate love,
Like before, without fear, and without sin.
And without a single regret, being unable to change a thing,
I'll still be able to adore it, like before.
SOPHIE. (*After a little consideration, and as if she's coping with a great deal.*)
Very well! If you want my heart to make this sacrifice,
It might be able to be harnessed,
But, at least, agree to my last requests.
I'll do everything to control this love
Which, you say, is dragging me towards the edge . . .
I promise you, Desfrancs, I'll fan its flame no more . . .
But let nothing separate us.
Especially do not arrange a more dreadful punishment;
Give up the thought of forcing that marriage on me.
I'll hate the husband whose title
Would insist on the vows that overwhelm me with terror.
At that price, beloved Desfrancs, my heart will become free . . .
At that price, I'll break the bond that offends you,
And sacrifice myself under your authority.
(*With a triumphant expression, and as if convinced that she has accomplished a great deal.*)
Are you satisfied with my courage?
Am I not worthy of you after all?
DESFRANCS. (*With a most tender pity.*)
How incredibly powerful is your delusion:
Sad effects of the influence
Of that flame in your impetuous heart!
Since, even in tearing yourself to pieces,
You don't deaden the feeblest glimmer of hope;
And how it convicts you with so much authority
When trying to prove to me you've overcome it,
You arouse it more vigorously. (*A pause.*)
But I require nothing more today.
I'll gently soften these tensions of your age . . .
In short, I'll talk about the desire I have
To make you happy and to see you at peace.

SOPHIE. (*Quickly.*) Peace! Ah, don't think that it approaches
my heart any longer . . .
Can the feeble change of heart your goodness grants me
Take the place of that sweet sentiment
Which, for me, had to arise, alas, in loving you?
(*Drawing near him timidly, tears in her eyes.*)
At least don't take this cherished image from me.
This entrancing picture will relieve my sorrow:
I need it to live.
Ah! This is my hand's attempt;
My heart directed it to create this moving testimony.
How far I was from thinking, in creating this work,
That it would not be the happy token
Of the most faithful and sweetest ecstasy.
(*She tries to take the picture. DESFRANCS refuses. Proceeding with resentment.*)
Ah! God, in my unhappy situation
I see that you still allow me nothing;
And you've never loved me!
DESFRANCS. (*Almost without hope, and holding her in his arms.*)
You lovely and excessively frightened girl,
Do not ask for proof of your offense;
It would soon cause regret
In my burning heart.
SOPHIE. Regret for loving me? Then what causes it?
DESFRANCS. (*Distressed to the highest degree, and stuttering.*)
Farewell, Sophie, I have to leave you.
I'm forced to shun you!
(*MADAME ARMANCE enters from the woods.*)
DESFRANCS. (*As soon as he sees MADAME ARMANCE.*)
Hurry, hurry, madame.
And if you can, have more influence
Over her than I. (*He goes into the house.*)
ARMANCE. (*False and malicious throughout the scene.*)
I think it's easy to guess
What's causing this disturbance...
Hasn't the husband destined for you
Made any impression on you?

SOPHIE. (*Very disheartened.*) Oh, that business is over . . .
Anselm and my guardian aren't considering it anymore.
ARMANCE. In that case, why are all my Sophie's senses
Affected in this way?
SOPHIE. (*Unable to control herself any longer; throwing herself
into her governess's arms; with cries of sadness.*)
Ah! My most loving friend.
ARMANCE. Ah! Why these fears all of a sudden?
SOPHIE. (*Very quickly, still in tears, and hidden in MADAME
ARMANCE's bosom.*)
Let my tears flow in your bosom,
I am in the depths of misery.
ARMANCE. You must know the charms I always use
To sooth your heart.
SOPHIE. (*Getting up, but still in despair.*)
I used to adore him . . . he abandons me . . .
Pity my frailty,
Lament with me my mistake.
ARMANCE. How is it that you kept this love a secret from me?
SOPHIE. (*Recovering herself somewhat.*)
There's a certain delight in silently pining;
What can you confide in someone
When you're hoping for it to happen?
It's in despair when the heart wants to unburden itself.
Ah! I loved him with too honest a passion.
ARMANCE. In this country is there someone he likes better?
Is he impassioned over another beauty?
Is it scorn? Is it infidelity?
SOPHIE. (*Still in tears.*) I don't know.
ARMANCE. (*After appearing to give it a little bit of thought.*)
For a long time, his old mistress
Knew how to arouse his tenderness;
Who says she still can't seduce him?
SOPHIE. (*Surprise, uneasiness, and interest.*) She's no longer
alive.
ARMANCE. But the heart is often still interested
In the object of an ecstasy
Which death has taken away from us.

SOPHIE. (*At first somewhat uneasy, then straightforward, and naïve.*)
It's certain that I've seen him find great pleasure
In speaking to me about her, my good woman!
Ah! If she's the one, well, I forgive him
Because she has nothing to do with me.
He sees a slight resemblance
Between my feeble existence
And that sweet object of his love.
Perhaps, enraptured by her beauty
Traces of which he notices on my brow,
He can burn one day for me, like he burns for her!
How I'd like to resemble her!
ARMANCE. Banish that hope. Such a blow is terrible
And I see that you're already terrified by it,
But you have to endure it.
SOPHIE. What do I hear? What? Is Desfrancs insensitive then?
In the long run, will I not be able
To overcome that insurmountable separation
Which fate, for the moment, seems to be offering me?
You don't like to flatter me,
Or you think my heart is a little too composed,
Since you dare to affect it to such a degree.
You're very cruel! Oh, never mind. Finish …
Say everything you can to smash and destroy
These unfortunate inclinations which I've kept for much too long.
I've suffered too much under their control;
Finish by breaking their bonds.
ARMANCE. I tremble to tell you
That emotion seems to be a frenzy;
It could become dangerous,
In this case, to remove the blindfold from your eyes.
One always cherishes the illusion!
SOPHIE. (*Very quickly.*) Oh! no, no. Speak. I demand it!
ARMANCE. You've only yourself to blame.
SOPHIE. (*Impatiently.*) You're driving me to despair with your delay.
ARMANCE. (*Cleverly building; the last line as strong as possible.*)

Well, you must be satisfied.
At last, this shameful secret
Must be revealed to you:
Cast far away from you that horrible fantasy,
There's no more time to nourish it.
Tremble at the danger which you were going to pursue,
The one your heart prefers . . .
The one you dare to love without blushing . . .
Wretched girl, he's your father!
(*As the words are piercing through her, SOPHIE has prepared the situation by shrieking out of fright down to the grass. At the last line, she falls on the grass without moving.*)
ARMANCE. (*Without being heard by SOPHIE who has lost her senses.*)
Ah! what a terrible and swift effect!
How costly was her mistake!
(*Looking at her.*) Death is painted on her forehead.
Yes, in the fit of rage that drives me,
Being able, like this, to gaze upon my victim,
Is, I feel, a very great pleasure.
But now, what am I going to do?
How to lead her to the trap that's being set for her?
After all, I want to get rid of her . . .
Time is pressing, and they're waiting for her.
I have to help her. For a moment
Let pity serve my anger.
(*She goes to her and shakes her.*)
Recover from this madness . . .
Come back to your senses . . .
And let's hurry away from this place
Where iniquity rules.
SOPHIE. (*Coming to.*) Ah! it's you.
(*In tears, she falls into MADAME ARMANCE's bosom.*)
Too cruel friend,
What a shock you gave me!
(*Getting up, and excessively woeful.*)
Forgive me for the vastness
Of the horrible sin where this mad passion

Was about to lead my youth . . .
And judge my repentance by my despair.
The bonds of duty alone, at last, lie heavy upon me;
Their weight terrifies me, and draws closer to destroy me.
Carry me away. Disregard my weakness.
Above all, let's hurry to escape.
ARMANCE. I have to agree with you.
But you'll have to make an appearance at the festivities
In spite of all that's happened.
SOPHIE. (*With fright.*) Me? Alas, can I allow myself some
enjoyment?
ARMANCE. Out of courtesy at least.
SOPHIE. Ah! But he'll be there.
ARMANCE. No. I'm telling you this to avoid him.
A package that's supposed to be delivered to him
Will keep him busy for the rest of the day.
Let's hurry.
SOPHIE. (*Distraught.*) Guide me. Conceal my offense.
Deaden the regret that's breaking my heart.
Hide me, if it's possible, from all of nature.
My presence offends it . . . and I disgust it.
(*She goes out, her face hidden in her hands.*)
ARMANCE. (*To herself.*) Ah! If my own love might be slighted
here,
I'll triumph in the end. I'll be avenged!
(*At that moment, SOPHIE finds herself almost facing
DESFRANCS's house, having gone there without looking where she
was going. As soon as she recognizes that fatal house, she turns away
from it with a gesture of fright, and lifting her arms up to heaven, she
goes into the forest. Here, MADAME ARMANCE is waiting for her.
MADAME ARMANCE supports her, and they disappear.*)

END OF ACT FOUR

PANTOMIME

Three or four men dressed in blue enter the village from the forest. A little while later, they leave following a peasant who is running away and who gets lost, along with them, in the mountaintops. Meanwhile, three or four other frightened peasants run down the footpath intending to warn him. The peasant who is being pursued reappears at the highest point on the mountaintop. He looks around, and sees nothing; to reach the woods more quickly, he darts from rock to rock and disappears into the forest.

ACT FIVE

JULIE. (*Running behind ALAN who enters first, carrying a bundle of letters; both of them coming out of the woods.*)
What's the matter, sweetheart,
Do you have to have so much to worry about
Even on our weddin' day?
ALAN. (*Indicating one of the letters.*) Don't you see that this is a message
My father told me to carry here!
It's for Mr. Desfrancs . . . or maybe even for the young lady
For she has a lot of them there, as you see.
JULIE. What could they have to say to each other
In this squabble . . . in such a way . . . and at the same time . . .
Still, they'd have to be pretty smart
To write each other such a lot of letters.
ALAN. Quiet! Quiet! I have to do my duty.
Ah! Do you think that they take the trouble
Of readin' or writin' the letter?
Somebody else always writes it for them
Then puts their name at the bottom.
That's how it happens that people in that position
Often do you harm.
JULIE. It's only a job to them.
ALAN. Dammit! It's always some fat-assed page
Who very often does nothing worthwhile,
But as long as he's successful in what he's doing,
He'll auction it off;
And since he puts it in the harvester
And his mind is always sharp,
It's done as if he's had nothing to do with it.
So, if I wanted to go take a trip
Into the country,
Anyway, after I left, when I was underway . . .
Wouldn't you write me letters?
JULIE. (*Pushing him away with her hand.*)
Let it be. Let it be, 'cause it's botherin' me.

Don't tell me these things, Alan darlin',
What could I do with my own hand?
I'd go find my great grandmother;
She writes like a monk!
And I'd tell her, here, here, Mad'lene,
Just tell him that I love him a lot!
ALAN. Well, that's not what's toddling around in my head.
I'm afraid that this damn celebration
Is going to bring misfortune to someone among us.
I thought I saw Madame Armance with Miss Sophie.
Both of them were going very far away
From where we were having the party.
As they were going out in that direction,
I saw the altogether subtle claim of a lover
Reading the look on her face,
I knew that all was not well.
(*He gives her the bundle of letters.*)
Here. I need to satisfy my curiosity:
I need to see what's going on.
JULIE. Don't go fighting alone against that brood.
Take Gregory and Big Cola.
Go on, sweetheart. I won't stop you
Since it concerns Miss Sophie,
'Cause I'd give my blood . . . my life
To save her from that disgrace.
That's all that concerns me.
Let me go with you, honey.
ALAN. These letters are important then.
Don't go . . . stay there . . . don't worry.
Especially, don't say a word to Mr. Desfrancs
About this conspiracy.
It'd put him in an awful mood!
It's probably just one of our countrymen,
That's the way it always happens!
JULIE. Take your father along.
(*ALAN exits toward the forest. Alone, holding the letters.*)
Forgive me, but that drives me to despair . . .
I've already been trembling over it,

Throughout my entire body!
That sweet, dear, little Miss Sophie . . .
How sorry I'd be my whole life
If someone were to do something like that . . .
Oh, well. Really! See how upset I am!
Let me go see why nobody's comin'.
(*She goes in the direction of the house. DESFRANCS comes out of the house and goes to her.*)
JULIE. (*Giving him the letters.*)
Mr. Desfrancs, here. Here's a letter
That my honey, Alan, told me to give you.
Everything's all ready for the party.
When are you coming to visit us?
DESFRANCS. (*Entirely occupied with the letter.*)
Yes, my child, go wait for me.
In a moment we'll go call on you.
JULIE. Oh, Miss Sophie is there already.
I'm expectin' you. Don't disappoint me!
(*She exits, skipping, into the forest.*)
DESFRANCS. (*Alone, reading the postmark.*)
It's from Paris.
(*Tearing the letter open very quickly.*)
I can hardly read . . .
All my brains are in my heart.
(*He reads rapidly and in a low voice. Then, at the height of joy.*)
Ah! It's all over. They're finally going to consent
To restore her birthright!
It's going to put an end to this awful secret
The effects of which were so dangerous.
You'll be able to call me your father.
I'm at the height of my desires!
(*A jumble of feelings in which one does not manifest itself more than another.*)
Oh, nature, now your holy law is made clear.
In the depths of my heart, I feel wasting away
Those feelings that now seem to me somewhat less vigorous
Than in those moments when your sovereign hand
Took pleasure in betraying us to the dreams of delusion.

Let me find Anselm. Let's go tell him quickly.
(*He meets up with ANSELM while trying to find him. ANSELM enters from the woods.*)
DESFRANCS. (*Energetically, and in the intoxication of a melancholy joy.*)
Ah! My friend, I was rushing to tell you
About the good news that just arrived!
She's their daughter ...
ANSELM. (*Quickly.*) Ah! God, hurry up and finish.
DESFRANCS. (*Giving him the letter, and still excited with the same feeling described above.*) Here, read. They agree to give my Sophie
Everything she had the right to expect.
(*As soon as ANSELM has read the letter, he gives it back to DESFRANCS who puts it back in his pocket, and continues speaking.*)
But my victory is imperfect;
You, alone, my friend, can make it complete.
ANSELM. (*Staring at DESFRANCS.*) After what's happened ...
DESFRANCS. (*Disturbed.*) Ah! You know her secret.
But dear Anselm, alas! Think better of her heart.
She'll have to give up her guilty passion
As soon as she knows the object of it.
Her feelings for me will become legitimate;
Introducing you, at that time, to complete my plans ...
Why would you be afraid to test
Whether the respect she's always had for you
Might not immediately be changed
Into bonds more sweet and passionate?
ANSELM. Frivolous illusion! Her heart is no longer
The master of this so-called change.
DESFRANCS. What are you talking about? What?
From the moment she knows about her life ...
ANSELM. (*Interrupting quickly.*) How little you know about the power
Of the feeling people call love.
The more you resist it,
The more it resists in turn.

I know that virtue will fight in her heart,
But be assured that her passion
Will only change its name.
Nothing is weaker than the mind . . .
Nothing is stronger than nature.
DESFRANCS. (*Firmly.*) She would have sinned against its
most sacred whisper.
ANSELM. That's only the lesser evil;
And your careful deception
Has allowed the greater evil to arise.
No, no, my friend. I cannot be bound
To your daughter by ties of this kind.
No. Immediately send her back to her family,
And let's both of us return to Bordeaux.
(*There is a noise in the forest; in a state of confusion, several peasants
climb down from and up to the village.*)
DESFRANCS. What is that? God almighty! What an awful
racket!
ANSELM. (*Lifting his eyes.*) Everything's in an uproar at the
village.
DESFRANCS. God! Once again, I foresee some new distress.
Oh, my Sophie!
(*The noise gets louder and becomes more distinct. The clatter of arms
and loud voices are heard. The confusion increases in the village and
along the footpath which leads to the base of the forest.
Dishevelled, SOPHIE runs up the Bayonne Road and darts like an
arrow into the arms of DESFRANCS; there she faints. She was being
followed. She escaped from the midst of the uproar; and even though
the noise has already been heard, the characters creating the disturbance appear only at the moment SOPHIE falls into DESFRANCS's
arms. This noisy crowd, bustling for a long time, enters only then. It
is composed of bailiffs' men and peasants. The bailiffs' men, swords in
hand, have a policeman leading them. They are vigorously resisting a
number of peasants, nearly equal to their strength, having WILLIAM
and ALAN as their leaders. The peasants retreat.
After the first attack has been repelled, some peasants with rifles, others
with sticks, appear and push aside the sharp ends of the swords. The
rear of the stage is filled with the rapid movements of this attack and*

*defense. Meanwhile, having come out of the village in terror, unable
to participate in this scene of horror, many aged members of both sexes
line the entire top of the mountain. They groan, lifting their arms up
to the sky.*
*This picture must be completely fashioned at the speed of light
and should stay active until the word "fright" [below]. As soon as
ANSELM, who is one of the principal characters, notices the fight and
sees who its object is, in order to further SOPHIE's action, he jumps,
sword in hand, in front of a group of bailiffs' men and speaks:)*[14]
ANSELM. Stop, you wretched men!
Respect this dwelling, and innocence, and me!
POLICEMAN. (*Coming forward with a document in his hand; at
first, to ANSELM whom he mistakes for DESFRANCS.*) We're not
the guilty ones!
Let this document dispel your fears.
(*Here, DESFRANCS leaves SOPHIE and entrusts her, still feeble, to
the care of JULIE, who hurriedly moved forward through the crowd
in order to look after her. As soon as DESFRANCS sees the order, he
signals his peasants to lay down their arms. They obey. The two groups
stay mixed together with no more acts of hostility.*)
ANSELM. (*Vigorously to the POLICEMAN.*)
Unravel the contradictions in these various proceedings:
One letter just this minute announced that Sophie
Could go in peace and rejoin her relatives;
And your order stops her and carries her off to Desfrancs.
(*Here, SOPHIE, having returned to her senses, is in the scene.*)
POLICEMAN. (*Sniggering.*) That letter was just a hoax,
Or, if you prefer, a warning.
(*Congratulating himself with stupid laughter.*)
We consider ourselves allowed to use these arms.
With them, we calm anxieties
And we proceed with confidence!
DESFRANCS. (*With nobility, decency, and contempt.*)
Get out. I take responsibility for Sophie.
You have my word and my life as a guarantee.
Go!

---

[14] At this point in the manuscript, Sade added, "This picture is the subject of
the engraving." Evidently, Sade was preparing for the production broadside or
planning a frontispiece for the publication of the play.

(*The POLICEMAN gathers his troops, and exits along the Bayonne Road.*)

DESFRANCS. (*To WILLIAM and ALAN.*)
Oh, my children, how grateful I am to you!
And how dear to me are your efforts.

WILLIAM. (*Going out, and to DESFRANCS.*)
Lookee here! In all of that, I'll bet you
There's more than what meets the eye!
(*To SOPHIE.*) I'd be careful, if I were you, Miss Sophie.
(*He goes out, but his son remains.*)

DESFRANCS. (*To WILLIAM.*) My brave and faithful friend!
(*Continuing, to ALAN.*) You too, Alan. You too.
(*He gives him money.*) How far this token is from what you
should be given.
Take it.

ALAN. (*Quickly, refusing it.*)
No! For shame! You're making fun of us!
Could I get any pleasure out of it
If I got paid for those punches?
Go on! Whoever sells himself
To defend his benefactor or his country
Is never anything but a bad friend.

DESFRANCS. (*Taking ANSELM's hand, and acutely preoccupied.*)
Anselm, alas! Let us never see so many
Virtues and so many crimes together!
Fate seems to take a perverse delight
In assembling them to crush us
With their thunderbolts!
(*Turning toward his ward, in the most violent state.*)
Well, Sophie!
(*SOPHIE reaches out to him; she wants to run into his arms but confusion, remorse, despair suddenly suppress the movement and she falls in tears into the arms of JULIE, who is facing DESFRANCS. This movement, the effect of which is distressing, should be performed with the utmost pathos and, in that, SOPHIE must make intelligible all the various emotions that trouble her soul.*)

DESFRANCS. Oh, cruel fate!

She knows everything.
(*WILLIAM enters, bringing in GERMON with documents in hand.*)
WILLIAM. Sir, see here's a criminal
Offending you, honor, Sophie,
Virtue, his duty, innocence, and heaven
All at the same time!
GERMON. (*Throwing himself at DESFRANCS's feet.*)
Oh, my beloved master, tear my life away!
DESFRANCS. (*Confused and worried.*) Get up. Explain this talk.
What have you done, Germon?
GERMON. I made an unbelievable mistake!
I agreed to help that enraged monster
But having been better informed about her treachery,
I ran away from her, cursing her days.
DESFRANCS. (*Impatiently.*) Who are you talking about?
GERMON. (*Still in tears.*) Why, Madame Armance!
Listen to that villain's revenge:
Everything her rage indulged in here . . .
There you are defeated and she's running off to Spain . . .
But, at the foot of the mountain, I was able to force her
To put back into my hands the evidence you see here.
(*He does not yet return the documents to DESFRANCS.*)
She used to adore you. Her foolish hope
Expecting to received some recognition,
Indulged in these crimes in order to thrive.
You preferred Sophie and her youthful features . . .
DESFRANCS. Reject that idea with horror!
GERMON. Ah! You couldn't conceal that passion.
Love her now. And in the depths of your soul
Open at last to the truth,
May love and fidelity arise in peace.
She's no relation to you. No. Hortense's daughter
Died in Armance's arms just after she was born.
Daily, you were waiting for
The touching fruits of your love.
There was a reward

For whoever could reconcile them with your impatience.
That monster lied to you.
DESFRANCS. What loathsome schemes!
GERMON. (*Eagerly.*) She gave you Sophie. A similar coincidence
Had placed her into her hands at Bordeaux.
Do not forgive her this vile deception!
ANSELM. (*Very surprised.*) What a coincidence!
DESFRANCS. Good heavens, what evil!
GERMON. She became guiltier and guiltier.
Everything that just took place
Is the shocking result of her violent love,
And I still tremble thinking about it.
She advised Hortense's family
And set them all against you.
She robbed Sophie of your kindness
To sacrifice her to those jealous ecstasies.
Ah! Avenge that terrible offence!
ANSELM. (*Aside.*) Oh! what a dreadful woman!
(*To GERMON.*) Ah, Germon, describe that hateful conspiracy
More clearly for us, and reveal
The social positions and the names of those
To whom Sophie owes her birth.
A secret emotion enlightens my love.
GERMON. The mother, sir, was called Isabelle.
Take a look at these documents.
(*ANSELM takes them and looks them over quickly.*)
ANSELM. (*Very quickly.*) Isabelle! Good heavens! Am I allowed such hope?
Oh, Isabelle's daughter. Oh, my beloved Sophie,
Let's not question it any longer. I'm the one who gave you life.
Embrace your father and behold your husband.
SOPHIE. (*In tears, throwing herself into ANSELM's arms.*)
How dear life is to me when I receive it from you.
ANSELM. (*Quickly, to his friend, and holding SOPHIE in one of his arms.*)
In offering her to me, you wanted me
To accept half of your possessions

Immediately, along with her.
I'm widowed. I'm free. I've no responsibilities.
In settling with me here, you'll take all of mine.
DESFRANCS. (*At the height of esctacy.*) Oh, dear Anselm!
(*To SOPHIE.*) Oh, my most loving friend,
What a blessed turn of fate.
(*To ANSELM.*) I welcome everything. In your good graces,
Sophie nor her husband will ever want for anything.
(*To SOPHIE, delicately and lightly.*)
Regarding our wedding: it's absolutely necessary
That we subject ourselves to the waiting period
That propriety demands.
I'm use to loving like a father and now I have to learn,
At your knees, how to love like a lover.
But soon, under the laws that your worship requires,
Since I've naturally returned to my initial condition,
Love is going to right the wrongs it used to inspire.
SOPHIE. (*To DESFRANCS.*) Ah! During that waiting period,
due to propriety,
May I become even more worthy of you!
Let everyone who follows us experience the effect
Of our sweet and happy destiny.
Let us forgive old Germon of everything he's done . . .
And let us leave Armance to her regrets.
(*Indicating ALAN and JULIE.*)
Let's tighten the bonds filled with kindness
For these young people
So that, eventually, with acts of charity, making us
Appreciate the worth of our existence,
Every day might rekindle the goodness
At the bottom of our hearts.

END OF THE FIFTH AND FINAL ACT

The Shyster

Introduction

Two manuscripts of *The Shyster* exist. The first called *The Double Deal; or, The Shyster* was sent from Cell Number 6 of Vincennes Fortress to Renée de Montreuil, de Sade's wife on 18 March 1783. The Marquis had been incarcerated through the efforts of his mother-in-law since 7 September 1778 in a maximum security prison, though as of 7 December, after three months of solitary confinement, he was allowed to walk in the garden twice a week and to have paper and pens to write as he chose. His wife was allowed to visit him in the presence of witnesses as of 13 July 1781 and evidently she had expressed a willingness to edit her husband's manuscripts. The letter accompanying the text of the play indicates that by 1783, Sade had already completed *Henrietta and St. Clair*, *The Madness of Misfortune*, *The Freak* (then entitled *The Inconstant Man*) and *The Twins*.

Like the finished copies of *Count Oxtiern* and *The Freak*, the second manuscript of the play now entitled *The Shyster; or The Magistrate of Long Ago* dates from 1810-1814 when de Sade was an inmate of the Asylum at Charenton. The original inscription, "They ought to regulate public morality, and they corrupt it; they're supposed to be guardians of virtue, and they become the helpmates of vice" was altered to a quotation from Dorat, a Pléiade poet, and a long introduction, comparing Sade's efforts in producing *The Shyster* to Molière's turmoil with *Tartuffe*, was added to the manuscript of the play.

Roulhac de Maupas, director of the hospital at Charenton, writing to the Abbé de Montesquiou, the Minister of the Interior on 7 September 1814 makes specific reference to the play as well as Sade's somewhat unorthodox activities at the asylum:

I have recently learned that he [Sade] not only was walking through the gardens at all hours and while the patients and convalescents were strolling, but that he habitually admitted them to his or Madame Quesnet's room,[15] under the pretext of having them read the newspaper. I've discovered that he had hired one of them, an honest but simple man, to copy, and to make other patients of the inside ward copy various theatrical works of his… I've discovered that one of his plays, entitled *The Lying Judge* [*The Shyster*] had been copied several months previously. The play being worthy of its author had horrified the one who told me about it.

Sade replied in a letter to Roulhac de Maupas dated 5 November 1814 in which he admitted that a Mr. Donge, the head of the Lottery Office, was copying various dramatic works which had been "accepted at various theatres and approved by the police." He urgently requested that Mr. Donge be allowed to complete his work suggesting that both author and copyist would "lose much by this interruption" and that the work should not occupy Mr. Donge "for more than an hour a week for two months."

Evidently, Sade's response produced the desired effect as there is no record of the Marquis being denied his request, and a letter dated 11 November expresses an "inexpressible need" for money, possibly to fulfill his commitment to his copyist. On the same day, Sade encountered a young doctor in the corridor at Charenton who described the Marquis:

Walking all by himself, with heavy, dragging step, most carelessly attired, in the corridor off which his apartments opened; never once did I catch him talking to anybody. As I passed I would bow and he would respond with that chill courtesy which excludes any thought of entering into conversation. . . . Nothing could have led me to suspect that this was the author of *Justine* and *Juliette*; the only impression he produced on me was that of a haughty, morose elderly gentleman.

---

[15] Madame Marie-Constance Quesnet (née Marie-Constance Renelle), an actress who was Sade's constant companion at Charenton. She had been granted permission to remain at the hospital as a "boarder."

At Charenton, de Sade's quarters were on the second floor opening on to the garden. In his biography of the Marquis de Sade, Lély
reports that the main room and small library were filled with dilapi-
dated tables and chairs, a marble-topped commode and a dresser
full of old clothes. Some two hundred and fifty books crowded the
three shelves that constituted de Sade's library. Among these were
a complete edition of Voltaire (in seventy volumes), the works of
Seneca, Suetonius and Tacitus, *Don Quixote*, Newton's *Principia*,
La Fontaine's *Fables*, Chateaubriand's *The Spirit of Christianity*, de
Sade's own *Aline and Valcour*, *The Crimes of Love*, and four copies of
his latest published work, *The Marquise of Gange*.

By the time Sade had completed the final manuscript of *The
Shyster* at Charenton, it had been submitted to at least four theatres.
Miramond, rejecting the play on behalf of the Théâtre Feydeau on
28 February 1791, commented that the plot was confusing and that
no one could ever approve of what St. Albon wanted his daughter
to do. In fact, he questions why Athénaïs should even masquerade
as Miss Selmours. If Philoquet is susceptible to the charms of a
beautiful woman, why cannot Athénaïs secure her father's victory
by pleading on *his* behalf? It is interesting to note that at this point
in the letter, de Sade wrote "that comment is right."

Between July and September of the same year, Sade attempted
to convince the administration of the Théâtre du Palais-Royal to
produce the play. On 31 August 1791, Gaillard,[16] with whom de
Sade had quarreled the previous year over *The Madness of Misfortune*,
replied that the work was unsatisfactory. His comments argued that
Philoquet was forgiven or absolved in some way in the denouement,
and that such a development would be "revolting and destructive
to the moral lesson" of the play. He offered to review the work provided that Sade would rewrite the last act. Apparently, the Marquis
affected some changes and resubmitted the play, for, on 6 September
1791, he received another letter, this time from Gaillard's secretary,
De La Beaume. After the usual preamble affirming the inability of
the theatre to respond as quickly as an author might like, and a plea
for patience, the letter lapses into patronizing politeness:

---

[16] Gaillard and Dorfeuille were the administrators of the theatre.

Sir, when he will have reviewed your new revisions, if they leave nothing to be desired, he will immediately inform you, and then send you a letter of acceptance.

If, on the contrary, it seems to him that the defects of your fifth act are still there, in spite of your efforts to remove them, he will have the courage and candor to tell you. It will not be an issue of your talent which is fertile and flexible, but of your subject matter and the way in which you develop your characters that makes a good fifth act impossible.

As there is no further communication between Sade and Gaillard, we may assume that the Marquis was put off by the secretary's reply. Still confident of the play's merit, he approached Langlois, the director of Théâtre du Marais, who responded that it was a bad idea to resurrect the past, and rejected the play on 7 November 1791.

It is clear why Sade was anxious to have his plays produced. Since he was given his liberty on 2 April 1790 by Degree of the National Assembly, he was in desperate need of money. A letter written to his lawyer, Gaufridy, early in January 1792, paints a clear picture of the situation. It had been impossible for Sade to possess "eight complete outfits of clothing . . . fairly good linen, a house which though small is delightful, pleasing enough to be admired in Paris . . . free entry to all the shows, and a measure of literary esteem, a circle of friends who are decent and most attentive to me" without "much expense, care, work, effort and pluck," all of which "inevitably" involved incurring debts. Because of financial obligations to Mme. de Sade, his ex-wife as of June 1790, he had no ready cash to settle his accounts and he badly needed the royalty income from his novels and plays.

On 1 April 1792, almost a month after *The Briber* was hissed off the stage of the Théâtre Italien by a Jacobin cabal, *The Shyster* was rejected by the Théâtre de Louvois. Two weeks later, when his family home was in danger of being destroyed after a resolution had been passed to despoil the houses of the old nobility, the Marquis penned an eloquent address to the Constitutional Club expressing loyalty to the French Revolution and signed himself, simply, Louis Sade. While de Sade was busy trying to preserve his ancestral home, the manuscript of *The Shyster* was lost. Finally, on May 1793, after his ex-wife and two sons had gone abroad as expatriates, after ten thousand prisoners were slaughtered, after the Sade estate had been ransacked and pillaged by the people of La Coste village, the Marquis retrieved the manuscript of his play. There is no indication that it has ever been performed.

The Shyster

Preface

THOUGHTS ON THIS WORK

In general, men are so evil and ridiculous that their most pressing interest lies in rising against the malicious philosophy that gives them a glimpse of getting caught.

DORAT[17]

Everybody knows what Molière proved when he tried to produce *Tartuffe*:[18] Superstition and unmasked bigotry were exposed to everyone's horror. Worthless branches and parasites of the respectable society that rejected them, nevertheless, did their utmost to use the play as an example of their own struggle. Bigots cried out "It's religion—it's religion itself being attacked, and it's even one of its most zealous practitioners who dares to ridicule it."

Nothing resembles slander like bigotry; both borrow the same mask, both make use of the same weapons, and both, as offspring of the same vices, produce more or less the same crimes. Consequently, a great many men were swept away; the malign influence of these two monsters of humanity corrupted an infinite number of minds. The play was vindicated and Molière had the pleasure of his revenge with this well-known and amusing announcement: "Mister Prime Minister does not want it performed."

Nevertheless, as the torch of healthy philosophy, sooner or later, succeeds in eradicating the shadows of superstition and ignorance, it soon becomes understandable that there is more danger in condemning such a work than in allowing it to be performed.

In reality, wasn't allowing the truly pious to suppress this comedy creating the suspicion that they might have the same vices and follies, since by their own request one was supposed to condemn a

---

[17] One of the poets of the Pléiade, and their mentor for many years.

[18] Molière first tried to produce the play in 1664. He subsequently rewrote it in 1667 and 1669.

work that divulged them? Producing it would prove, to the contrary, that they were not open to ridicule, that the man decried in the play could only be a hypocrite who assumed the appearance of virtue better to disguise all his vices, and that it was simply art, established as a school for moral behavior, that blackened with its brush those who disparaged religion. Many wise churchmen to whom the author read his work, perfectly convinced of this truth, and not recognizing themselves or anyone like them in the character of Tartuffe, easily understood the creation coming from Molière's pen and consequently enlightened the indecisive monarch and the play was performed.[19]

It can undoubtedly be seen as something very bizarre for permission to have been granted at the King's theatre to unmask the religious hypocrites while these same people were ruining millions of the King's subjects in the Languedoc and Cévenole[20] districts. What is also quite astonishing is the fact that these false devotees were laughing at Versailles at the same time they secured the revocation of the Edict of Nantes.[21] Odd occurrences undoubtedly, and accordingly, the man [Tartuffe] can only be a product of them.

Does anyone want another product of the time in a different style and of much less significance? Here it is: a work so far from *Tartuffe*, so prodigiously inferior to that masterpiece, which, nevertheless, finds itself obliged to use the same means of defense.

Fools cry out in horror, "What an outrage!" We hear them saying, "Behold the whole body of the judicial system attacked." To the lively outcries of these good men, we will respond like Molière: What? No, sirs, the play does not portray a group composed of France's wisest judges, nor does it attack the temple of justice simply because it was the thing to do at the time. If we should be inclined to do such foolish things, we don't need to defend our work, we need to be treated as fools. The object of our attack is the rascal who slips through society and disgraces it. It's the moth that eats through the

---

[19] The play was finally performed in 1669 and had an initial run of thirty-four performances, a record for the time.

[20] Languedoc was a province in southern France, the capital of which was Toulouse. The Cévenole district was comprised of the Cévennes mountain range in the south of France, populated by a great number of Huguenots.

[21] Louis XIV revoked the Edict of Nantes in 1685. This resulted in all religions except for Catholicism to be forbidden in France and a subsequent exodus of French Protestants (Huguenots) to England and the Low Countries.

fur, not the fur itself we're after. And beyond that, we seek permission from all the respectable jurists, ancient and modern, to bestow the guilty on the public. That venerable body (knowing quite well that we are portraying a ridiculous situation, and consequently not any of them, and creating personal, not political satire) will not only authorize our work, but will even allow its members to come occasionally to the performances and lighten up the august severity they use to engender respect—if this respect could be engendered by something other than their personality—by their position— their office—their integrity, their sublime duty, in a word, which so greatly endears them to the state. Let me add, in conclusion, that the magistrate whom we are drawing belongs to the long ago; it is impossible to see anyone like him in our own day. Enough on a subject that shouldn't concern us.

Now let's talk about the work itself.

To those zealous defenders of the rules of drama (funny how we've just been talking about this sort of thing), those who think they can ramble erroneously without retribution, we say that we have not committed an offence by causing the action to take place alternately at the homes of Saint-Albon and Philoquet. The twenty-four hour rule (established according to the great principles of nature and the real absurdity of prolonging beyond this limit an action which the spectator spends only two hours viewing) logically gave birth to the rule of unity of place. But every time that the action finds itself only having the limits of "the compass of one city which could be traveled through two or three times in twenty-four hours," it does not appear deficient either to verisimilitude or to the rules to put your action in the different locations you might find necessary within the compass of this city. To enforce the opposite any longer would cruelly restrict the public's pleasure in a genre whose satisfaction today makes variations more necessary than rules. "It's no trouble," says Marmontel,[22] "to go from Paris to the Capitol[23] as early as the first act. Between the first and second acts, it's even less trouble to go from the Capitol to Brutus' house."

We have no need to demonstrate that we are within the rules regarding the unity of time. The action is pretty close to twenty-two

---

[22] Jean-François Marmontel (11 July 1723 – 31 December 1799), playwright and member of the *Encyclopediste* movement who enjoyed the patronage of Madame de Pompadour.
[23] Toulouse.

hours. The first three acts occur somewhere between two and four in the afternoon, and the last two, the following morning before noon. Likewise, there is a single action, and although the story is intricate, it is nevertheless easy to recognize the unity of action and the inevitability of the dénouement in connecting all the threads together. The plot is rather complicated but it is so well developed throughout that we are not the least bit apprehensive that it will be in any way hard to understand. All of La Chaussée's[24] plots are very complicated in a convoluted way, and no one as yet has ventured to complain about them. Both the story and its development are entirely original. We've found it takes less time to write a story than to plunder three or four, following the exalted example of our modern *plager-wrights!*

The second act is in a new style. Those who have not experienced in the past an audience with a great lord or with a magistrate will not understand these foolish assemblies, where people, while waiting for the master of the house, form little groups and chat among themselves, independent of a more elevated conversation held by certain influential individuals near a fireplace or in a hallway—without which, certainly, these two speakers would be heard by the rest of the people as if they were speaking before an audience. Those, I say, who have no use for that environment, will be better off not watching the second act; but the precedents exist, and those who know them will understand us. The scenes of this act will perhaps be found a bit long. In consideration of this apprehension—this is hardly the time to say that we have made sacrifices. Nevertheless, they exist. Moreover, the vanity of not losing anything that comes out of our head will not cause us to imitate the custom of putting leftovers in the text as *variants*. The public already has enough of what we *know* belongs in the play without wearing them out with what we *think* is too much. Besides, there is not a single one of these scenes that would not have served us in the development of the main character. And what does it matter in the end if the character should be discovered through action or dialogue, so long as his development is solid, all of his traits are sufficiently marked, and the rhythm of the play suffers either nothing, or very

---

[24] Pierre-Claude Nivelle de La Chaussée (14 February 1692–14 May 1754), French dramatist who blurred the lines between comedy and tragedy with a kind of tragicomedy called *comédie larmoyante*.

little? You don't always have to focus on the main character to get to know him; most often you use the characters surrounding him. This is so true that we are very certain of the general public's aversion to Mr. Philoquet after the attractive scene between Valville and Lisimon, even though Philoquet doesn't say a word or even appear in the scene.

Someone perhaps someday will cut out a few of these scenes—he'll be making a mistake. There's nothing useless in a work of this kind, nothing which does not serve the plot, or is without proper motivation. Molière and Regnard[25] were full of these grotesque scenes. Some provincial acting company, or even a few in the city, who for their own convenience would want to lop off a few of them, could not do it without hurting the end of the play and without offending the good taste of true theatrical connoisseurs.[26]

2

Many people will say, "The author of this play is a man who lost his case. He's got an axe to grind." These people are mistaken—but what good does it do to protest here? They'll never believe it! Since people are interested in the personality of the author, they ought to examine his paintbrush carefully and see if gall has diluted his paints—as if it were possible, in a word, to make a scoundrel any more rose-colored! It was said that Molière was an atheist because he created Tartuffe—but it was the Tartuffes who said that, just as it will be the Philoquets here who will accuse us, at least, of high treason in the second degree. And what really humiliates them is the fact that we will never respond to their outcries. As a mirror-maker said to a hunchback who was complaining about his reflection, "Really, sir, I think it'll always look bad, so long as you've got that hump!"

Philoquet,[27] in short, is a character found in nature, as dangerous a beast as we have (not created but) captured—put a name to—and who has yet to bite us. We have had to furnish him with

---

[25] Jean-François Regnard (7 February 1655 – 4 September 1709), after Molière, the greatest comic playwright of the seventeenth century.

[26] This statement is rhetorical. The play was never performed.

[27] A combination of *philo*, a Greek work meaning *lover of*, and *quete*, the French word meaning *collection*, i.e. money.

specious reasoning that may be considered too hard to believe and, especially, too well punished to really catch on. You have to let vice speak its own language if you want to see vice punished in the theatre. And what stumbling blocks there are for those of us who attempt this kind of painting! Is it too rose-colored? It's nice and corrects nothing. Is it too black? It's rejected. This question has to be settled since no one ever expects to see great scenes on the stage while these obstacles exist. It is not the pretty side of vice that needs correcting, it's the atrocity. From this single abomination naturally flows emotional situations which can help the playwright show the dangers of evil behavior. If you forbid the playwright to expose this evil conduct, in the open, whether it be in words or in action, how will he ever reach his goal? How can he disprove or punish vice, if he is mute or inactive?

We have portrayed a father begging alms at the feet of his son, that ungrateful and merciless son, correctly suspecting that the old man is his father, and shamelessly sending him off to an asylum. From another perspective, we show a lover throwing himself at his rival's feet asking for his mistress in marriage. In both of these seemingly opposing plots, the situations should appear as novel as they are interesting. Other playwrights should have worked so hard!

The character of Athénaïs[28] will probably appear enigmatic because the story of the soul is an enigma to most people, especially to those who don't have one. It is drawn in the finest colors of the play, with strokes that are imperceptible but always true. Women will take to it better than men. Their supple and delicate feelings will reconcile them quickly to all the nuances of the character, and they will find nothing incongruous in it. Athénaïs is a very gay, very lively, singularly tender and sensitive creature. Such are the souls where nature has placed the cradle of virtue! Could it be said that her despair in finding herself to be the innocent motive for treachery does not express itself fully enough in words? We venture to believe the opposite. Perhaps she even says too much. Great sorrows are not verbose; a single word paints them, a single gesture characterizes them. Permit us to end this treatise with an example of what we're talking about, found in an act of beauty so impressive that, to a particular point, the story will appear either germane or

---

[28] A combination of Athena, goddess of wisdom and Thais, a famous courtesan.

a digression (since they're totally different things, we are not at all afraid of either boring or displeasing you in narrating this story).

Louis XIII passing through Moulins wanted to find out the news about the Duchess of Montmorency who, for ten years after this monarch had cut off her husband's head,[29] had lived there in seclusion at the Convent of the Visitation. Moulins was the city where she had buried the ashes of her beloved husband (the only man she had loved in her life) under a superb monument, a constant object of curiosity for tourists. The Duchess is discovered in a place close to the mausoleum. The envoy respectfully fulfills his master's orders. This woman—as beautiful as she is charming—looks at him with tears flowing from her lovely eyes. "Madam," says the gentleman, full of concern, "what should I tell my master?" "You'll tell him that you saw me," then turning toward the mausoleum she says, "you will tell him that I still weep for him." This is the stuff of tragedy.

---

[29] Henri II, Duke de Montmorency was beheaded in 1632 for his participation with Gaston d'Orleans in a plot against Cardinal de Richelieu.

The Shyster

or

The Magistrate of Long Ago

Verse Comedy
in
Five Acts

CHARACTERS

Mr. De Philoquet, *the magistrate of long ago*
Mr. De Saint-Albon, *father of Athénaïs*
Lisimon, *an unknown old man*
Valville, *Athénaïs's fiancée*
Athénaïs, *affianced to Valville, and Saint-Albon's daughter*
Barrière, *Mr. Philoquet's secretary*
Dubois, *Mr. Philoquet's valet*
Lafleur, *one of Saint-Albon's servants*
Mr. Hipocrène, *a playwright*
Mr. Canzonnetti, *a musician*
A young milliner
A police officer [*The manuscript indicates that these last characters are non-speaking parts*]
Two bailiff's men
A fencing master
A dancing master
A lackey

(*The play takes place in Paris, 1774, alternately at the homes of Mr. Saint-Albon and Mr. Philoquet.*)

ACT ONE

(The setting is a simple salon in the home of Mr. Saint-Albon.)
VALVILLE. Lafleur, is Saint-Albon awake yet?
Can I go in to see him now?
LAFLEUR. Sir, I don't think so.
He went to bed very late; important business
From which nothing can distract him
Keeps him busy night and day.
VALVILLE. I know all about it, Lafleur,
He's working for me and my happiness.
Because, my friend, ever since I was a child,
He was the one who soothed the scourges of my sad existence,
Took me to live with him, and raised me as a son.
And because of his successful upbringing
I was able to acquire the sweet name of son-in-law,
And attain a state in life I could hardly have hoped for.
His paternal endeavors filled the gap
Left by a father, swept away by terrible misfortune.
Alas, I owe him everything, and my gratitude
For this most tender bond is very great.
LAFLEUR. Sir, if you can believe the household gossip,
His daughter Athénaïs . . . excuse the innuendo . . .
Means more to you than the sincere friendship,
And pure feelings that you have for her father.
VALVILLE. No, I love Saint-Albon without self-interest.
My friend, duty . . . kindness . . . justice,
His very existence demands my gratitude.
LAFLEUR. And his daughter?
VALVILLE. Is lovely! Oh, I know that!
I hope to bind her to me in happy wedlock;
Eh! Who could see her without falling to tears?
Who could resist, alas, her myriad charms,
Combined in so many different ways?
He'd have to be a machine or standing in irons.
So wild a gaiety, and yet such tenderness,
So charming a smile! But the thing no one can imagine

Is her generous heart.
It's said that the image of heaven is in her soul.
(*A noise is heard.*)
Someone's coming. Leave the room. It must be Saint-Albon.
Yes. It's the father of the girl I love.
SAINT-ALBON. (*Entering.*) Lafleur, leave us. It is absolutely necessary
That I speak in private with my dear friend.
LAFLEUR. (*Leaving.*) Very good, sir, I'll tell everyone to say
That the master of the house is not to be disturbed. (*He exits.*)
VALVILLE. (*With passion.*) Ah! father . . . ah, sir, forgive this rapture.
It comes from my heart!
SAINT-ALBON. No, no, you're not wrong
To call me your father . . . that's what I always want to be.
I'm replacing the one you were unable to know;
I'll complete his responsibilities. Listen to me, son,
You know that I've been working on
A single project for some time now.
Nothing has been left to chance.
During the course of our travels, from which
We've just returned, a very learned lawyer
Was preparing the case with the greatest of care.
It's a matter of your rights to the estates in Burgundy
Which some stupid probate lawyers
Want to dispute unmercifully.
So much greed is blinding!
A similarly troublesome affair forcing your father
To escape to an island off the coast of England,
You know, is the reason you're in my hands.
I'm afraid that his destiny has run its course;
I've been unable to learn anything about him for a very long time.
Stopping by the mansion where I was living in Flanders,
He only had the time, in the name of friendship,
To entreat me for your life, my affection, and my pity.
I respected him too much not to be moved by his tale
Of a legal mishap, for which he was hardly responsible.
He then gave me an important document

Which made him the heir to the estate in question.
Since it came to him as a bequest, which he had hidden
Mysteriously, no one could take possession of it
During his disastrous litigation. You can be certain
At the moment, the Selmours want very badly
To get that title, now in my possession.
Their lawyers are contriving very unjustly
To uphold their rights without any foundation.
We will undoubtedly refute them, but
One small point continues to worry and annoy me.
Common practice indicates that I have to engage
A Mr. Philoquet as judge for the case.
He's a man rich in esteem, but wicked in person,
Enjoying pleasures more than his business affairs.
He would delight in reducing entire families to nothing,
In his disreputable spare time.
Ashamed of the apparel that distinguishes the magistrate,
He is seen everywhere dressed effeminately, in fancy clothes,
Talking about games, operas, melodramas, horses, jockeys,
Antiques, and music, but never the law.
That's not my kind of man!
VALVILLE. And it's not possible
To entrust the management elsewhere?
SAINT-ALBON. I can't demand that.
These men take turns; my request to go against precedent
Would be laughed at and denied. Besides,
There isn't much time, tomorrow's the hearing.
What's worse, I didn't think about all of this beforehand,
And I'm nervous about the outcome. Ah! I've reason to be.
But there's still a way for me to become privy to the man.
I'm going to set a trap for that scoundrel,
To probe the part of his heart beset by debauchery.
Selmours, our adversary, has a daughter living in Paris;
Philoquet doesn't know her at all. I want Athénaïs
To go to his office and pretend to be that girl,
And Marton will follow her, like one of the family,
A mother, an aunt, or whatever she likes.
Cleverly then my daughter will inquire into

The provisions of the subject under litigation.
As beauty rules and directs him,
I'm certain that Athénaïs' charms will immediately
Incline the judge in their favor,
And the lack of integrity he reveals in this endeavor
Will raise my beaten soul up from the sewer.
Because of the evil I believe he possesses,
It's our last resort, my friend, and it must be done today.
Well, do you approve?
VALVILLE. (*Innocently.*) Too young and too trusting,
I can't decide . . . but I would have doubts
About using what seems to me such a dangerous disguise.
SAINT-ALBON. As far as I'm concerned, my young friend, I
have none.
Valville, if I lived among savages who were
Virtuous and straightforward, I would agree with you!
I know I would find goodness there, my friend.
But I live among people, honest and civilized,
Less jealous of virtues than the art of faking them,
And who try to replace what they cannot attain
With false appearances made to dazzle us;
To prevent our being duped, we must be cautious of everything.
The great art in the world is to dissemble;
If you're born into the high-life, the fools and rogues
Will take advantage of you soon enough;
If you're a low-life like them, they'll destroy you.
VALVILLE. Ah! That's enough to make a misanthrope out of
you,
But your heart . . . that honest heart which
I've had the pleasure to study
Should not, and cannot doubt the existence of virtue.
In short, if the project does not sit well with me at all,
Sir, only blame the ethical lessons,
The decent examples, the simple and pure morals
Which I've discovered while living with you.
SAINT-ALBON. I would blame myself for these underhanded
methods
If they were directed against a good man;

But in this case, we find the most despicable vice.
We have to stop its effects mercilessly.
To deceive who deceives us is a very light offense.
Do I have to say more? Well, read this letter;
Before receiving it, I was able to take the liberty
Of exchanging my suspicions for proof
Since I had already taken certain steps
To appraise the value of this individual.
But to top it all off, this arrived later. (*He gives him the letter.*)
VALVILLE. (*Reading.*) "Do you know, Sir, the man who's in
charge of your case? Don't be taken in either by his extravagance,
or by his reputation. He's the most dangerous scoundrel in all of
Paris. He is susceptible to all sorts of temptations. Don't believe
me; prove them for yourself! Some personal reasons force me to
remain anonymous, but as soon as you have unmasked the villain,
I will introduce myself as your best of friends."
(*Continuing.*) He doesn't give his name? Why the secret?
When someone is doing you a favor,
What good is so much affectation?
(*Giving him back the letter.*)
Ah! Too often, cruelty knows how to grind the glass
To magnify the fears of the unfortunate.
SAINT-ALBON. (*A bit peevishly.*) Really, my dear friend, ideas
like that
Come from closing your eyes to the truth.
VALVILLE. I'll be quiet, and guided by you.
But are you absolutely certain that he has no memory
Of your daughter? Because I believe
He knows your family.
SAINT-ALBON. At most, I've seen him
Maybe three times in all; if I had known him personally,
He would never have been the judge for my case.
But he couldn't know Athénaïs,
I'm very certain of that.
VALVILLE. Very well, but the Selmours?
SAINT-ALBON. No, the father in Auvergne is confined to a
wheelchair,
And the daughter in Paris lives with a relative

Who hardly lets her out of the house. I believe it's an aunt,
And Marton will play that solemn role.
VALVILLE. Sir, if you'd like, I could play it better.
SAINT-ALBON. Are you crazy? What! Is your jealousy
Trying to turn us away from this course of action?
Use your head, Valville.
VALVILLE. Ah! Sir, that scoundrel
You're describing may be making me
Legitimately suspicious!
SAINT-ALBON. Oh, heavens! You're insulting
My daughter! Ah! My friend, I bet
That you wouldn't want her to know that!
I hear her approaching. Valville, come on,
Talk to her and reassure her in this business.
VALVILLE. I tell you, sir, I'm extremely uncomfortable with this
whole thing.
SAINT-ALBON. (*To ATHÉNAÏS who enters.*)
Come in, Athénaïs. You know my plan.
Would you believe him, daughter? He feels uncomfortable about it.
His tenderness alarms him. He's jealous, I tell you.
To cure his madness, persuade him to have more trust in you.
I'm going to be on the lookout for our man,
And as soon as he returns, I'm sure somebody will tell me. (*He exits.*)
ATHÉNAÏS. What, always distraught? Is it true then, Valville,
The heart of Athénaïs doesn't soothe you at all?
VALVILLE. Oh God! When you're in love like I am,
Rivals make you tremble, and you see them everywhere.
What you were saying? Oh, yes, I admit it,
I am jealous of everything . . . of the flower that adorns you;
I envy the air that refreshes you when you breathe in
And the air that you purify when you breathe out.
Forgive the jealousy, it's nothing to worry about;
My love simply creates it out of weakness.
Yes, I'm afraid of everything; because it would destroy me
Should that awful lawyer fall in love with you!
ATHÉNAÏS. Well! I'm going to try to make that happen, and a
comic scene

In this case, would suit me better than a tragic one.
In everything you do, you need naturalness
And truth, that's essential.
VALVILLE. You're a comfort.
ATHÉNAÏS. And you're really strange
To blame me rather than praise me.
What I'm doing, Valville, is out of love for you.
My love is so true that, just between us,
If Philoquet offered to chain me up forever,
My soul wouldn't oppose it in the least;
I'd go as far as I could, within the bounds of modesty,
To convince you that my passion for you is real.
VALVILLE. (*Very agitated.*) I'm not leaving you alone with him.
ATHÉNAÏS. I'm telling you,
Everything is going to work out fine for both of us.
Maybe even better. Come on, don't be nervous.
VALVILLE. Why nothing could be more convenient . . .
This great idea just came into my head.
I look pretty good as a girl; remember you used to always
Dress me up as a princess when we were children.
You know that I've recited poetry a hundred times
In falsetto, and with hardly any problems.
Eh! Well, I'll try it, I'll be your guardian angel!
ATHÉNAÏS. Really, my dear, that's a stupid idea!
I don't love you any more, you're too jealous.
To be suspicious of your mistress is only self-love:
When that feeling is drawn to the extreme
It is born of pride more than romance,
And at my altar, that pride is incinerated by my passion;
You don't know how much of a sacrifice I'm making
In letting him violate the holy bonds that tie us.
VALVILLE. Ah! How many times you calm my woes with a
single word;
And how this hand knows how to dry my tears. (*He kisses her hand.*)
(*SAINT-ALBON enters quickly.*)
SAINT-ALBON. Not a moment to lose, come on, leave as
quickly as you can!
Our man has just gone back to his office.

VALVILLE. (*Quickly.*) Sir, it's been decided. I'm going to be the aunt
Who has to chaperone her this afternoon.
Oh, please, agree to it. The scene will play much better.
I'll be able to tell you about everything that happens,
Since I'll be keeping my eyes on him.
SAINT-ALBON. Oh! As far as I'm concerned, I agree.
(*To ATHÉNAÏS.*) Forgive his stupidity.
ATHÉNAÏS. (*Gaily.*) Why, I won't pay any attention to it,
And I'll laugh at his clumsiness,
Father, at every moment, whether I want to or not.
VALVILLE. (*Quickly.*) Oh! No, no you'll see.
SAINT-ALBON. Very well, make him happy.
He adores you, my daughter, and even when he makes mistakes,
His heart, which is tender but naive, serves as his excuse.
Fly without further delay to our gentleman-at-law,
And come back soon to tell me of your success.
ATHÉNAÏS. Count on us, father. Ah! I'm getting a very keen pleasure
Out of this foolishness, even before the fact!
VALVILLE. (*Leading ATHÉNAÏS out.*)
You see, sir, I am less frightened now;
A person can do anything when he's in love!
SAINT-ALBON. (*Alone.*)
Oh, likewise set your mind at rest about everything else!
Valville, don't you know how much you mean to me?
It would certainly be useless for me to argue with you
About what your delightful heart knows it so richly deserves.
All right. If I have taken pains to bring you up,
Your good-natured virtues are my reward.
Don't be at all afraid that my choices were guided by self-interest,
Nor fear the flowing chaos of our fragile laws
Whose art of equivocation has created a labyrinth
Which leaves to the unfortunate, only their futile complaints,
And to us, for being outside of it, only a slender thread,
Which wealth has carefully woven into gold.

END OF ACT ONE

ACT TWO

(The setting is MR. PHILOQUET's study. The room is decorated tastefully and extravagantly. On each side of the stage there are two desks, one covered with women's attire, the other with books, stamps, ancient artifacts, and busts. MR. HIPOCRÈNE is seated next to one of the desks. The upstage area is occupied with a musician playing a harp, a dancing master, a fencing master, a millinery saleswoman, and by the door, an old man dressed in black, looking terribly sad. Those who are not working are chatting at the rear of the stage, but a feeling of respect will be stamped on everyone's face when the lawyer appears. Proportionately, as he grants his audiences, those who have been received will retire and the others will approach in a semi-circle to obtain the same indulgence in their turn. At the end of a short interval, DUBOIS enters under the pretext of putting something in order in the room. The first person he meets is the old man at the door.)

DUBOIS. *(Talking to the old man.)*
This awful man is still coming to bother us;
Mr. Philoquet is going to kick him out soon.
(To the MILLINER, examining her merchandise.)
Are these hats designed according to the latest fashion?
MILLINER. They're the best we have.
Look at these flounces with ribbons and sweethearts;
One could say that Zephyr himself is making them flutter in the air.
They'll please the master.
DUBOIS. It's for your own good;
You know what he does when he's happy.
(To the author who is still seated)
Mr. Hipocrène! Ah! Unfortunately,
Aren't you the author of the play today?
MR. HIPOCRÈNE. *(With emphasis but without moving.)*
If you please, Mr. Dubois, do not confuse me
With those miserable specimens from the sewers of Parnassus;
My verses are better chiseled, my style is more concise,
The subjects I write about, simpler and better chosen;
And, so that the public mind doesn't wear itself out,

Often, just like with art, I don't use any plots.
OLD MAN. (*Humbly approaching DUBOIS.*) Sir, I would like . . .
DUBOIS. (*Sharply.*) Wait a minute.
Mr. Philoquet is going to be here in a moment.
(*BARRIÈRE appears.*)
If you're in a hurry, there's Mr. Barrière,
His counsel . . . his right arm . . . in a word, his secretary.
(*When BARRIÈRE enters, everyone bows to him; he gives each the feeling of protection. He is dressed in riding clothes and boots. On one of the desks he places a large portfolio made of rose satin embroidered with silver. The old man pushed away by DUBOIS approaches him, but he is rejected, again with the greatest insensitivity, and the unfortunate man returns to his place at the rear of the stage, but always remains in sight. The author and the MILLINER likewise go to the back.*)
BARRIÈRE. (*To DUBOIS; both of them occupy the forestage, oblivious to the characters in the scene, and speaking in a manner not to be heard by them.*)
To work like a dog for just a hundred louis!
I could give them to you in the mood I'm in.
DUBOIS. Give them to me, give them to me, sir, and may you often get
Whatever can equal such a sweet windfall for me.
BARRIÈRE. (*Peevishly.*) Why, decide for yourself if I'm wrong.
The case is profitable for one of the parties;
He was a humanitarian and without any haggling
He pays me the customary bribe.
Now, as for myself, following my instincts,
Right away, I look into what the other side
Would pay me in advance to balance that amount.
I was sure of myself . . . and if this second man
Had acted without any hesitation as he should have,
He could have had at least a forged will,
And some document misplaced on his behalf.
Our own client would become the patsy
And he wouldn't even be able to complain about it. So, I set about
To carry out the matter with dignity,

To mask our duplicity expertly.
Suddenly, nothing at all to do with the case at hand,
Our client's pretty sister comes to ask for some advice.
The master sees her, becomes enraptured, and with a cautious voice
Tells me to work only for his 'honest' client.
I would have still followed the other adventure,
And renounced the absolute integrity
That guides me in all things, for a short time, anyway:
But he wouldn't hear of it. Really, my friend,
I've become virtuous in spite of myself!
A plague on Paris with his beautiful Helen!
See how the sex impedes our every step;
You sweat blood to get a little money,
A pretty face appears, and it's to hell with the business!
DUBOIS. (*Bantering.*) Ah! it's ridiculous. You've a right to complain.
BARRIÈRE. So much so, my dear fellow, I'm beginning to fear
That I'm going to leave here the same way I came.
DUBOIS. (*Ironically.*) It had better be hot weather at least, since you were naked,
If I remember correctly; and if it's cold and damp,
And you have to leave in as light a uniform,
I'd feel really sorry for you.
BARRIÈRE. Yes, yes, make fun of me,
And yet you can be sure that I'd be earning nothing
If I weren't practicing, with such versatility,
A trade which requires great skill . . .
(*He steals DUBOIS' s handkerchief. DUBOIS who notices this reclaims it while BARRIÈRE continues talking.*)
In the practice of slight-of-hand!
In short, I would have been ready to sprout
Wings on my feet like Mercury
For the master, when Lucifer tempts him.
Oh, damn the art of causing virtue to waver.
I don't know, really, how I sustain
A manner so robust as I have at the bar,
But, thank God, nature has given me

The talent required for more than one daring enterprise.
It's the only way to live in Paris!
And since every day, everything we encounter is extravagantly expensive,
We need to learn how to be extravagant. (*Taking him aside.*)
But to the subject at hand. Tell me,
Where is the mysterious letter I received yesterday?
It's important for both of the parties here
To understand one another.
In this unsigned letter someone is begging me,
Encouraging me to weaken the interest
Already taken in Saint-Albon's case
At the trial tomorrow.
And if I carry it off, it says that I'm guaranteed
Two thousand écus in cash. The business is lucrative.
They also add at the bottom of the letter
That today the Selmours (the Selmours, you hear me),
Who have been in litigation for some time now
Against Saint-Albon, are coming to see our master.
DUBOIS. Well, what's he supposed to do about it?
BARRIÈRE. I don't know . . . everything's still shady in this affair;
I've got good reason to believe that awful old man . . .
(*Showing, or rather, secretly indicating to DUBOIS the individual who is standing at the back of the stage.*)
Happens to have a part in all of this underhanded dealing.
In serving Saint-Albon, it could be very possible
That he could serve us.
DUBOIS. It's incomprehensible.
BARRIÈRE. Yes, I can well imagine that you don't understand.
And what will become of you, when you know
What he's after? (*DUBOIS is frightened.*)
I tremble when I think of it!
To recover, (he claims) some goods left behind in France
In the hands of a brother, dead for some time now.
But, if we follow the thread of our master's situation,
(*He counts the three points on his fingers.*)
—That his father is missing,

—That the treasure he has comes from a dead uncle,
—That the names are alike . . .
(*He raises his eyebrows, then shrugs.*)
My dear fellow, in these fiendish times,
It takes a lot of effort to figure out what we're really supposed
To inherit. It's only after the fact that I am opposed
To hanging on to twisted threads for a very long time.
We have the grounds: he'll die of misery,
Before declaring the tender name of father . . .
But it would be better nonetheless to keep him at a distance.
DUBOIS. Isn't it necessary for the gentleman's mind to be
convinced?
BARRIÈRE. Yes, but once again, I've taken care of all of this.
Maliciously, I've cast a great deal of suspicion
About the father he doesn't know on to that old man . . .
That's more than he'll need to justify the reasons
He has to hate him . . .
DUBOIS. (*Interrupting him; nervously.*) Well, yes, but maybe . . .
Why let him in?
BARRIÈRE. It was both to find out
The real object of his intentions,
And for us to decide on his claims.
Now it is clear that we must use the greatest caution
In dealing with the old man's property.
The rest is my affair, and I assure you
He'll be long in the tooth before getting the goods.
DUBOIS. (*With a very skillful delivery.*)
Sir, people have really done you justice
In these affairs. For deceit, fraud, pretense,
For cheating in every way possible, for the art of confusing
people,
Spying, betraying, lying, distorting the truth,
Disrupting a marriage or stirring up the struggle
Between a father and his son, between a son and his mother,
For violating all their rights and stripping men to the bone,
Nobody, I'm sure, will ever match your abilities.
BARRIÈRE. (*All puffed up with pride.*)
Do you know what trick I used to prepare for the trial tomorrow?

I wrote an anonymous letter to Saint-Albon
As soon as I received the letter yesterday.
I spoke to him somewhat frankly about Mr. Philoquet.
I offered in two words the evidence of my assertions
If he wanted to play round-robin with the proof.
DUBOIS. (*Honestly surprised.*) An anonymous letter?
BARRIÈRE. That surprises you?
Why, today it's the means that one employs
Among gentlemen of honor to disguise an affair . . .
I use it to the best advantage. I know how to counterfeit
Handwriting and style with so great an art
That I even fool myself.
DUBOIS. There's a lot of skill that goes into the art of being a crook!
You really make it an obsession.
There ain't no flaws on you!
(*Making a gallows with his hands.*)
Your abilities, sir, will lead you to high places.
But why that letter?
BARRIÈRE. (*Relating the details slowly.*)
Eh! To confuse the issue,
So that Mr. Philoquet would appear nothing but a terrible scoundrel
To our Saint-Albon who trusts him with tight-assed integrity.
Because whatever the evidence may be,
After we're through manipulating it,
Not even an angel will be able to defend himself.
As soon as the first shot is fired, he'll yield;
And, incidentally, Saint-Albon will turn himself around
And start bribing the right people,
Or, the master, having lost interest, will maneuver the case
Assisted by my documentation, so that Selmours will win.
And shoved in the middle of all of this,
Finding himself without a single resource,
Our old man will not dare to have the truth unraveled.
The Selmours, someone wrote me, are going to support this;
That's more than enough to make our wise Mr. Philoquet
Start double crossing his client from now on . . .

May that damned old man . . .
(*Pointing to him.*) That old devil,
Who ought to have an interest in Saint-Albon's victory,
Give up his house forever!
And may I, without delay, without any hitch,
Put two thousand écus in my pocket for his troubles.
Do you understand me, now?
DUBOIS. It's becoming clearer . . .
You have borrowed your ghost from hell.
You'll repay him . . .
BARRIÈRE. Good, good! You, wait for visiting hours,
And if like always, they crowd you and beg for
The honor of being introduced to the secretary,
Bring them to me without a fuss.
I will accept nothing without giving you a commission.
(*Emphatically.*) And you will participate in the laurels of my glory.
DUBOIS. Take care that the laurel doesn't turn into the Cyprus
tree!
Often you see the port but the reefs are very close by.
In the unfortunate event of a shipwreck, sir, never mind my share,
I don't want to finish with such a display.
For almost a hundred years, the Dubois and their children
Have always died in their beds in a very Christian way,
And I certainly do not have the vanity, sir,
To implicate my family in this kind of indiscretion.
Be that as it may, I'll, nevertheless, risk slander
And try to facilitate your delightful scheme.
If somebody comes, he'll have to be close to death to escape me--
It's not people like us who are bamboozled.
Be quiet, be quiet. I hear the master. I'm off on the lookout.
(*PHILOQUET enters grandly.*)
PHILOQUET. (*To the jockey.*) Ah! I'm worn out by that
English horse:
My ass hurts and I've got a headache.
(*To BARRIÈRE.*) How did this happen? Didn't you break in the
beast?
My very dear squire, you're awfully careless.
BARRIÈRE. No, no, this time, sir, I've got an excuse.

I was trying to mount her, not expecting anyone,
When up came some people who had been reduced to poverty.
You know quite well that they wanted to speak to you, sir.
PHILOQUET. I know . . . I know nothing! Why talk law to me,
When I'm talking cases?
BARRIÈRE. (*Playing for pity.*) It's just that they were dying of
hunger.
PHILOQUET. What do I have to do
To get it through that thick skull of yours
That you're supposed to serve me before my clients.
(*To the MILLINER.*) Are these the hats that Madame Bertin
sent me?
Where are the Italian flowers? I want to see them.
MILLINER. In the big box right here, sir. Here they are.
PHILOQUET. (*Pulling out a rose and holding it close to the young
girl's face; to BARRIÈRE.*) Why, these aren't fresh, take a look at
them.
The bloom on this child causes them all to fade.
BARRIÈRE. It's because, at the very least, she's very pretty.
MILLINER. Sir, if you please,
Make your decision quickly and let me leave,
Because they scold me when I'm gone so long.
PHILOQUET. (*Continuing to examine the flower.*)
With so much to choose from, I should be confused,
But making choices is my business.
In this box or that, there will always be roses
That I can inspect. Hence, I can run about,
Compare, publish my ideas on the subject . . .
(*Sniffing a rose.*) And even watch that blossom,
My pretty child, without the slightest insult to anyone.
You can see that a magistrate is a good judge of character.
Come on, don't sulk any longer, you'll be soon on your way.
(*To the musician who comes forward.*)
Of course! I want her to sing at the Opera.
Mr. Canzonnetti, try out her organ.
MILLINER. Look, I don't want to be made into a tramp.
PHILOQUET. You know what they say: a lady is a tramp!
CANZONNETTI. Let's try a little song.

MILLINER. Sir, take or leave what you've been offered
And let me go. I have to get back home.
BARRIÈRE. (*To PHILOQUET.*)
She's really quite lovely. Look at that ass.
PHILOQUET. Her body is spectacular. Why do you rob me
Of the pleasure of hearing you sing?
MILLINER. But I haven't any voice, sir, I assure you.
PHILOQUET. Nature gave you everything you have.
Why would it deny you a voice?
(*Looking at the harp and at CANZONNETTI.*)
Accompany her song
With the melodious tones of that sweet instrument.
MILLINER. Oh, God, how I'm trembling!
CANZONNETTI. And very incorrectly I'll bet.
MILLINER. I'll obey up to the point it becomes painful!
(*The MILLINER sings accompanied by the harp; tune: to be selected.*)
Since I am, at this moment, perhaps
Close to the perils of seduction,
A powerful God must preserve my being;
I place myself under his protection.
Though you want my feeble mind
To pay no attention to your clever traps,
When virtue knows how to unmask vice,
Its lying art quickly loses all of its power.
If, by misfortune, I acted imprudently
In coming alone to confront this danger,
Instructed at least by my experience,
This lesson will chastise me.
PHILOQUET. Of course, I'm sure our tramps would like
To have the soft and pure timbre of this child.
BARRIÈRE. (*Softly to his master.*) Did you hear what she just said?
I don't think you should plan on seducing her ...
A child is teaching you. Ah! I'm ashamed for you.
PHILOQUET. Be quiet, shut up.
MILLINER. Sir, they're waiting for me at home.
I'm going to leave.
PHILOQUET. A moment, I beg of you.

I have to pay you. (*He gives her a role of 50 louis.*)
MILLINER. Ah! I thank you. (*Noticing that the sum is too much.*)
But you've given me too much. It's only ten louis,
And this is fifty.
PHILOQUET. (*Confused.*) Ah! fifty? . . . Eh, well, yes.
MILLINER. Sir. . .
PHILOQUET. Keep it, keep it. I have a receipt for it
And your eyes have signed it silently in my heart.
MILLINER. (*Giving back the roll.*) I never accept what I don't
deserve.
PHILOQUET. (*Taking out the ten louis and giving them to her;
she leaves, bowing from where she is.*)
What, so young and so wise!
BARRIÈRE. I would have never believed it.
I'm going to go with her to investigate this mystery.
(*To his master.*) Your soul is a stranger to such events.
Isn't that true, sir? And I also admit
That examples like these are very rare in places like this.
PHILOQUET. Very well! Will this music be finished soon?
CANZONNETTI. It's been finished and refinished for some
time now, sir,
And whenever you want, we can rehearse it.
PHILOQUET. Remember to resist temptation,
And when the moment arrives, take great care to say
That it was my art alone that produced it.
Let it be well documented that you had nothing to do with it.
Here are twenty-five louis to keep your mouth shut. (*He gives
them to him.*)
CANZONNETTI. (*Quietly the first line. Then strengthening his
voice. To the others in such a way that whoever is in the room can hear
him.*)
Ah! You can always be sure of my discretion!
And who would be surprise at the effort, sir?
Everybody knows that you surpass me in music.
Your abilities in this matter are so well-known. (*He exits.*)
(*The DANCING MASTER and the FENCING MASTER come
forward.*)
PHILOQUET. Lessons today? No, I'm can't take them.

(*He takes out checks from one of the drawers in the desk on the left.*)
Here are your fees. I've been waiting for you.
I'd be really sorry if you knew
All the wonderful pleasures I have to give up for work.
It's the piling up of these damned cases
For which I am alone responsible! Ah! I have no doubt at all
That your hearts would honestly pity me.
Goodbye, dear friends, tomorrow for certain. (*They leave.*)
PHILOQUET. (*To the author who comes forward.*)
Might I inquire, sir, what business brings you here?
HIPOCRÈNE. (*Respectfully giving him a notebook.*)
The hope of explaining this child of my imagination,
Both serious and light, it is a little piece
In the form of comic symbolism.
PHILOQUET. Ah! That's a fresh idea!
What do you mean, sir, by comic symbolism?
HIPOCRÈNE. (*With a flute-like voice.*)
It's as one would say an allegorical sketch
Performed on stage in a clearly obscure manner
Offering to the eyes, two senses: one true, the other less certain.
It's a new genre which my muse is toying with—
No one is eager to be viewed in this way,
Seeing that your typical asshole, carried away with pride,
Only thinks his best side is what he really looks like.
Very often he's mistaken; someone laughs about it, or carefully
Distracts his eye from looking only at his best side—
And in such away he becomes an easy mark for satire.
PHILOQUET. It's your first attempt? . . .
HIPOCRÈNE. No, sir, no indeed,
I've written a play for every kind of drama.
Did I say a play? At least ten, and I share them with everyone.
The Théatre Français, the Italians, the Boulevards, the Ambigu,
The Vaudeville, the Opera. I've appeared on all the boards.
You can see me today, by command, at some prince's,
Tomorrow, with a crash, I'm playing the provinces.
And I have all the skills, I don't lack a single one.
PHILOQUET. What? You do as well in each?
HIPOCRÈNE. Equally well, sir. Either farce or parody,

Or the art of tragedy or comedy,
A character piece, or tearful drama,
Melodrama or spectacle. . .
I am the same in all, nothing gets in the way of my genius.
The muses have nourished me from the breast of Minerva,
And their learned harmonies dictated the verses
With which I inundate the court, the city, and the world.
(*Softly and mysteriously.*) Pegasus and I drink at the same
fountain,
That's why I got the name Hipocrène.[30]
PHILOQUET. Ah! Sir, what an honor! With such rare talents
You ought to be assured of brilliant success.
HIPOCRÈNE. The public is ungrateful.
PHILOQUET. That vindicates you!
HIPOCRÈNE. You can be certain at least, and I'll swear to it,
That of all my plays, the masterpiece
Is the one I'm dedicating to you.
PHILOQUET. You're dedicating it to me?
HIPOCRÈNE. I've taken the liberty,
I hope you'll forgive me. I praise your virtues
And your rare abilities insufficiently,
But I know how you have to act with great men.
PHILOQUET. (*Skimming through the dedication.*)
Let's see, let's take a look because I'm afraid . . .
(*He reads aloud.*) "Sir . . . the stars that shine in the heavens shed,
on our glory, rays less exciting than those which your profound
lights pour out today on the arts. The powerful protection with
which you honor them . . ." (*He reads the rest silently and continues
quickly after mumbling two or three words.*)
Like an angel,
I love the truth but I hate praise.
(*He throws the notebook on one of his desks.*)
What is the lucky plot that you have chosen?
HIPOCRÈNE. A reconciliation between father and son.
PHILOQUET. That seems worn-out.
HIPOCRÈNE. No, no, the setting is new,

---

[30] In Greek mythology, Hippocrene was the name of a fountain on Mount Helicon, formed by the hooves of Pegasus, and supposed to be a source of poetic inspiration. A literal translation of the word "hippocrene" is "horse's fountain."

I included in there a nice ordeal for a judge.
To seduce him, I put in a lovely lady on her knees,
But he resists everything, just like you would do.
It will delight you. I've leapt with the flight of an eagle,
I'm discovering the talent that's been stifled by the rules;
I'm deviating from them a little.
PHILOQUET. I find that delightful.
In the eyes of the wise man, rules are the death of pleasure.
Imitate Shakespeare and you'll be sublime;
Show us the victim, in tears on the scaffold,
Before our English eyes, tear out his entrails,
Make his cries heard, make his blood flow.
In horrible dungeons in the midst of shadows,
Suspend swords and ominous torches
With scraps of flesh or on piles of corpses;
These are the nimble blossoms of a great talent!
HIPOCRÈNE. Soon I'll match this marvelous model . . .
Hidden in my studio, at this very moment,
Is a subject that surpasses my original idea.
(*Softly and mysteriously.*)
Fifteen deaths . . . and I've set it . . . in a hospital.
PHILOQUET. (*Embracing him, enraptured.*)
In a hospital, sir! You are a great man,
And you have to name me as your patron.
(*Mysteriously.*) Tomorrow you'll receive a lovely letter
Informing you of the time for a meeting at my house.
You will leak it to all the newspapers in France
So that each one will have plenty of evidence
That I am patronizing you and that you're patronizing me.
(*He slides him a roll of gold.*)
HIPOCRÈNE. (*Bowing to the floor and putting the gold in his pocket.*)
I'm eternally grateful for the commission! (*He exits.*)
PHILOQUET. (*As the OLD MAN approaches.*)
What? This old man is always following me and bothering me!
The poor enjoy hounding the rich!
Well, what do you want? I've already told you
Your case looks bad, and even so, you're going to court.

Why, I can do nothing about it. Your lawyer is lying to you.
Must you always waste my time?
I'm too busy to deal with the flimsy anxieties
Of interminable litigants!
OLD MAN. (*Noble and dignified.*)
It's not for that reason that I entreat you,
And soon I will have given up all of my cares.
Age and despair at last have opened the door for me
And my refuge is ready in the arms of death.
I'm not at all asking for the things that my old age
Can no longer enjoy . . . without regret, I leave them.
Yes, I abandon them to the guilty heir
Who knows how to use them much better than I.
(*As forcefully as possible.*)
Ah! I'm only asking for a very feeble service.
I'll tell you my situation, without any deception.
(*Fighting pride.*) My distress is at its worst . . . for the past four
days
I haven't been able to support my old age.
(*Tears fall from his eyes.*)
Everybody leaves your company heaped up with riches.
Is it the poor alone who are excluded from your generosity?
Is misfortune, then, a crime in your eyes?
Be frightened of inflicting the sting of remorse upon it!
Look at these hairs, turned white out of misery.
Perhaps they will paint you the memory of a father?
You have certainly enjoyed so sweet a thing . . .
For a moment, imagine that he kneels at your feet;
There, I'm falling. Oh, just God, come open his soul,
Let him attend to the distress which I lay at his feet.
Heaven do not punish him with terrible torment
For seeing the tears of an unfortunate old man without being
moved!
(*A movement of weakness makes him bend at the knees.*)
I'm dying . . .
PHILOQUET. (*Without moving, but nevertheless without
harshness.*)
Stand up, we'll take a look at your case.

For the present, there's nothing I can do.
My heart is not deaf to the sound of misfortune,
But a person who listens to his heart is always a fool.
The concerns of our king have caused
More than one home for the poor to be opened in the city,
And my credit will prevent them from refusing you.
Go, give your name there and don't come back. (*He exits.*)
OLD MAN. (*Alone and in despair.*)
Yes, I will spare you my presence forever.
You will never see the author of your birth,
Ungrateful and wretched son. But if I gave my name,
Needless trouble ... alas! Useless plans!
God! For my revenge ...
Whenever you have the lightning ready ...
Take only moment to separate him from his head ...
And permit me, oh, God of heaven, to die
Before hurling your very just thunderclaps!

END OF ACT TWO

ACT THREE

(*Mr. PHILOQUET's study as in Act Two.*)
BARRIÈRE. We're rid of him! I shouted like the devil,
But we won't see that unbearable man any more.
Oh! You were really crazy to lure him here.
PHILOQUET. By doing that I was hoping to uncover
everything.
BARRIÈRE. I think, for once, he's closer to buying the farm
Than arguing about who's going to inherit it!
(*The next line in a 'country' dialect.*)
Mr. Candebas, your country cousin,
Is going to sustain the shock with a brow that's calm and serene;
I went to see him the other day. Really nothing surprises him;
And I doubt that the tides of the Garonne
Have ever tossed up on their shores a Gascon . . . more Gascon!
(*The next four lines in a 'country' dialect.*)
You might just as well (he says to me) send the money my way
Since I'm the only heir; I don't know of anyone else.
And I'd never be able to drink in the Garonne again
If that rascal loses me a single cent.
PHILOQUET. But what if we discover he's not the legitimate
heir?
BARRIÈRE. What of it! Dubourg, your uncle, was really very
smart
In not leaving everything to you.
I've rummaged through his papers, all are in safe keeping,
And nothing can dispute your claim;
But it'll take a few charitable donations to the Gascon.
Pay him well, sir, since he's useful to us.
PHILOQUET. Do whatever you want, I'll take your word for it.
BARRIÈRE. (*In a false and smooth-tongued manner.*)
Sir, you have too much confidence in me!
PHILOQUET. You never take advantage of it; I trust you
implicitly.
And your friendship convinces me of your prudence.
BARRIÈRE. (*Playing on the mention of friendship.*)

I'm devoted to you more than you think...
(*He wipes his eyes with a handkerchief.*)
And I will do for you ... enough said;
But, sir, we have to get rid of the old man.
PHILOQUET. That son-of-a-bitch.
BARRIÈRE. Oh! It's very easy to do ...
Hell, we get him in trouble with the law,
Our little pranks turn out successfully,
You know they will ... and then ... to help him out
Your weighty influence on the hands of justice
Would put him in jail immediately.
Yes, as we say between these four walls,
"Everything in due process"—and if conscience
Should bring you some memories of a father ...
To calm your regrets,
Just think of all he'll gain being locked up!
You won't see him calmer or more peaceful
Than spending his days in that happy refuge.
PHILOQUET. (*Interrupting quickly.*)
Your morality is heavenly ... it's worthy of you,
Do you know that often you go even farther than I do?
BARRIÈRE. Good, good, that pleases me. Practice, study ...
(*In a silver-tongued manner.*)
The wrinkles in the human heart made it a habit with me.
Besides, think about it, you have time,
I never deal well with violence ...
My spirit ... my frankness inclines me toward leniency.
Think about it, sir, it's what you taught me.
PHILOQUET. It's a delightful way of freeing ourselves
Of that irksome fellow.
BARRIÈRE. Then tell me, who do you expect
To speak in favor of, tomorrow at the trial?
PHILOQUET. Eh! Saint-Albon.
BARRIÈRE. Don't trust
That foul Saint-Albon. I've always told you
It would be a greater benefit to you to work for Selmours;
That old bastard insists on talking against Selmours ...
I don't know. All that seems to me like a plot

And we don't know where it's leading us.

PHILOQUET. Make every effort to figure it out.

BARRIÈRE. He doesn't have an explanation for the second affair.

But tell me, sir, didn't you have a brother?

PHILOQUET. A brother? Me?

BARRIÈRE. Yes, you.

PHILOQUET. Why, I don't know anything about it!
When my father left, I still seem to remember
There was talk that he took his youngest son
With him to England.

BARRIÈRE. That's your brother then?

PHILOQUET. (*Carelessly.*) You think so?

BARRIÈRE. (*Repeating peevishly.*) You think so?
(*Getting angry.*) Undoubtedly, and I really think
You have to desert your old Saint-Albon.

PHILOQUET. (*Considering it coldly.*)
If I let you, oh, thread the needle,
You're going to sew life into my whole family;
It's an original talent, worthy of your mind,
To bring the dead to life.
Your generosity just gave me a brother,
Tomorrow, a dear uncle, the next day my mother.
And I'm going to be grateful for your manipulations,
Dancing in the middle of everything like a little monkey.
This brother you're so worried about? What does he matter, after all?
If he's alive, he's still a younger brother.

BARRIÈRE. Eh! Yes, but everything connects,
And you will see, sir, that I am totally right
In plaguing you to reject Saint-Albon.

PHILOQUET. So be it, for the moment, sir, since you think it's useful;
I've become very amenable to betraying my duty.

BARRIÈRE. Duty must be sacrificed to happiness.

PHILOQUET. And which case is that? For fear of forgetting it,
I was waiting until tomorrow to take a look at it.
All work annoys me . . .

But can my decision be changed?
BARRIÈRE. Yes, sir, undoubtedly.
I will so weaken the sense of it in my notes
That no one will be able to understand what the trial's about.
The Selmours are going to come to see you.
PHILOQUET. (*Disturbed.*) Eh! And what will I say to them?
BARRIÈRE. Well, you'll act like you're taking part in their scheme,
Like you're strongly against Mr. Saint-Albon,
Like you're siding with them in everything.
They'll leave happy, and I'll take care of everything else.
(*The flow must be very swift.*)
DUBOIS. (*Starting to shout offstage, running in very quickly.*)
Sir ... Sir ... Sir ... a celestial beauty ...
(*All through the scene he makes several gestures to BARRIÈRE to make him understand that there is money to be had.*)
No, never have we seen anything so perfect.
(*Stressing the following line.*)
She's here to beg a favor.
PHILOQUET. (*Deaf from DUBOIS's shouting.*)
Who? What? Speak, asshole!
DUBOIS. (*To his master.*)
Who? You ... What? Their trial ... two of them I tell you,
But one truly, sir, is a beauty!
The other is a little worse for wear. You could get used to her
Nevertheless; and really if the aunt wanted ...
And since I have the authority to be of help in these things,
I'd make her win her case unanimously.
BARRIÈRE. (*At the same time as PHILOQUET.*)
Speak more clearly!
PHILOQUET. (*At the same time as BARRIÈRE.*)
Will you speak, jerkoff?
DUBOIS. (*Sill making his gestures, and shouting softly.*)
Eh! It's about the Selmours against the Saint-Albons.
To make myself understood then, do I have to shout?
BARRIÈRE. And the niece is pretty?
DUBOIS. Oh! Shit, yes. Pretty
Isn't the word. She is like nothing

That's ever appeared here to win a case.

BARRIÈRE. (*To his master.*) Sir, I have nothing more to say to you now,

Love and money are both going to advise you;

Avoid the details and change the subject.

They're coming. Let's clear out.

(*They leave by the side of the stage opposite to the entrance of the ladies.*)

A LACKEY. (*Announcing.*) Miss Selmours.

(*Enter ATHÉNAÏS, pretending to be Miss Selmours, and VALVILLE in drag, as Madame Selmours, her aunt.*)

ATHÉNAÏS. You see before you two timid litigants,

Cruelly ashamed to trouble you.

But, knowing you, we are not afraid

To put your noble equanimity to the test.

VALVILLE. (*Softening his voice throughout the scene.*)

A person is of service to a judge when he offers him

The good fortune of being just.

PHILOQUET. Alas! It is so rare . . .

And we're so remotely involved in the cases themselves . . .

That a person can only understand them with the greatest difficulty.

(*Looking at himself and his room.*)

Why, I'm really sorry about the mess stacked up around here.

You've made me notice because you're so stacked yourself.

I'm not making excuses . . . you just surprised me!

It's Venus descending to the palace of Justice.

ATHÉNAÏS. (*Looking around the room.*)

A person would think rather she was in the temple of the three Graces.

PHILOQUET. (*To ATHÉNAÏS, staring at her.*)

Only when you're here.

(*To the two women.*) Ladies, please sit down.

(*They sit. PHILOQUET sits next to ATHÉNAÏS. VALVILLE, who was sitting next to ATHÉNAÏS, is forced to get up and find another place to sit.*)

PHILOQUET. (*Continually to ATHÉNAÏS, and very softly.*)

You want to tell me what this is all about?

Out with it! Being unable
To help you immediately just makes me wither away!
ATHÉNAÏS. (*To VALVILLE.*) Aunty, explain our situation to
Mr. Philoquet.
VALVILLE. No, no, you'll speak much better than I, my dear.
ATHÉNAÏS. (*To PHILOQUET, simpering.*)
I am at a loss, but they say you're taking
Such a keen interest in Mr. Saint-Albon.
PHILOQUET. As soon as a person hears a word out of your
mouth,
How can he have any other interests but yours?
Have you ever thought about that?
ATHÉNAÏS. (*As above.*) That's charming ... it makes me blush
. . .

(*Raising her eyes to him, trembling.*)
But the severity of the laws of Justice ...
PHILOQUET. (*Bent toward her and looking at her passionately.*)
Soften when your eyes temper their power.
We put the balance in the hands of beauty;
Venus and her child adjust it in turn,
And for us, Justice is Cupid's daughter.
VALVILLE. Come on now, give him the details, give him the
details, niece.
(*To Mr. PHILOQUET.*) We're taking too much of your time, Sir.
PHILOQUET. Ah! For me, times like these just seem to fly by.
ATHÉNAÏS. I am the daughter, sir, of the Marquis of Selmours;
We don't know why Saint-Albon is disputing
Our inalienable rights to the property in question.
Before he left the country, Valville's father
Was never able to secure them for him.
PHILOQUET. (*A little surprised and hiding his discomfort the best
he can.*)
What? Valville's father left the country?
And where do they say he found protection?
I didn't know that man had gone in for a change of climate.
ATHÉNAÏS. Why, they said he went to England.
PHILOQUET. Did he take Valville with him?
VALVILLE. He left him in the care

Of a good friend, sir, so that no one could intercept
The secret he was so justifiably keeping.
PHILOQUET. And the friend's name is?
ATHÉNAÏS. (*Mincing as above.*) Mr. Saint-Albon.
PHILOQUET. (*Hiding his uneasiness as best he can.*)
You learn something every day! Ah! That's really ridiculous;
Instead of telling me everything, a man pretends, he keeps
secrets.
That's a big mistake already . . . for Mr. Saint-Albon.
Please continue.
ATHÉNAÏS. (*Absently.*) Ah! You're too kind.
(*Stressing the details.*) Now then: when this man left France,
All his property was confiscated . . . as a means of protection . . .
This guy comes along, they say, with an inheritance
Which could not be confiscated by the government.
We know perfectly well that any connection he has to that father
Is only in his imagination.
Since everything was seized, except for that estate,
Will it undoubtedly return to the real heirs?
That seems to us, sir, entirely incontestable.
VALVILLE. Saint-Albon must be an amazing man
To venture to doubt such a fact for a moment.
PHILOQUET. (*To VALVILLE.*) I agree with you, the facts are
conclusive.
VALVILLE. Meanwhile you have to try his case?
PHILOQUET. Whether I like it or not!
I've never been able to get rid of it.
But seeing the facts so clearly today . . .
I'd keep it only with great reluctance.
VALVILLE. Can you quit the case?
PHILOQUET. No, but when you pronounce judgment,
You can glide over certain facts in such a way
As to benefit the opposition.
ATHÉNAÏS. (*Quickly.*) Ah! Sir, will you condescend to be our
friend?
(*She pretends to shed tears.*)
We're very grateful! If you only knew the rest . . .
I'm the one . . . I'm the one who'll settle the case!

PHILOQUET. Good heavens! You're crying? What misfortune
pursues you?
My soul is moved and touched by your sadness.
Ah! I would give my life to dry your tears.
ATHÉNAÏS. (*Crying.*) If he wins, Saint-Albon, generously, but
to my misfortune,
Offers to compensate my father with a merger of the properties
Over which they've been quarreling. This will be accomplished
Through a disastrous marriage, against which my heart rebels.
He plans on giving me to Valville, the heir to his estates,
And money chains me to these unfortunate bonds.
PHILOQUET. You don't love Valville?
ATHÉNAÏS. Ah! God, I hate him
And death would be less distressing in my eyes!
He's jealous, cruel, tyrannical, and suspicious.
PHILOQUET. We'll snatch you away from this dangerous step.
(*Softly and tenderly.*) Will you give me something of value for my
trouble?
ATHÉNAÏS. (*Soft and mincing.*) My best quality is my gratitude.
PHILOQUET. (*As before.*) And your heart is free?
ATHÉNAÏS. (*Speaking with her eyes.*) It certainly is;
But it didn't used to be. Money
Has to direct our lives to such an extent
That there are no ties at all I wouldn't sacrifice . . .
VALVILLE. (*Impatient, and softly.*)
If you don't stop, I'm going to tell him everything.
(*Aloud.*) Niece, you don't have to go into such great detail
For the gentleman about certain things, do you?
(*Softly.*) And about others . . . much less . . .
PHILOQUET. (*To VALVILLE.*) No, no, I can read between the
lines.
(*He goes back to speaking softly in the same way as ATHÉNAÏS to
the end of the scene.*)
If you succeed in your expectations,
Will a fellow be able to conquer your inclinations?
ATHÉNAÏS. (*Still playing passion.*)
When I owe everything to you, could I defend myself
Against the palpitations of a grateful and tender heart?

PHILOQUET. And your father ...
ATHÉNAÏS. (*Like before.*) Very well! If we win,
He'll give me my freedom ... and from there ... we'll see.
(*Very softly.*) But my aunt has to agree to it ...
(*Sadly.*) And I doubt between us, alas, that she'll consent.
VALVILLE. (*Impatiently.*) So, sir, what's your diagnosis of the
case?
PHILOQUET. (*Getting up quickly and throwing himself at
VAVLVILLE's feet.*)
In your hands alone, Madame, rests the success of this case.
Ah! Condescend to grant me your lovely niece
And whatever his expectations may be, Saint-Albon will never
Get a plug nickle out of any of this.
VALVILLE. (*Getting up with as much speed as bewilderment,
stammering.*)
Sir, it's an honor to know you ... but don't do anything
About this affair until tomorrow.
ATHÉNAÏS. (*Rising also to end the interview and covering as best
as she can VALVILLE's distress.*)
All will depend, sir, on the way you handle the case.
Come see us tomorrow and you'll be satisfied.
(*Bowing to him.*) We've taken up enough of your time.
We will not take advantage of your good nature any longer;
For a fellow like you in this business, time is money:
And you ought to regret what you're losing with us
When you know how to use it as well as you do.
(*The women get up. PHILOQUET takes ATHÉNAÏS by the hand
and leads her to the door. She prevents him from going any farther.*)
MR. PHILOQUET. (*Alone.*) She's delicious! And how
interesting!
How each of her glances expressed tenderness!
She loves me ... that's certain ... and I'm crazy about her.
Oh! Mr. Saint-Albon you are making a big mistake
When it's time to plead your case, not having on your side
Such a tight little ass, such creamy skin,
Such roguish eyes, such sex-appeal ...
Or don't hire me as your judge!
Still, the more I think of it, the more I see it's possible

That I have a very obvious brother in that Valville.
It seemed to me, however, that I've always been told
That my father took him along when he left.
When we're in the courtroom, if Valville is my brother,
The old man in the case can't be my father . . .
Certainly, then, they'd be reunited.
Let's consider a worse-case scenario for the moment:
This man we're talking about . . . exiled from France,
Has a strong resemblance to my very dear father,
And if it's the same man, it is more than likely
That Valville is my brother.
Let's make use of that. Then, this contrivance
Of my father, in a word, this terrible injustice
To have left such large estates to this younger brother,
Cries out for revenge. We'll argue it that way for starters.
(*BARRIÈRE, running in.*)
PHILOQUET. (*Enthusiastically.*)
There you are, Barrière. Ah! I am intoxicated.
Work, yes, work for the Selmours very skillfully.
They're right. Love just proved it to me.
BARRIÈRE. (*Looking at him dubiously.*) Conscience?
PHILOQUET. (*Leaving the room.*) Is deaf. Eh! Am I able to
prove it?
Love levels all and its heavenly whisper
Softens the nature in all of us.
BARRIÈRE. (*Alone.*) He's right, really, I agree with him.
It appears to me that today, at last, everything is cleared up.
The matter is no longer in question, we're home free.
Good, the stronger the obstacle the brighter my talent shines.
I answer to him for everything, if he follows my instructions . . .
Besides . . . I can cleverly profit from the confusion.
His daily expenditures amount to six hundred pistoles[31] . . .
And my earnings . . . six hundred . . .
Why, to pledge their good faith,
His creditors handed me a bill to the bearer;
(*He looks at it.*) Good luck in the end serves me well.
I get back all the money my master spends . . .

---

[31] A pistole is a unit of currency worth about 8 US dollars. Six hundred would be equivalent to
$4,800.

Seeing me, prudently, make the most out of nothing,
Will shock no one. Today everybody knows
The property the father was manipulating
Has more than one son involved!

END OF ACT THREE

ACT FOUR

(*The setting is at the home of SAINT-ALBON for the remainder of the play. The OLD MAN, going by the name of LISIMON, is onstage with SAINT-ALBON.*)

SAINT-ALBON. Don't concern yourself with those under-handed dealings,
Heaven is just, my friend. At least it soothes
The horror of your misfortunes as it reunites us.
(*The two friends embrace.*)
LISIMON. Philoquet is capable of a great deal . . .
And I'm frightened of his influence;
The appropriation he's going to make
In the case legitimately concerns me.
My friend, he can only take advantage of me,
And since authority supports a wicked heart,
Vice is in the ascendancy and innocence is in chains.
SAINT-ALBON. Be that as it may, take refuge in my house.
Here you'll be cared for by your beloved Valville,
His heart will not betray you.
He's a young man for whom I have great esteem.
But now, my friend, continue telling me about the "big secret"
Which made you conceal the fact that Valville had a brother.
LISIMON. In my best judgment, Saint-Albon,
My old heart was concerned only
About the trial and the money for my sons.
The property I concealed was considerable;
Fearing that they were attachable along with my goods,
I thought I'd be able to hide the property and the children
With the same care. I scattered all the evidence.
In addition, very wisely perhaps, I wanted
The children never to recognize one another.
In this way, each one played his part without having to fear
The disastrous outcome of the trial.
Then, when I brought Valville here to you
I told you the eldest son was dead.
Only Dubourg, my brother, knew the real facts.

He helped me up to the day he died.
Back to what I was saying:
What an effect your absence had on me.
For a long time, the word was you were out of France.
SAINT-ALBON. We were travelling at the time ...
LISIMON. I had no other way
Of becoming acquainted with the heart of my eldest son
Whose horrible behavior was completely obvious
Than to hide my identity as his father.
SAINT-ALBON. Shouldn't he have recognized that the plaintiff
Was the single author of his good fortune?
How, then, did you appear before him?
If you were no longer in control of the situation
Through the office of father or sole heir,
How were you able to get his attention?
LISIMON. I went to see him as if he were the kind of judge
People go to for their final appeals.
Dubourg had stressed the necessity
Of concealing name and rank forever,
And since Dubourg was dead, no one was able to discern
Where the property he was keeping for me, came from.
That uncle, who so liked Philoquet, made out a false will
In favor of a cousin, a distant relative
Someone dug up on the banks of the Gascogne ...
He was informed of everything and only had to lend us
His name if he wanted to make a case.
Then Philoquet would get everything with nothing to fear.
Then as I said, I didn't want to be recognized,
As much for him as for myself, since I created the interest
In reinvestigating Dubourg's estates;
But now the Gascon's suing and getting his day in court.
And there's Philoquet!
He and his secretary have no greater delight
Than entangling all the threads of the case.
And there I was with my sacred rights, dying of hunger,
And no one wanted to see it all cleared up.
Perhaps somebody bribed him?

SAINT-ALBON. Ah! It all should have taught him a lesson!
The mere voice of a father has so much control over us,
It's a secret spell that entraps us so well
That the impulse to fight it is useless.
Come on, I don't want to keep you any longer
From the pleasure of embracing your son.
That pure heart, trained in virtue since childhood,
Is going to make up for the tears you've shed.
He doesn't know who you are.
You can surprise him and enjoy his reaction . . .
But first of all, let me take care
Of an important matter before I forget.
(*SAINT-ALBON rings, a lackey enters.*)
SAINT-ALBON. (*To the lackey.*)
Someone is going to arrive looking for Athénaïs
Under the name of Selmours, La Brie. Please take the trouble
To tell all of my selvants that today,
Instead of Saint-Albon, Selmours is the name of the household.
(*To LISIMON.*) Tell my son to come in. Excuse me, I'm giving
him, you see,
A name, to which he will have all rights,
Without any reservations, until the end of time.
LISIMON. My friend, that reinforces my own tender attachment to him.
SAINT-ALBON. (*To VALVILLE who appears in man's clothes.*)
Valville, allow me to leave with you the gentleman here.
You know the distress that weighs upon me today.
Please show him, for a moment, the hospitality of our home;
I'm only leaving to work on your behalf.
LISIMON. Saint-Albon loves you dearly; he adores you as a
father.
VALVILLE. Ah! The feeling is mutual. I love him, I respect him
. . .
LISIMON. I've been told he's giving you his daughter.
VALVILLE. Yes, if our case is successful.
LISIMON. What, if you lose, you're no longer his son-in-law?
Is he that concerned with money?
VALVILLE. Oh! No, sir, no, no, don't be suspicious

Of the most loyal heart one could imagine.
But, in losing my case, I wouldn't have any money.
Can I make his lovely daughter
Share in my humiliation?
LISIMON. (*Moved.*) Ah! Ah! I understand;
And I certainly applaud such sentiments.
If the case is lost beyond hope
There you are, alas, reduced to poverty!
VALVILLE. (*Nobly.*) The greatest poverty, Sir.
LISIMON. And will you endure it?
Will you know how to sustain such terrible distress?
Misfortune is an awful test for a man.
Now and then, in prosperity, the soul is incorruptible,
Virtue can defend itself against the shallows of deceit;
But it withers in the midst of misfortune.
VALVILLE. (*Full of pride and nobility.*)
No, no, when a soul is strong and courageous,
It's the same even in the middle of a storm;
And in time, its strength and peace
Conquer the inflexibility of fate.
LISIMON. Ah! How noble your soul is . . . for such a young
man
To muster such spirit and refinement . . .
So what are you planning to do
If your case turns out badly? I'm interested.
VALVILLE. I'll seek honor in the fields of glory forever . . .
That is, if I can banish from my memory
My mistress, friendship, and happiness.
LISIMON. How, without any money?
VALVILLE. Since I'm anticipating such profound bad luck
In whatever money the trial leaves me,
I've put some money aside, you see, sir, in a strong box.
LISIMON. (*In a frank and friendly manner.*)
And the strong box is very full?
VALVILLE. Oh, yes, I've got a hundred Louis.[32]
But don't say anything about it.
With that money, I'll defy misfortune,
I'll imitate the fate of my poor father.

[32] A Louis d'or is a French monetary unit worth 24 livres, or $120.00 in US currency.

LISIMON. Then your father was . . . is he unhappy?

VALVILLE. Ah! Undoubtedly he was and his misfortunes were terrifying;

He was a victim of jealousy and slander his whole life.

LISIMON. Do they believe that his very troubled destiny has been fulfilled?

VALVILLE. We think so, sir. Saint-Albon believes he's dead.

LISIMON. (*In the greatest contained ecstacy, and grabbing his son's hand.*)

Dear Valville, they're all lying to you. He loves you, he's alive.

VALVILLE. (*With the greatest agitation.*)

Oh Heavens! Please tell me where he lives.

I'll be ever in your service . . . no, I'll be ever in your debt

If you'll lead me to where I can embrace him.

LISIMON. What you desire is not yet possible;

Know merely that he is alive, and that he loves you.

VALVILLE. (*Quickly with concern.*)

Then his misfortunes continue, so that he must stay away!

Isn't fate tired of persecuting him?

LISIMON. No, since he is still on the coast of England.

(*Looking at him.*) And what's worse, Valville . . . he's in trouble.

VALVILLE. (*Agitated.*) God! What are you telling me? He didn't know

That I had any money? Take me to him.

I want to go help him if he's in distress.

Ah! Don't prevent me from being useful to my father.

(*Taking Lisimon's two hands with the most shameless rapture, and holding them.*)

Sir, don't leave. I'll be back in a minute.

LISIMON. (*Alone.*)Where is he going? Good Lord, I've escaped my boundaries,

I'm no longer in control of myself. God, by your power,

Were you able to put so much of a difference between my two sons?

I must continue the disguise a moment longer.

VALVILLE. (*Enters, with a purse in hand which he gives to LISIMON; he is winded, scarcely able to talk; he speaks with the greatest speed and energy.*)

You will see to it, sir, that my father gets this.
(*At LISIMON's refusal.*)
Ah! It's all that I have. No, no, I'm giving it to you.
Who knows . . . good Lord, who knows
If maybe it's exactly the amount of money he needs.
And yet, I still want to hold on to it a single moment longer!
That would be opposed to the beloved laws of nature.
Damn him who resists their sacred bonds,
Damn him who can imagine a pleasure
Greater than the one I'm about to enjoy!
LISIMON. (*Abandoning all restraint.*)
There is one greater . . . you're about to know it;
I am unable to hide myself any longer.
Valville, embrace your father; he is in your arms.
VALVILLE. (*Enraptured.*) Ah! the voice of my heart did not
deceive me.
LISIMON. I can hardly endure so tender a moment.
Oh! What a virtuous son fate has just given me!
VALVILLE. Saint-Albon knows all about this?
LISIMON. Yes.
VALVILLE. What a kind heart he has.
Always looking out for my happiness!
LISIMON. I must go find him. I have to leave.
VALVILLE. Eh! Why, father, why must we separate so quickly?
I'll follow you everywhere, nothing will prevent me.
Nothing, no nothing can ever tear me away from your arms.
(*They go out arm in arm.*)

END OF ACT FOUR

ACT FIVE

VALVILLE. (*Eagerly.*) Athénaïs, at last I've found my father!
My happiness is so great that I can't keep quiet about it.
Come and share my incredible ecstasy!
ATHÉNAÏS. Is it indeed true, Valville? Oh! God what good
fortune!
Between the two of us, alas, the happiness of your life
Will begin to grow from now on, without trouble or jealousy.
We'll hope for that at least, if that monster in his rage
Doesn't destroy us with all of his foul deeds.
VALVILLE. Clear up this mystery for me.
You meant what you said about me to Mr. Philoquet, didn't you?
I can see through these nice little tricks of yours.
ATHÉNAÏS. When you're happy you always pick on me.
VALVILLE. Happy, yes I am, but perhaps only for the moment.
ATHÉNAÏS. Why?
VALVILLE. (*Sighing.*) Ah! They're passing judgment on us,
And we're going to discover
Our unhappy state.
ATHÉNAÏS. Why must it be unhappy?
VALVILLE. It's what I always fear.
ATHÉNAÏS. And if untimely fate
Gives this affair a sad turn?
VALVILLE. I would undoubtedly leave.
ATHÉNAÏS. (*Galled.*) Ah! That reassures me;
That's some love!
VALVILLE. Eh! What? Would you like that?
ATHÉNAÏS. Yes, I would like for you to finally understand me,
For you not to act so foolishly weak anymore . . .
(*Throwing off all restraint.*) To want to test the heart of your
mistress!
And between offering me the pleasure of being dependent on
you,
Or the enjoyment of seeing you in complete possession of me,
You didn't always happen to provide me with the hope
Of a plan for doing away with your quick temper.

No you don't love me!

VALVILLE. How can you think that,

When, inside me, there is not the power to express,

To describe, Athénaïs, the full extent of my passion!

Ah! I hope that one day you'll understand my soul.

In hearing nothing but happiness here

Could I lead you by the hand into my misfortune?

Remorse . . .

ATHÉNAÏS. (*Cutting him off quickly because she sees PHILOQUET.*)

God! I see that shameless monster,

I have to calm myself to endure his horrible presence.

Everything is going to work out. Don't desert me.

(*PHILOQUET enters wearing black, believing he is at the home of the SELMOURS.*)

PHILOQUET. (*Still thinking he's speaking with Miss SELMOURS.*)

I hastened, miss, as soon as I could

To free your mind from fear and embarrassment,

To prove to you my respect, my love, and my passion.

With the report I'm drawing up, it's next to impossible

For Saint-Albon to get all the money.

I've weakened the grounds that he objects to so well,

That without any delay, he's going to lose his case unanimously,

And success is guaranteed for Mr. Selmours.

(*Softly and tenderly to ATHÉNAÏS.*)

Will you condescend, alas, to always bear in mind,

Or at least allow me to flatter my memory

With the delicious prize you offered for the victory?

ATHÉNAÏS. (*Returning to the character she played in Act Three.*)

Certainly you have not counted on me in vain,

As it was agreed, sir, you will be repaid;

I will not be ungrateful to your heavenly services,

You have, I feel, made great sacrifices;

Integrity, honor . . .

PHILOQUET. Only myths;

People don't pay much attention to those trifles.

All the hidden bonds that use to captivate men

Are powerless today; in this day and age,
Integrity consists in helping your friends.
A person must reserve his intelligence for that alone.
Everyone has a right to be a victim:
It's well known, and what does it matter
Since calamity has to fall on someone!
And, considering people in general,
The choice in the eyes of fate would be perfectly even;
What does it matter . . . then, say, whether it's Peter or Paul
Who experiences the wrath of God.
That it's immaterial is so true, so accepted
That to question it now would be laughable.
Now, I'm just asking if, under the circumstances,
A person is wrong in trying to stack the odds
In favor of the people he wants to work for?
What about integrity? You've got to get rid of it.
We aren't living like our ancestors anymore.
We must be masters of their opinions,
And philosophy has the right to rule them.
ATHÉNAÏS. You're a philosopher?
PHILOQUET. Yes, I love to judge people,
To infect them with my morals and ideas;
I love to see them guided by some real principles!
And I detest superstition to such a point
That I would rather close my eyes to the evidence,
Which I believe in a great deal . . . than risk accepting
A deadly prejudice that I'd have to depend on.
If you want, I'll woo you . . .
I'll focus your attention on some infallible theories.
The adorable Selmours will be my Aspasia,[33]
I'll be her Socrates.
ATHÉNAÏS. Ah! Thank you
But to continually add to what I owe you,
To constantly double the weight of your goodness, sir . . .
It's really putting me in an awkward position.
How will I ever repay you?
PHILOQUET. God, you know the prize I expect,

---

[33] Aspasia was a Milesian woman involved with the Athenian statesman Pericles, and famous for her intelligence and wit.

Can't a person see you for a few minutes without a witness?
(*Leering at VALVILLE.*)
Who is this young man? Just looking at him, he seems ...
I'm not mistaken ... eh! yes. He looks like
Your aunt. Oh! No. Damn me, the resemblance is striking.
VALVILLE. (*Brusquely.*) Eh! I expect so since I'm her nephew.
PHILOQUET. (*Embarrassed but still looking at him.*) The aunt's
nephew.
VALVILLE. (*As above.*) Eh! Of course, the aunt's.
PHILOQUET. (*To ATHÉNAÏS.*) He seems to have a rebellious
nature.
ATHÉNAÏS. I'd like to give him to you to mould a little.
PHILOQUET. All right, I'll mould the nephew with pleasure.
VALVILLE. That's not a very reliable commitment.
PHILOQUET. But tell him, first of all,
To have a little respect for his elders,
And to go away when he clearly sees
His presence can only be offensive or annoying.
ATHÉNAÏS. It's because he's stubborn!
PHILOQUET. Must it be as I anticipated?
Then he's really going to pay for his foolishness,
For as the child of Mars as well as Justice,
I neither fear nor tolerate my enemies.
You'd better stop me from going too far ...
It's in your best interest.
ATHÉNAÏS. (*Frightened.*) Sir, don't behave so unreasonably.
VALVILLE. (*Coldly.*) Let him, let him do whatever he wants,
he's not dangerous.
(*Enter SAINT-ALBON, LISIMON, A POLICEMAN, and
BAILIFFS.*)
SAINT-ALBON. (*Quickly to VALVILLE.*)
Finally, my good friend, we can both be happy.
The swindler has been exposed. Lone justice shines ...
Your rights have been acknowledged.
PHILOQUET. (*Confused and at a loss.*) But at least I expected ...
SAINT-ALBON. (*Indicating the policeman.*)
Yes, in a moment, the officer, here, is going to tell you all about it.
PHILOQUET. A policeman, bailiffs, what does this all mean?

SAINT-ALBON. That it's finally time for the crime to be punished.

You're the first victim of your own circuitous justice.

POLICEMAN. Hear your fate: the court deprives you of your civil rights.

SAINT-ALBON. The world knows about your heinous crimes.

You had poorly understood your respectable duty,

Very poorly carried out, sir, the incorruptible post

To which you had been appointed.

Happily, the office has not been entirely ruined by you.

No: you were endowed with a soul too vulgar

To have contaminated its sacred character.

If human laws make up the public safety,

If their observance is the seal of the society,

The heart of a judge their holy trustee,

Then those very laws become the sanctuary of all virtue.

Many happy examples shine everywhere,

Imitate their great qualities, exposed before our very eyes.

(*Indicating LISIMON.*)

You know your crimes . . . this worthy old man

Who was only a despicable being in your eyes

Either because of foolish pride, or because hearts

Hardened to misery by corruption

Have no longer a clear sense of their function . . .

This wise man, in short, sir, is your father.

Valville is your brother and it's Saint-Albon,

And not Selmours who owns this house.

Now, get out.

VALVILLE. (*To SAINT-ALBON and making a tender move toward PHILOQUET, immediately repelled by him.*)

Who, him, sir? He's my brother?

PHILOQUET. Oh, nature!

Yes, I felt your voice, perhaps not very securely,

Since my heart doesn't speak to me about things like that,

Your judgment was delivered in too grand a style.

The goddess of Justice whom you quote will fashion my defense,

(*To everyone while going off with the policeman.*)

And I'm going to call down her power against you!

I expect she'll provide me with a refuge
Against the disgusting traps being laid for me here.
SAINT-ALBON. (*Angrily following PHILOQUET.*)
Ah! Get out, vile wretch, and go be an example
To those who, like you, dishonor her temple!
He was callous to the very end. (*LISIMON enters and speaks.*)
LISIMON. What have I heard, my friend? God, what an
ending!
SAINT-ALBON. (*Indicating VALVILLE. LISIMON is
unhappy.*)
May this happy child console your old age;
I join him to my daughter and their lively affection
Will set aside misfortune in the winter of our years.
(*He joins them together.*)
Ah! Live for one another, my beloved children!
ATHÉNAÏS. (*With nobility.*) But we must delay the wedding,
father,
So I can repair some knots on a father's chain!
(*LISIMON makes a tender gesture thanking ATHÉNAÏS.*)
LISIMON. (*With feeling.*)
As for me, I'm going to give Philoquet my support and advice.
Even though he's a criminal, he's still my son.
SAINT-ALBON. (*Very quickly.*)
Ah! Is a person supposed to excuse these fiends and help them,
Or feel sorry for them and protect their evil ways?
The time has come to be happy, Frenchmen.
You have driven away so much horrible abuse . . .
And in the end, justice, pure like the heavens,
And her laws reflecting divine virtue,
Both paid their respects to you.

END OF THE FIFTH AND FINAL ACT

Jeanne Laisné
or
The Siege of Beauvais

Introduction

The Marquis de Sade wrote *Jeanne Laisné*,[34] his only tragedy, in 1783 at Vincennes Prison, nearly a year after he completed the manuscript of his *Dialogue between a Priest and a Dying Man*, and a year before he was transferred to the Bastille. He first discusses the play in a letter to his wife on 26 March 1783 and indicates that his one act comedy, *The Bedroom*, was written as a companion piece. In Sade's *Descriptive Catalogue of 1788*, the play is mentioned with the note: "This is the piece of history when the women defending the city of Beauvais, during the reign of Louis XI, made Charles the Bold, Duke of Burgundy, raise the siege." A note dated 1813 on the manuscript reveals that the Marquis received permission to recite the tragedy to members of the staff of the Bastille in 1787 during his incarceration at that fortress, and that a first reading of the play took place at the home of the Governor's mistress, in the presence of the actors Saint-Prix and Saint-Fal.

It was through the efforts of Saint-Prix and Saint-Fal, along with those of Mademoiselle Raucourt, the actress, that the Marquis gave a reading of the play to the Committee of the Théâtre Français on 24 November 1791, a month after his *Count Oxtiern* was produced at the Théâtre Molière, and five months after his notorious novel, *Justine, or the Misfortunes of Virtue* had been published.

---

[34] Sade's play was inspired by *Siège de Calais* (1765) by Dormont de Belloy (Pierre Laurent Buirette), and *Siège de Beauvais, ou Jeanne Laisné* (1766) by Jean-Louis Araignon.

Unfortunately, the Committee rejected the play by a vote of eight to five, and three of the five who voted in favor of the play wanted significant changes made to the text. Writing a hundred years later, Apollinaire suggested that the play was turned down because King Louis XI was a heroic figure. His point is well taken. In 1791, a heroic king named Louis was an unwelcome figure on the French stage!

On 21 July 1798 the Marquis de Sade sent an open letter to the *Journal of Paris* in which he claimed to be the first to discover that the heroine of the siege of Beauvais was Jeanne Laisné not a woman named Jeanne Hachette, and cited letters patent of Louis XI as irrefutable proof. On 1 October, the following year, Sade sent a very long letter to Goupilleau de Montaigu to prevail upon him to use his influence as deputy of the Republic to insist that the Théâtre Français produce *Jeanne Laisné*, a play guaranteed to stir up patriotism:

> In a word, citizen deputy, as the first of my offerings, I propose to you a tragedy in five acts, a work most capable of exciting the love for the fatherland in every heart; and you will agree that it is at the theatre rather than somewhere else that we must revive the almost extinguished flame of the love that every Frenchman owes his country; there is where he will be convinced of the dangers that would exist for him should he fall back into the hands of tyranny. He will carry home the enthusiasm and teach it to his family, and its effects will be so much more durable, so much more passionate than the momentary inspirations of a newspaper article or proclamation because at the theatre, he learns the lesson by example, and he remembers it.

The failure of the Marquis's impassioned plea inaugurated another period of misfortune for Sade. His financial problems were aggravated by the refusal of his elder son to provide him with money. His eyesight deteriorated to such a point that he could no longer see to write and was forced to spend three months of the winter accepting charity at the Versailles Infirmary. Otherwise he would have, as Sade wrote, "died at a street corner." In a letter to his lawyer dated 26 January 1800, he describes his unfortunate condition:

Dying of cold and hunger in the public infirmary of Versailles for the past three months. It is Sunday today. When you went to mass I hope you at least asked God to forgive you for lacerating me, slicing me up, and torturing me as you have been doing these three years now.

By April, the Marquis de Sade had left the infirmary. The remainder of the year saw the publication of his play *Oxtiern* and his collection of stories called *The Crimes of Love*. On 5 April 1801, as a result of the furor surrounding his latest work, Sade was once again imprisoned, this time for the rest of his life.

Jeanne Laisné laid dormant for several years until 1813 when Sade again attempted to secure a production at the Théâtre Français. He argued that the theatre had accepted the play in 1791, subject to certain alterations. Having completed the changes, he felt confident in submitting the play a second time. The final refusal, which ultimately arrived in Sade's hands in February 1814, had little good to say about the play. The reader's report sarcastically questioned the Marquis's manipulation of historical fact and cited the mayor's behavior as highly improbable. It also suggested that the theatrical effects called for at the end of the fourth act were the province of melodrama, not of tragedy, and coyly advised that the play would be better served written in prose and produced at the Ambigu (a theatre devoted to melodramatic spectacles). Finally, the report quibbled over the poetic text and argued that much of the dialogue was not even good prose.

Though a long prose essay appended to the manuscript dealt with most of the objections to the play, the Marquis de Sade, now in his seventy-third year, did not pursue the matter further. Instead, he readied the manuscripts of *Adelaide of Brunswick* and *Isabelle of Bavière* for publication and gradually began to exhibit signs of weakness. By 1 December 1814, he had completely lost the use of his legs, and the following day he died of "pulmonary congestion." His will, made at Charenton on 30 January 1806, expressly forbade a Christian burial and ended with these words:

Once the grave has been filled, it shall be sown over with acorns so that all traces of my tomb may disappear from the face of the earth, as I expect my memory will be wiped away from the minds of men, except those few whose affection for me has continued to the last, and of whom I take a pleasant memory to the grave.

JEANNE LAISNÉ
or
THE SIEGE OF BEAUVAIS

Verse Tragedy in Five Acts

> Let us carefully note these various
> Examples, and one day, let them prove
> To the eyes of the world,
> How fidelity, glory, and bravery
> Were at all times the virtues of France.
> *Jeanne Laisné*, V

CHARACTERS

Matthew Laisné, *the mayor of Beauvais*
Jeanne Laisné, *the mayor's daughter*
Loiset de Ballagny, *chief military officer of Beauvais, and commander of the garrison*
Chimai, *spy for Charles the Bold, Duke of Burgundy, in charge of a secret mission*
Old de Pile, *an elder of Beauvais and head of the town council*
Young de Pile, *Old de Pile's son, in love with Jeanne*
Torcis, *a gentleman from a neighboring town, hurled into the public square at the time of the siege*
Morel, Vilpreux, Saint-Yon, *head conspirators and friends of the mayor*
Coucy, Champlit, Dautrey, *spies for the Duke of Burgundy, but disguised as Royalists*
Emily de Pile, *Jeanne Laisné's friend, old de Pile's daughter*
Lord Chabanne

Count of Dammartin, *general of the French army camped outside of Beauvais*

Laval, Maillé, *Young French officers in Chabanne's army*

Citizens of Beauvais

Soldiers of the garrison

Detachments from Chabanne's army

A group of officers

Squires

(*The action takes place at Beauvais.*)

ACT ONE

(*The entire play is set in a very large public square, surrounded by Gothic stockades. At the rear of the stage is the Town Hall whose courtyard is marked by twisted gothic columns. To the right, a street leads to the battlements; this is where all of the commotion occurs since it is the side threatened with attack. To the left is the Bresle Gate, one of several entrances to the city. That side will be designated as the Bresle side throughout the play. The action begins in the middle of the night of 8/9 July 1472. Everything is calm and the stage is in darkness. Only by the fourth scene of Act One does it begin to get brighter; the change in illumination should be virtually imperceptible to the audience. Various guardsmen leave from the interior of the city to take their positions on the battlements. COUCY, CHAMPLIT, DAUTREY enter, arriving from the Bresle side and wandering in the shadows.*)

COUCY. (*In a low voice.*)
Let's stop a moment, friends, for too much boldness
Could betray the triumph of our plans.
With its thick veil, the dark and tranquil night
Has masked our footsteps from the city guards.
Give thanks to destiny for the success
Our plans have found against all probability.
Champlet and Dautrey, both of you go wait for me
At the bottom of the battlements;
I'll meet up with you there to steal again
To the camp where Charles, filled with suspense,
Desire, fear, and hope, stands counting the minutes.
(*He motions for the two fighting men to leave.*)

CHIMAI. (*Coming from the courtyard opposite the direction in which COUCY is walking. COUCY stops as soon as he hears a voice.*)
Before the torch of the divinity
Who guides us
Hurls its brilliant flames all over the world,
Laisné intends to meet me here in private
To talk about the consequences of
The plan. I'll wait . . .

COUCY. (*Having stopped walking, listening.*) Who's talking?

CHIMAI. (*A little emotional.*) On these premises, some old man
. . .

COUCY. (*Quickly approaching CHIMAI.*)
I know the voice that's knocking on my ears . . .
It's he, no doubt about it. Oh, Chimai,
It's Coucy. Calm yourself; embrace your friend.

CHIMAI. Is that you, Coucy? Heavens! Why this strange behavior
Within enemy walls? Speak up. What are you
Doing here? Has Charles renounced his plans?
Is he concerned about the quantity
Of men he needs to be successful?
Does he doubt my ability?

COUCY. Ah, you know how he is!
No matter what the plan, his fiery heart
Wants to be convinced immediately
Of its success. He fears that in Beauvais
Someone might have resisted your desires.
He who wants to serve the state must be
A miracle worker!

CHIMAI. Yes, I will succeed, you can both be sure,
And tell him I'm expecting him tonight
Within these walls!

COUCY. Excuse my asking, but the duke's impatient . . .
Chimai, why were we able to get into
Beauvais tonight, with no resistance?
The courage of these tired folk is weakening,
That's evident.

CHIMAI. Make no mistake about it:
Nothing can match their wisdom or their strength.
Perhaps, cast down by such great enterprises,
Their soldiers, without fear, enjoyed a little rest.
What in the world were you expecting, at
Such a propitious time like this?

COUCY. If fortune foretold success so easily
The task of war would be like planting flowers!
That Charles would love, impatient as he is.

CHIMAI. (*Taking him aside.*)
Coucy, the mayor should be here in a moment,
Then you can carry back a real response
To our master ... perhaps one that will calm
A bit that temper that's too full of fire.
While waiting, my old friend, let's think about
The serious undertaking that brings us
Again together.
(*They come forward, completely onstage.*)
Night favors us and we can, dear Coucy,
Converse here without the slightest danger.
Has Charles remarked how, at the heart of the storm,
These overburdened people still keep their courage?
These brave inhabitants, these burghers and soldiers ...
Does he see how passionately they greet death?
Tomorrow they will meet certain defeat
But today they arm themselves for victory.
The spirit of the French is always steadfast!
As long as he serves his prince, he fights
And dies content.
And in the meantime, friend, these civil wars
Devour his land and cover it with ruins.
COUCY. Terrible afflictions certainly!
Such woes with which the evils of the day
Perpetuate themselves!
If, on the field of Mars, war seems attractive,
In its own backyard, it only causes tears!
CHIMAI. When John was facing defeat in the fields
Of Poitiers,[35]
He needed a worthy son, a brave warrior ...
In short, Philip, the only hope of France,
To revive the passion and bravery of old.
When he rewarded the precocious exploits
Of his younger son, by giving him
The glittering endowment of Burgundy,
Friend, would he had foreseen what vile crimes
Were to follow that disastrous gift!

---

[35] King John II of France was captured at the Battle of Poitiers, fought between France and England on 19 September 1356.

Everything is due to Maupertuis[36]
And that fatal string of wars, misfortune,
Murder and hatred ... revolutions which
Because of idle claims put a Lancaster
On the throne of the Valois. My friend,
I tell you, all of this brings Frenchmen back
To that unlucky time ... that dreadful loss.
There's where their spirit, crying for their heroes
Departed from the bosom of their flags.
COUCY. But Charles VII at least redeemed so many wrongs ...
If Louis XI, in a word, if Louis is as wise
Or less ambitious ...
CHIMAI. Say less false, less crafty,
Less apt to enjoy the idle pleasures
Of crushing his vassals.
No sooner had he been crowned in Paris
Than his dishonesty compelled them all
To get out of his way ...
And those who were honored by his father
Spend their days begging for alms while he rules.
Charles thought himself secure because of promises,
But Louis, still deceitful, lied to him
And gave refuge to that fiery Warwick[37]
Who, three times in a row, rendered the kings
Victorious and criminal.
No guarantees, nothing in writing, friend,
No promises restrain that autocrat.
And so, as a result, he severs ties,
Breaks faith, hurts feelings, offends relatives,
And betrays human dignity with his
Vulgarity in word and deed.
With nothing left to try but force of arms,
Charles seeks to compel the renegade
To respect his oaths more honestly,
To observe those checks and balances
Obediently maintained by all great kings.

---

[36] In the manuscript, Sade noted that Maupertuis was the true name of the Battle of Poitiers in 1356.
[37] Richard Neville, 16th Earl of Warwick (22 November 1428 – 14 April 1471), known as "Warwick the kingmaker."

To reach this end, you see, our noble lord
Has just scattered the lilies on the banks
Of the Somme. He's marching toward the Seine,
And according to his plans, he'll attack
Paris as soon as he has taken Beauvais.
(*Looking at the city.*)
Surprised . . . confused that such a feeble place
Should still oppose his army with such force,
He sought to know if its fidelity
Was comparable to its temerity.
The most important issue, first of all,
Was simply making certain of the mayor;
You know that I've been working secretly
For some time now, to settle that important
Business.
(*Taking COUCY aside; mysteriously.*)
His vanity has finally won the day . . .
I'm working for this most ambitious man,
And marrying his daughter!
COUCY. Oh, heavens! What a sacrifice!
What! Chimai, are those ties worthy of you?
CHIMAI. Is it just a matter of debasing
Myself than raising her to my own level?
If you could see the beauty that inspires me,
Coucy, if you could know the dignity
In that noble heart; if you could hear
Her open up her soul in conversation . . .
If you could see her captivating eyes
Fastened on your own. Yet, more than anything,
It is her courage that impresses me.
I think she's Venus, but disguised as Mars.
Still unaware of what her father plans,
Looking noble, yesterday she said,
"Ah, if I feared that Beauvais could be taken,
My friends and I will just have to defend it.
I know them, father, and I guarantee
That they would all die to avenge their country."
From her eyes, then, suddenly a flame

Emerged, surrounding her entire soul,
Engraving upon it with its fire,
My friend, the features of courage and love.
I can see that Laisné is approaching;
His problems are frightening to him.
Ah! How often, dear Coucy, do we find
In a scoundrel's heart the duty that betrays
A soldier!
(*MATTHEW LAISNÉ enters. The three actors in this scene must
modulate their voices in deference to the critical situation in which
they find themselves; they speak softly for fear of being overheard.*)
MATTHEW LAISNÉ. (*Quickly to CHIMAI, without seeing
COUCY.*)
I ply my steps here with terror, Chimai.
We've been discovered. God, I'm paralyzed
With fear. Yet, there's no evidence. I doubt
They know the real reason that brings us here.
(*Becoming nervous.*) Who is that soldier? Where does he come
from?
CHIMAI. It's Coucy . . . he's on our side. There's not
A single detail we should keep from him.
Our nervous prince has dispatched him to us
To learn if he can trust you after all.
What shall he reply?
MATTHEW LAISNÉ. (*Quickly.*) Let him tell Charles
That in spite of all our circumspection,
Someone has discovered all our plans.
No matter. Let him come ahead. When he appears,
Immediately, the city will surrender
To his colors.
CHIMAI. You hear him, Coucy. Accept his fealty.
MATTHEW LAISNÉ. (*Putting his hand in COUCY's.*)
Yes, I will serve you. Here, I pledge my faith.
Accept it, my lord, and don't be concerned.
Through my efforts, you have friends in Beauvais.
COUCY. (*Eagerly.*) I'm going to tell all of this to the duke.
(*Pointing to MATTHEW.*) He'll be glad to know that he's still on
Our side.

The troops will be here in about an hour.
MATTHEW LAISNÉ. (*To COUCY.*)
Prevent this attack, if you can, Coucy.
Our battlements are all prepared for Charles's
Arrival. The city is open to you.
I've sworn . . . I've promised to hand over all
Our goods to you; don't bathe them in the blood
Of our inhabitants. And I implore you,
Above all, call upon the duke to wear
The colors and the armor of the French.
COUCY. I willingly consent, if the duke agrees.
MATTHEW LAISNÉ. (*Very rapidly.*)
Those trifles will spare us the loss of blood.
Our citizens deceived by the likeness
Will offer no resistance to your men.
CHIMAI. Still, cautiously, I add another word:
Should he be deceiving us, the city
Will answer for it immediately.
MATTHEW LAISNÉ. Don't worry about anything; you have
My word. My heart is only interested
In your success. Trust in my words, not idle
Gossip. Why would I betray you now?
Wouldn't I live to regret it?
CHIMAI. (*To COUCY, quickly.*) My friend, go find Charles . . .
COUCY. Ah! With pleasure. (*COUCY exits by the Bresle Gate.*)
MATTHEW LAISNÉ. (*Having heard a noise coming from the
side opposite where COUCY is exiting, he goes to see what it is. The
day begins to dawn. He returns to CHIMAI.*)
It's some of our citizens, sent to meet you.
Allay the suspicions they have about us.
CHIMAI. Yes, I'll try to dispel all of them.
MATTHEW LAISNÉ. It would be dangerous if someone
thought
That I was guilty.
CHIMAI. (*Looking at the crowd coming forward.*)
Who is that old man
In the middle of them?
MATTHEW LAISNÉ. It's de Pile,

One of the councilmen, attended by his son.
Méru, Rohant, Saint-Yon and young Torcis;
Morel, one of our men, a kind and faithful
Friend; then a few officers and merchants
From the city. There's the one who's most suspicious:
Loiset de Ballagny, commander of
The garrison.
(*Enter OLD DE PILE, YOUNG DE PILE, LOISET DE
BALLAGNY, TORCIS, A group of Merchants, among whom is
MOREL, the governor's escort, a troupe of officers and soldiers.*)
LOISET DE BALLAGNY. (*To CHIMAI, boldly.*)
My lord, we have a right to be surprised
By your presence in our city.
Upon arriving here, immediately
You should have had an audience with the council.
CHIMAI. (*Boldly.*) I thought that I could free myself of that
Rightly believing that a man like me
Should be excused from ordinary rules,
Especially when he carries in his hands
Either war, or something far more pleasing
To Beauvais: the end of all our troubles
And the olive branch of peace. Rather
Than placing a time limit on our conquests,
Dread the misfortunes hovering over your heads.
Attacked, with no sign of relief, defeated
On all sides, ready to be interred
Beneath your war-torn battlements,
How do you intend to stop the victory
Of a prince, successful on all sides,
Crowned in glory everywhere?
Rather, you should fear that the conqueror
Of the fields of Montlhéry,[38]
The master of France, and soon of Paris,
Will be disgusted with your impudence,
Drag you with his cart around the square,
And reduce the town to wilderness,
Thus setting an example for the world.
When he speaks from the heart, with humbled pride,

---

[38] On 16 July 1465, Charles VII defeated Louis XI at the Battle of Montlhéry.

Requesting that you save yourselves the trouble
Of being ravished by his greater strength,
You should fall at his feet, without delay.
OLD DE PILE. Before replying to such arrogance,
And pointing out the madness in your pride,
We demand you tell us, Chimai, without
Evasion, anger, or misunderstanding,
Why there is so much secrecy.
When negotiations are in process,
We call a truce and put away our swords.
However, you've been here for some time now,
And we still hear the roar of Charles's cannons.
The loss of life incurred during this time,
Evidently does not satisfy him.
CHIMAI. Shouldn't he perceive, before he stops,
If you plan to maintain your feeble claims?
LOISET DE BALLAGNY. We haven't been reduced to such extremes
For him to think that we'll cast down our weapons.
As long as ten among us still can carry them,
He'll never conquer us without a fight.
Made callous by him to the sting of war,
We know how to withstand and subdue misery;
Dawn has risen thirty times upon
These tottering walls, entrusted to my care . . .
Joined together in this dark enclosure,
Our lives are hampered by a thousand sorrows . . .
Yet, not a single one has found the way
To give up his responsibilities.
YOUNG DE PILE. Had Beauvais been destroyed . . . ah! Had it been
Reduced to dust . . . (*Vigorously taking his father's hand.*)
They'd find the son beside
His father. Brothers, sisters, old men, children,
Each would die, one on top of the other,
Creating new obstacles with their bodies,
Rather than accept your ignominious
Proposition.

LOISET DE BALLAGNY. (*Quickly.*) How does he expect to govern us
When every day our farmers irrigate
Their crops with the water from their tears . . .
When women hold their injured daughters close
Against their breasts and pray to God for vengeance
Against that hateful and fierce oppressor!
Does he expect to rule over us amid
So great an uproar? In the midst of tears
Drowned by the sound of battle? What he didn't
Anticipate is that crime creates terror:
People hate the chains of a destructive
Tyrant,
And severity only engenders hatred.

CHIMAI. If he doesn't pity your misfortunes,
He can double them.

TORCIS. I agree, but we've made up our minds.

OLD DE PILE. Whatever has been attempted against us,
Nothing can prevent Beauvais from fighting
To defend itself.
It will never be taken and . . . (*Putting his hand on his heart.*)
A tyrant never will be master here.
(*To YOUNG DE PILE.*) More than once, my son, I filled your head
With virtuous deeds that glorify our name.
Therefore, if a traitor was among us,
Swear to me, you'd kill him right away.

YOUNG DE PILE. I place the vow into your hands, my father,
But cast away that terrible idea.
These are the days of virtue, not of crimes.
(*To CHIMAI.*) No, my lord.
Charles will not take Beauvais in our lifetime.

CHIMAI. The provisions: food and ammunition,
They're bound to run out. Have you considered
The terrifying panic that will be
Created when they do?

TORCIS. We only have one fear: of all misfortunes,
The most frightening for us is to surrender.

YOUNG DE PILE. When a man wants to defend himself,
Eagerness can always urge him on.
Great people will do anything for fame.
(*Indicating the battlements and the streets.*)
These rocks, those houses will provide the ammunition,
The poorest foodstuffs will work wonders for us,
And we will all be happy here regardless
If the king, our master, finds our efforts
Satisfactory.
CHIMAI. (*With the greatest pathos.*)
Let more apparent evils move you, friends;
Let your spirits tremble about more
Immediate dangers.
Which of you will endure the certain sight
Of the soldier bounding over your walls?
Once he has gained admittance to the bosom
Of your home, what will destroy his rage?
There, bound by no laws except murder and indecency,
See him, animated with the horrors of death,
Massacre the children in your arms,
Without remorse, and measure his conquest
By the extent of his gruesome crimes.
See him show no pity in his choice of victims.
See him tear out the entrails of your women,
Trembling with their sides half-open, alas,
Trying to hide underneath the furniture.
Nothing gets the better of his wild soul.
A torch is in his hand and curses on his lips.
See him profane those beloved sanctuaries;
See the angry flame dart through the air
Presenting to your tender souls only a
Worthless mass of cinder and debris.
If you don't tremble at these hideous sights,
You're crueler and more barbarous than they are.
OLD DE PILE. (*Quickly, expressively, passionately, and vigorously.*) No!
You seek, in vain, to agitate our feelings.
No, you will not succeed. We shall see death

Upon the battlements; no one among us
Will therefore feel the sting of those indignities.
You will get rather tired of our resistance,
That strength you think we cannot muster here
In our defense. You ask about the women?
Anyone who wants can lend a hand,
Regardless of the danger.
And you will see our brand new heroines
Conquer, or die beside us on the ruins.
You've heard our thoughts about the situation;
We make them known to you so we'll die happy,
Sure that, envious of our distinguished deaths,
Our neighbors will speak well of us, when they
Show the place to our French fighting-men:
"That's where the heroes of Beauvais once lived."
LOISET DE BALLAGNY. (*To CHIMAI.*)
In the meantime, you can make known to us
What it appears your master wants of us.
CHIMAI. He'll let you live provided you, your elders,
Soldiers, women, and children go to his camp
As suppliants to call upon his mercy
And swear forevermore to renounce France.
LOISET DE BALLAGNY. (*With a marked gesture of indignation, followed quickly by a cry of joy expressed in the first word he utters.*)
Friends, enough! Let's go back to our walls,
Thanking Heaven, by sweet and pure vows,
For all the many obstacles we face . . .
For to them God has added such a strong . . .
CHIMAI. Such a strong what?
LOISET DE BALLAGNY. (*Quickly.*) A sense of honor, my lord,
Which you continue to offend in us,
But which escaping from these odious traps
Will show the future that we are more worthy
Of the only prize that can exist
For people like us:
Inner peace and a good reputation.

My lord, you cannot leave the city walls
Until after the attack has taken
Place, and only so that you can see
How our citizens do their duty here.
When we triumph, tomorrow, perhaps
At evening, we will send you to your master
To see if he has learned that he cannot
Impose his will upon these worthy Frenchmen
Who fight for the honor of their king.
(*Boldly, to CHIMAI.*) You've heard what I had to say.
(*He goes to the rear of the stage with the others.*)
CHIMAI. (*To BALLAGNY.*) I'm right behind you. What an
ordeal!
How can I stop my heart from being moved?
Today, he'll suffer all the desolation
That he's ever been afraid of.
(*He joins the crowd and everyone exits right, toward the battlements.*)
MATTHEW LAISNÉ. (*Alone, returning to the Town Hall.*)
Ah! I'm a thousand times more unfortunate than he!

END OF ACT ONE

ACT TWO

JEANNE LAISNÉ. I can, of course, my dearest Emily,
Describe the troubles of my life to you.
The feelings for me that your brother has,
His love's but a reflection of your own;
The greatest good we relish in this world
Is seeing that another soul responds
To ours, and shares with us our pains and sighs.
Tell me,
What is that stranger doing here unarmed?
His presence on these premises alarms me.
He spends too much time alone with my father ...
They must be busy with important matters.
Yet, Charles's war machine does not stop thundering
Even though they're in negotiations.
If the talks were done, there would have been a truce
And we would not be overwhelmed with gunfire.
In this age of deception, of intrigue,
A person is afraid of everything ...
Yes, I'm afraid that man's taking advantage
Of the power he seems to hold over my father,
That he's corrupting him, making him act
Contrary to his duty and his country.
I'm overwhelmed with terror. Speak, I beg you,
Just tell me without pretext or deception,
What can we conclude about these schemes?
EMILY. The stranger has not spoken to my father,
Head of the council, colleague of the mayor:
He should have made his purpose clear to him.
I won't conceal that people are suspicious,
Not about your father ... they trust his honesty;
They're trying to clear up the shady schemes
Of the young soldier who's lying to him.
They think that he's the bearer of bad news.
JEANNE LAISNÉ. (*Trying to suppress an idea that she regrets having had.*)

If he wants to trick us, he wouldn't dare
Negotiate such business with my father.
That would be illogical. I feel there's
No reason my mind should fear that man.
(*Returning to her initial thought, as if in spite of herself.*)
Oh, my dear Emily, whatever he tries,
Whatever his purpose, or his vile desires,
We and our friends must vigorously oppose
Any scheme he'd possibly propose
To deliver this town into the hands
Of his false-hearted master. Promise me
You will persuade the women of Beauvais
To join us in noble opposition.
EMILY. Heavens! What in the world do you mean?
JEANNE LAISNÉ. To save our country . . . to protect it
From the rage, from the indignant fury
Of an audacious conqueror, who'd vainly
Promise to watch over it, but who would
Destroy it, once it's under his control.
Look at the horizon glittering
With flaming cities, consumed in his wrath.
Hear the air resounding with the cries
Of every one of his unlucky victims,
Sacrificed as he profanes both God
And nature.
We saw them, you know, those wandering families,
Whose dying faces were tainted by hunger,
Worn by poverty, haunted by death.
Having seen the proof of their misfortunes,
Do you want us to follow their example?
Do you want such strife within our walls
To attack our hearts with its foul stench?
Whether Charles captures us, or wins us over,
Remember that he'll have to burn, defile,
And annihilate, without remorse,
These hearts in which so many sorrows reign.
EMILY. What steps can we take to avoid these evils?
JEANNE LAISNÉ. Resolve to perish, rather than surrender!

We share in the danger of our citizens:
If through fear or weakness, they allow
That young stranger to have influence here,
We'll share in the defense of our walls with them.
We'll imitate their courage . . . boldly attack all evils,
We'll fight in front of them and become heroes.
We'll rush to battle like the gladiators:
You have to break the bondage of misfortune
At its heart!
Ah! Don't you feel your heart leap, Emily,
At the sublime endeavor I've just introduced?
Don't you feel your tears flowing, and your soul
Elevated by the dear and sacred
Names of honor and country? Like me,
Can't you feel your soul become inflamed
With courage and passion?
EMILY. What?
Do you count bravery among our virtues?
Is our sex entitled to victory?
JEANNE LAISNÉ. (*Rapidly, only stressing the final line.*)
You must believe that woman always has
The right to merit glory. And you must
Believe that she is only truly great
When she knows how to rise above herself,
When she can prove it to such self-applauding
Rivals who humble and insult her,
By doubting, without cause, her noble courage.
You must believe that, whenever she needs them,
She possesses the same virtues as
That proud sex which oppresses her today.
EMILY. (*Eagerly.*) I'm enraptured by your spirit. Well . . .
If I were certain of it . . . yes, I will
Inflame their hearts with your aversion to
This foe of both our people and the state;
And most of all, prepare our sex for battle.
JEANNE LAISNÉ. (*With enthusiasm.*)
Oh, glorious moment! Memorable day!
Surely, I'll be fortunate enough

To show our haughty enemy the woman
Who can inspire love for her country.
And if I thought that France was watching me,
Even for a moment, as I venture
Into battle; if my master were to
Praise my feeble efforts ... on that day,
I'd be prepared to die a thousand times.
EMILY. What of my brother who returns your love?
JEANNE LAISNÉ. (*Very quickly.*)
Speak less of love and act more like a patriot.
When the enemy is far from Beauvais,
When we have destroyed its deadly efforts,
Then we'll speak of love. But now, my soul
Is focused only on the purpose that
Provokes it. Glory is the only thing
I see. It is my one and only law.
The only love I feel is for my king.
Someone's coming. We should slip away.
Go, keep your word, excite the women's spirits.
Let them do as I do and run off
To show their husbands, children, and posterity,
That they can fight, conquer, and die, just like men.
(*Enter CHIMAI.*)
CHIMAI. (*To JEANNE.*) May I detain you for a moment?
JEANNE LAISNÉ. (*Continuing upstage.*)
My father is the one you want to see.
Perhaps I could go...
CHIMAI. (*Interrupting her.*) Ah! Don't be afraid.
Can nothing stop you from running away?
JEANNE LAISNÉ. (*With pride.*) Perhaps I must.
(*Seeing MATTHEW LAISNÉ enter with MOREL.*)
My lord, here is my father.
No doubt you both would rather speak in private,
So I'll leave you alone. (*She exits with EMILY.*)
CHIMAI. (*Alone.*) Ah! God, nothing can win her over!
(*To the MAYOR as he enters.*) She hates me, friend.
MATTHEW LAISNÉ. Chimai, to surround her
With bonds from which her heart cannot escape,

To win her heart . . . to captivate . . . to please her,
Make use of that dexterity, that talent,
That skill that you knew how to use with me.
If you can make a French-born citizen
Betray his country, rather than defend it,
If you could deaden, through your skill, the voice
Of patriotism in my soul, Chimai,
You can have your way with anybody.
Come on, stop looking quite so secretive.
You've just seen how impulsively,
Defiantly the crowd behaved in trying
To separate us;
Let's not force them in any way to watch us
Even closer. I'll take charge of everything.
CHIMAI. (*Going out.*) Very well. I'll leave you. Think about our
Plans, about yourself, about my feelings . . .
And look for ways, throughout the day, for me
To serve your interests, Charles, and my beloved,
All at the same time. Everything is in
Your hands.
MATTHEW LAISNÉ. I'm overwhelmed with misery!
Forgetting one's responsibilities
Always leads to crime. I'm living proof
Of that, and my destiny is cruel.
Have you ever seen such eyes, Morel?
They seem to penetrate inside my head.
They seem to me confused, embarrassed, solemn;
I'm crushed beneath the weight of their perplexity.
It terrifies me.
That must be one of the effects of crime.
The criminal fears . . . dreads everything around him;
A virtuous look, the thing he can't abide,
Is the first weapon hurled to punish him!
Nothing can express my terrible distress.
I sold myself for my beloved daughter,
And all I see is that she cannot tie
The knots my pride sought to provide for her.
MOREL. Flatter her to pacify her courage.

She's young, she's eager, and you can believe,
That at that age, prone to the ebb and flow
Of passions, she will always give way to the
Sweetest inclinations of her heart.
Present her with the extraordinary
Alliance with Chimai. Then, praise his name,
His possessions, his titles, his courage;
Add to the courtship your legal authority:
When a father commands, he must be heard!
MATTHEW LAISNÉ. Alas! Don't you foresee what she will say?
MOREL. Nothing that you could not refute with ease.
MATTHEW LAISNÉ. (*Sadly.*) And how do I absolve my guilt, my friend?
MOREL. By looking for reasons that justify
Your behavior; thinking long and hard
About the loathsome conduct of a despot,
An overbearing prince, who, for his pleasure,
And in his own interest, creates for us
The intricacy of a thousand different
Miseries.
Fill your heart with his wicked injustice,
With his cruel suspicions, with his shameful
Lies toward the Duke of Guienne,[39] his noble
Brother.
Look at the bitter harvest of his madness!
Are you the only one whose heart intends
To abandon that prince and betray
His cause? Released from fealty, like you,
Because of the harshness of the bridle,
Subjects, friends, relations, even vassals
See nothing more in him but a shadow
Of power, which each one of them would like
To destroy, in short, they all compel you
To finally stop carrying the banner
Of a prince who brings you so much misery.
You have all of France lying before you:
Let its example serve you here. And bear

[39] Charles de Valois, Duc de Berry (26 December 1446 – 24 May 1472).

In mind that never is a subject bound
To one whose rights are only won by force.
MATTHEW LAISNÉ. (*Quickly and passionately.*)
You're wrong, friend. You don't seem to understand
That a Frenchman must always serve his master.
It's not our place to scrutinize his power;
To love and serve him, that's our only duty.
When we disregard it, nothing in us
Can extinguish the horrible cry
That overwhelms us to avenge the sin.
MOREL. Well, your affairs . . .
MATTHEW LAISNÉ. (*Interrupting him, poignantly and sadly, still full of concern.*)
They're the reason, I confess,
That my sacred oath has been undone.
I knew it was wrong . . . but I was won over.
I've given my word, what's done is done, and I'm
Resigned to it. Courage is putting new life
Into Vilpreux and Saint-Yon. Ah! I forgot
An important point about the plan:
Find a spot in some secluded tower
From which you can see far into the distance
Without being observed.
There, when you see the Burgundians appear . . .
You'll recognize them by their French regalia.
They're wearing it to trick us. Ah! Morel,
I'm frightened. Heavens!
To resign my city to the enemy!
With that idea, all hell breaks loose within me.
My heart is weak . . . you see how I am trembling,
Such offenses weren't designed for me.
No matter. There's no time. I gave my word.
I say, when they appear with cannons roaring,
With guns and swords, whose battle noises ought
To produce different feelings within me,
By three very distinct knocks . . . oh, my heart!
You'll let me know, at last my crime's complete.
Seeing the terrible distress that crushes me,

(*Taking one of MOREL's hands.*)
Remember, when a coward dares betray
His honor,
He's already punished in the depths
Of his heart.
MOREL. Cast away regret, strengthen your soul;
Let paternal love fill you today,
And to persuade your struggling heart, consider
That often, virtue is born of a crime.
MATTHEW LAISNÉ. (*Interrupting him.*)
I see de Pile. Farewell, I fear his violent
Disposition,
And I doubt I can endure his presence. (*He exits quickly.*)
MOREL. (*More slowly.*) I'll follow you.
(*Enter OLD DE PILE, AND YOUNG DE PILE.*)
OLD DE PILE. (*Stopping MOREL's departure and addressing
him resolutely with a riveting delivery.*)
I've disturbed a secret meeting:
Could you tell me what it was about?
MOREL. (*Uneasy and distressed.*)
Certain precautions the mayor wants to take
To help us to defend ourselves more ably.
OLD DE PILE. (*To his son, taking advantage of MOREL's
discomfort.*)
Look at how the forehead of a traitor
Shows all the horror of his cruel soul.
(*To MOREL, dispassionately.*)
Go on. We'll see in combat if the two
Of you are who you are supposed to be.
MOREL. (*Leaving.*) Let each citizen prove himself like us
In the face of enemy fire.
OLD DE PILE. (*Following MOREL with his eyes.*) Traitor!
(*Firmly, to his son.*) Think about the promise you just made me.
YOUNG DE PILE. (*Resolutely, to his father.*)
It's sacred to me; father, you can count
On it. Your fear is pointless.
OLD DE PILE. It's justified. Wait . . .
(*He goes to take a look around.*) I want to see if anyone can hear us.

(*Returning to his son.*) Do you love your country?
YOUNG DE PILE. Ah, you know my devotion:
All my blood, if need be, will be shed for it.
OLD DE PILE. Today, it's not a matter of your blood,
But if its voice is dear to you, you must
Suppress the voice of the brazen impostor
Who is going to betray his cause.
Matthew is the traitor.
YOUNG DE PILE. (*Taken completely by surprise; then firmly.*)
Him? You must be mistaken.
It isn't possible.
OLD DE PILE. Haven't you observed
His quiet demeanor, his aloofness,
His desire to entertain Chimai ...
Their secret meetings ... private conversations ...
What do you imagine could be keeping
An envoy here so long?
What could be clearer? He's betraying us,
I tell you. No one dares to convict him
Of it and that's what bothers me.
The scandal would affect Morel, Vilpreux,
And all the other traitors he corrupts with them.
Haven't you just seen how this vile business
Overwhelms them?
It's been decided, therefore, in these matters
A sword was needed to arrest the crimes.
(*He gives him a sword.*)
Here. Thank God for giving you the honors.
Because of your heartfelt passion to serve,
You've been chosen to avenge the traitor.
Now's the time to act.
YOUNG DE PILE. (*Refusing the sword.*) Who? Me? Good
Lord, why me?
I'd rather die. Father, without distress,
Can you command me to perform this deed ...
This terrible revenge ...
When his daughter is my only hope?
Don't force me to go to this vile extreme.

Am I the only one here who could possibly
Carry out this loathsome crime? No, no!
OLD DE PILE. (*To himself.*) I suspected as much. Oh, wretched
father!
(*Aloud, with rage.*) Very well. It's over! Go, unworthy
Citizen,
Since you dare not punish the conspiracy
By means of this distinguished crime, consider
Yourself banished, coward. Get out of my sight.
Your base and perjured soul opposes me
With arguments of love. Does love outweigh
The duty that you owe your fatherland?
Love should only be kept in a heart
To draw the ties of honor closer there,
Never to break them!
YOUNG DE PILE. (*In tears.*) Oh, I implore you,
Put a higher value on the person
I adore. If I have any virtues,
Her heart is the hearth that cleanses them.
If ever I've shown courage in your presence,
Father, my valor is her work alone.
My arm distinguishes itself in battle,
So I might earn a little fame to merit
Her. (*Recoiling in horror.*)
You'd order me to kill her father!
OLD DE PILE. (*A cold anger at first, becoming an impassioned
wrath.*)
I order nothing. I've nothing to say,
In circumstances such as these, except
To curse you.
Ignite the torch of such a lovely wedding
With the sparkling fires of your country
In flames. Go. Run.
Fly to the altar to confirm your bonds
Written with the blood of all your fellow-
Citizens. And
Disowned, disdained, discarded, prone to hardship,
Abhorred in Beauvais, in France, all over the world,

May your days be repulsive, ever fraught with guilt,
And misery upon misery lead you to your grave.
YOUNG DE PILE. (*Out of his senses.*)
Very well. Your anger fortifies me
And makes up my mind.
Place the dagger in my murderous hand.
Either it will pierce the traitor's heart
Or this breast, and end my life of sadness.
OLD DE PILE. (*Giving him the sword.*)
The treachery is certain, and you must
Pursue it. Sure, my son, that one is only
Worthy of life, when he can constantly,
No matter what the cost,
Be of useful service to both honor
And his country. Goodbye. (*He goes out.*)
YOUNG DE PILE. (*Alone, the sword in his hand.*)
I promised to commit this heinous murder!
I must obey. Oh, girl beyond compare,
I will plunge this steel into the heart
That gave you birth.
But, yielding to the weight of my remorse,
The hand that could commit so vile a crime,
Will soon carve out your image from my broken
Heart.
Go on, Heaven, convince my dismal soul,
That it can, by way of crime, move on to virtue.

END OF ACT TWO

ACT THREE

(*MOREL, followed by SAINT-YON and VILPREUX enter from the Brestle side. Quickly crossing the stage on their way to the City Hall, they meet MATTHEW LAISNÉ coming out of the building.*)

MOREL. We were just informed of Coucy's success.
Before dawn could shed light on their footsteps . . .
(*Indicating one of his companions.*)
Saint-Yon saw all three of them, full of power
And passion, scaling the heights of our walls.

MATTHEW LAISNÉ. (*Uneasy.*)
Ah! Every day Chabanne and his few men
Storm the barricades at Charles's camp.
Who knows how they'll fare?

MOREL. I know nothing more about it. But
We're pressed for time, Laisné. I've noticed that
De Pile has strong suspicions against us.
I'm afraid of his fanaticism
And his uncompromising patriotism.
We've got to do something about it soon.

MATTHEW LAISNÉ. How can we?
What could so few do against so many?
Let's wait for Charles, without fear or concern.
The art of conquering the weak is trickery,
No other arms are needed. Nonetheless,
However this turns out, it's absolutely
Necessary that I tell my daughter
About it. Good Heavens! There she is.
Leave us alone, my friends. As for discretion . . .
It hurts your pride, but helps in getting even. (*He sends them away.*)

(*Enter JEANNE LAISNÉ.*)

JEANNE LAISNÉ. (*With that kind of joyful calm that signals the approach of the moment when a person is about to perform a good deed.*)
My lucky day is finally dawning, father,
At last, today is going to spread the glory

Of your daughter and the name of Laisné
For centuries to come.
I'm going to march to victory by your side:
I'll share in the laurels you'll acquire.
I've prayed for them, now I'm here to collect them.
MATTHEW LAISNÉ. You'll find that I won't easily consent
To passion that's as vain as it is useless.
Listen to me. Control this deadly fervor.
I blame it on your age and not your heart.
A woman isn't made for bold endeavors:
She was born for peace and not for war.
Don't expose yourself to certain danger.
Do you expect your weak arms to defend
Our walls? Leave their defense to our soldiers.
Marriage has arranged for you a sweeter,
Softer duty. Sacrifice the right
Of engaging in a useless battle
To your more sacred duties, work more worthy
Of you.
JEANNE LAISNÉ. (*As confused as she is surprised.*)
I will tell you, in all honesty,
That I was not anticipating any
Opposition in this matter, by the
One who gave birth to those feelings in me.
I'll never forget all that I owe you,
And yet, forgive me, if you are my father,
You can't deny my country is my mother.
I have every right, then, from now on
To take an interest in the precious duties
Deeply impressed upon me by my mother.
In your opinion, women were made only
To give pleasure. What? Does not a person
Give pleasure through virtuous behavior?
I am certain that we should be valued
For the holy feelings in our hearts,
Rather than the empty outward features
Given us by nature. You tell me
Glory's never felt a woman's touch?

Has there not been a time within the century,
When either the greatest exploits, or
The bravest deeds that history acclaims,
Have been due to just a single woman?
It seems to me that these words should be welcomed:
A woman was thus useful to her country.
Ah, let me imitate her. My one hope
Is to receive, like her, a crown of glory,
And likewise, to bring honor to my country.
MATTHEW LAISNÉ. She has paid dearly for that fatal glory!
JEANNE LAISNÉ. She was clothed in it. Ah! What else
matters?
MATTHEW LAISNÉ. Do you want to immortalize yourself
In such a way?
JEANNE LAISNÉ. My heart is ready to try anything.
Just to equal her, I am prepared
To sacrifice my life. What good is living
Without loving your own native land?
Whoever does not work on its behalf,
Is ruining the best days of his life.
Whoever dies for it will live forever.
MATTHEW LAISNÉ. (*Extremely moved, his words are hurried
and marked by annoyance.*)
Stop this stupid chatter. In the light
Of our real interests, this demented glory
Troubles your father. You know Chimai:
Every day, before your very eyes,
He pleads his master's claims here in the city.
And those claims, more sacred than your own,
Deserve to be treated with respect.
Borrow Chimai's noble sentiments,
And offer him your hand as a token
Of the love I bear him.
JEANNE LAISNÉ. (*Horrified.*)
Chimai, my husband? Favorite of a prince
Whose madness ravages the countryside,
Who, binding us more tightly with his chains,
Continues every day to shed the blood

Of our countrymen.
What? Could you, my father, give your daughter
To someone on the side that would destroy
Your property, your family?
Could you have thought that I would pledge my faith
To anyone who'd force you to betray
Your people? Don't insult me like that. No.
Instead of sharing in these shameful schemes,
I'd rather die immediately at your own hand.
MATTHEW LAISNÉ. (*Aside.*) Oh, Heavens! I've said too much.
(*Aloud.*) Very well,
Ungrateful child, stop challenging the laws
Of nature.
My fate is in your hands, you know about
Our plans. Go!
Make known those dangerous secrets to your people.
You've nothing more to do to crown your life,
To even better serve your holy country,
Than to expose your father to the blade
Of the executioner. Go on.
Don't falter in the least. You'll put an end
To my misery. My noble child,
Think of the remarkable achievement
Of turning over to the state a crushed
And beaten, culpable old man. This touch
Is necessary for the fame you seek.
End my life, more glory will be yours.
One more offense will crown your victory, Jeanne,
As my unworthy blood secures your fame!
JEANNE LAISNÉ. (*Overwhelmed.*)
What language, sir! And what have I discovered?
I cannot argue with you for my heart
Has suffered too much. Did I hear correctly?
Have I now a father who is guilty
Of rebellion,
Who, separating his interests from mine,
Breaks all the bonds of nature between us?

(*Gathering her strength.*)
Cruel man, pity my excessive sadness;
Pity our misfortunes, pity yourself.
Look at the sad fruit of your ambition,
Look where its indiscretion is leading you.
(*Disturbed, quickly.*) If there's still time . . . there's still time, dear
father,
Hear the prayers of your most faithful daughter
For you to reconsider this betrayal.
Otherwise an awful shame will stigmatize
Us all. Ah! Crime doesn't pay!
Good Lord, stop at the edge of the abyss.
Look at all your relatives, your friends
Denouncing you for those horrible fires
With which you alone will have destroyed
The country. And, alas, your daughter! Lonely,
Dishonored, and branded with your disgrace,
Not daring to raise her eyes without
Seeing her disfavor stamped on faces
Everywhere . . .
Shame will leave its guilty scar on all
Your race. Our poor name will be but whispered
With the same horror as the names of criminals!
You are incapable of this vile crime.
Chimai has tricked you; he alone is guilty.
Forget the promises you made today.
On you will fall the shame, on him, the glory.
What have you to say against our master?
Cherish him, he's worthy of respect:
Never has his noble heart forgotten
A single good deed.
(*Seeing her father reject that idea.*)
Very well. Forget about his claims
And only think about honor . . .
You obeyed his laws for forty years.
A moment's error and you lose the fruit
Of your obedience.
(*She falls at his feet in tears.*)

Beloved author of my days, dismiss
My fears; allow yourself to be affected
By the sight of my tears.
I ask nothing but that you give up
What will ultimately disgrace you.
Father, either kill me with your bare hands,
Or swear to serve the motherland with me . . .
To love me and to follow me through danger,
To defend with us our crumbling battlements;
Defy the danger! Ah! Your daughter's ready
To protect you with her own frail body,
And she'll die before she'll ever leave you.
(*She gets up, frightened of the person who appears. Enter MOREL.*)
MOREL. (*To the MAYOR.*) Duty calls.
MATTHEW LAISNÉ. (*Taking JEANNE's hand as if to stop her from speaking.*)
There's no more time, my daughter.
There's only one way you can save your family,
And that's to keep quiet about everything.
In other words, to do what I tell you.
Obey me. I'm right behind you, Morel. (*They exit together.*)
JEANNE LAISNÉ. (*Alone.*) Obey? Good Lord!
When he commands me to commit a crime?
His decree debases me. No longer
Is it legitimate. De Pile is coming.
He looks upset.
Despair is painted on his troubled brow.
Ah! I'm trembling.
YOUNG DE PILE. (*Aside, still in the wings.*)
Oh, heavens! His daughter . . . my beloved!
The cruel weapon drops from my unsteady hand,
And nature, outraged at this, the height of horror,
Removes it from the criminal and thrusts it
Into my heart. No matter. Let's proceed.
JEANNE LAISNÉ. (*Approaching him, trembling.*)
In these hardly peaceful days, the chances
Of our seeing one another seem
Remote. And though we might be speaking now,

This is not the day for us to be
Together. What do I see
In your eyes? What somber and sullen looks?
You're running from me. You're afraid to talk.
You can't even look me in the eye!
Speak to me. God! Tell me what's the matter.
You make me tremble.
YOUNG DE PILE. Who? Me? I'm looking for a traitor. There's
no
Need to worry.
JEANNE LAISNÉ. (*Trembling.*) What do I hear?
YOUNG DE PILE. What's wrong?
JEANNE LAISNÉ. Ah! Calm my nerves.
Everything frightens me about you.
YOUNG DE PILE. Where's your father?
JEANNE LAISNÉ. By the city walls.
YOUNG DE PILE. (*Eagerly.*) When will he return? I need to
see him.
JEANNE LAISNÉ. (*Impatiently.*) Then, answer me, what brings
you here to see him?
YOUNG DE PILE. The most sacred of tasks, and every feeling
A reprobate enjoys in these cruel times.
(*Showing her his sword.*) Look, this will decide the destiny
Of the guilty man. I was considered
Capable of punishing his crime,
And proud of the honor of killing him.
I see his footsteps...he was in your arms...
JEANNE LAISNÉ. (*Forcefully, disguising her anxiety under the
appearance of great control.*) Give me that sword.
YOUNG DE PILE. (*Distracted, trying to get away.*) No.
JEANNE LAISNÉ. (*Detaining him.*) At least, listen to me.
YOUNG DE PILE. (*Impatiently.*) Well?
JEANNE LAISNÉ. (*Her speech builds slowly.*)
I thought you were more generous, more sensitive . . .
I thought that I was loved, and that my life
At least would offset your loathsome intentions,
Your very irrational intentions.
When one crime is committed, a new crime

Will never punish it or stop its effects;
Rather, to avenge the destiny
Of that important elder, all his friends
Will arm themselves immediately against you.
Let the state handle its own affairs.
Now I'm appealing only to your heart . . .
Let it listen. So, without remorse
Was your hand going to strike down my father
Right in front of me? What of our ties?
Those loving bonds we've shared since childhood?
Were you indifferent to them? Or were you
Going to offer me, perhaps, your hand
Still stained with blood as you withdrew your sword
From my father's heart? Oh, I was wrong
To think you were such a sensitive soul.
I see it now, that soul is capable
Of crushing me, with no fear of the most
Terrifying evils! Very well,
Go, punish him . . . that miserable old man;
Go, plunge your murderous hand into his breast.
I can oppose the madness that guides you
No more. (*Offering herself to him, boldly.*)
But see how it must reach his heart:
Before you stab the one whom I revere,
You will pierce mine in your deadly fury.
I will be a shield for my father's heart.
Come on, come on, then, without apprehension,
Without fear or trembling, stain with blood
The altar of our childhood promises.
You have betrayed them, scorned them, say it, wretch,
When you wrongly agreed to commit patricide;
Deceived by claims less sacred than my own,
You pledged your honor to annul our oaths.
Sever them without delay!
I consent to it. Who's stopping you?
Why hesitate when the victim is ready?
Consummate the crime, complete your task...
(*Quickly, taking advantage of her beloved's tears.*)

Nature takes its revenge on my behalf:
It just touched your heart. Throw down that sword.
I will restore all my affection to you . . .
My arms are open, come, weep for your crime.
YOUNG DE PILE. (*Throwing down the sword.*)
I knew only too well that, softened by
Your tears, I was going to detest such violence.
You win at last, and my affected soul
Belongs to you alone, not any country:
Instead of a killer whose sword you feared,
Enchain a lover, Jeanne. He's on his knees. (*He falls to his knees.*)
JEANNE LAISNÉ. (*Lifting him up.*) Get up. I don't in any way intend
To insult our country;
I love it more than you; my dearest wish
Is to die for it in these final hours,
Trying to defend it.
And I'm going to prove it to you.
YOUNG DE PILE. I know your plans. I couldn't be aware
Of them without experiencing a
Divine respect for you, which renders love
More pure and its fires more passionate . . . but
I don't agree with your sublime desire.
Promise your lover to preserve your life,
And not increase the horror of our sad
Misfortunes with the torment of worrying
About such important matters.
JEANNE LAISNÉ. (*Firmly.*) I will in no way make a coward's promise,
But I'll show you how troubled my heart is
About what you were to enact today.
Don't interrupt; listen, and follow carefully:
Your blind youth was very badly misguided;
You see how it was won over to villainy.
To change the course of crime, whatever it is,
Should someone make use of another crime?
Guided by reason, leave to spiteful souls—
Very often liars, and always dangerous—

The job of proclaiming the people's will, and
Permitting crimes so they can be prevented.
These appalling methods which show weakness,
Insulting virtue, Heaven, and discretion,
Only ever magnify misfortune.
They would dirty your hands. Refuse the honor.
What the people are afraid of, friend,
Is very real: my father is betraying
Us, but he is in no way guilty.
No. He wouldn't know how to be.
Chimai is tricking him. That traitor—agent
For the Duke—
He alone has been responsible
For everything.
Their evil endeavors must be stopped.
Their plans must be destroyed. My father must be saved!
That is the only way to serve honor,
Our citizens, the country, and the law,
All at the same time. There is no skill
In punishing wrongdoing, but in stopping
It before it happens.
The man who thinks that he can correct evil
By means of criminal acts, who thinks that torture
Or the dead man's blade render a man
Virtuous, correct, and purified,
Is but a vile fraud, lying to nature!
Dare to share the dangers of my plan.
Despite the troops atop our battlements,
Fly to the French camp. Chabanne is in charge . . .
Show him the way to flaunt his bravery:
In short, risking your life, serve as his guide.
(*Indicating the side of which she is speaking.*)
Not far from Bresle, you'll see two short roads
Which lead from Chabanne's camp to the city.
Tell him he must take them; and to set
His mind at ease, so that he'll deal with you
Without knowing who you are, put your
Fate in his hands, as a pledge of faith.

The Bresle Gate will minimally be guarded,
The imminent attack is very far
From it; and it's too close to the French camp.
Those who would betray us will not use it,
At least, I wouldn't expect them to.
But don't tell them that my father's guilty,
Just tell the generals that it's absolutely
Necessary to put out the fires
That Chimai ignited in the town.
Make sure they hurry; they have to move quickly.
In the meantime, fighting in the breach,
Astonishing the enemy with our
Unusual bravery,
We will establish ourselves in spirit
And in valor!
YOUNG DE PILE. You want to fight?
JEANNE LAISNÉ. I have to, dear de Pile.
Everyone must help defend the city.
If we save it, my father would be pardoned,
But if Charles takes it, he would be condemned.
Chimai succeeds, and from that moment on,
Everything is shattered. So you see
The sacred reasons for which I must fight:
I must defend my lover and my father,
The honor of my country and my own
Personal glory.
That unimportant blood I shed so willingly,
Couldn't serve a better cause!
Were I to have another life to sacrifice,
I'd give it up for so handsome a prize.
YOUNG DE PILE. I still dare, nonetheless, to ask you, please
In no way to expose yourself to danger.
Preserve your life for the good of a lover
Who's about to risk his own life eagerly
To save your honor and defend his country.
JEANNE LAISNÉ. Do you think that those reasons are less
worthy
Than my life?

Don't I, like you, have those precious duties?
I want to fulfill them. They are both
A thousand times more sacred than the life
That I detest.
YOUNG DE PILE. Ah! Then at least preserve your life for love.
JEANNE LAISNÉ. (*Passionately.*) Instead of softening me, in
your own way,
Arouse . . . excite in me the flame of passion
That burns in my heart for these sacred tasks.
Reflect, a moment, man worthy of my love,
Upon the supreme happiness of dying
For your king . . .
Of seeing our names renowned through history,
To convince the world that love of glory,
The first component of a Frenchman's honor,
Surpasses every feeling in our hearts.
See our names resound from age to age,
Taught to patriots as metaphors
Of honor, cherished by posterity,
And purified through immortality.
Do you believe a life of indolence
Or the deceitful charms of idle tenderness
Could, in the future, equal in our eyes
The enviable death to which we're heading?
Don't even think about it. Whoever
Confines his life to this inconsequential
Moment on the earth,
Whoever doesn't know how to survive
The oblivion of death, has not
Recognized the majesty of man!
It's time for you to go.
YOUNG DE PILE. What a charming task!
Some deity is filling me with tears.
From the bottom of my heart I worship
This divine endeavor.
How my heart delights in serving it.
I'll have punished the crime and saved the victim;
I will have served the state, without committing

Another crime!

(*He takes a few steps as if to leave. JEANNE LAISNÉ stops him; she experiences a kind of terror which she would rather hide from him; gradually she recovers her composure.*)

JEANNE LAISNÉ. Wait. A person trembles for a lover . . .

Everything is frightening when you're worried . . .

If I were with you, I'd be less afraid.

Going outside the walls you'll be a target:

Their arrows will dart around your head.

I can worry at least . . . but they will miss you;

This loving kiss will keep you safe and sound.

(*She kisses him on the forehead.*)

Go on, now, and may nothing stop you.

YOUNG DE PILE. Love, with such a feeling in my heart,

I'll face danger and death without fear.

(*He starts to go. Returning to JEANNE as if compelled by an urge over which he has no control, he takes her in his arms, and lifts his eyes toward the sky.*)

Protect her, Lord, she is your masterpiece,

A composite of the most noble virtues!

What example can we offer man

Hereafter, if in raising her to heaven

You take her away from us?

(*JEANNE is moved; her tears begin to flow. YOUNG DE PILE embraces her ecstatically. He lets go of her arms, falls back into them, tears himself away a second time, in tears, and rushes toward the Bresle Gate.*)

JEANNE LAISNÉ. (*Alone.*) Oh, these are sad times for a tender heart!

I am calmer, nonetheless. Ah! Preserve him,

Almighty God, protect him, hear my prayer:

Watch over my beloved, he's worthy of you.

In exchange, if you like, take my life

But save my father and my fatherland.

END OF ACT THREE

ACT FOUR

(*MATTHEW LAISNÉ abruptly comes out of the City Hall leading his entourage. LOISET DE BALLAGNY, entering from the battlements with his escort, stops LAISNÉ in his course and grabs him by the arm.*)

LOISET DE BALLAGNY. (*Quickly.*)
Stop shouting. Calm yourself for just a moment
So you can talk to me. The rest of you,
(*Addressing the mayor's companions.*)
Leave him here with me. Go show your courage
Atop our walls which are under attack.
When the nation is so tragically
In flames, it's best to quarrel as a soldier.
(*The conspirators exit.*)
(*To the mayor.*) Well, you've been carefully avoiding me;
I've been watching you for some time now,
Not without concern, or certainty
That the voice of honor imprints terror
Upon the soul of every guilty man.
MATTHEW LAISNÉ. A guilty man?
LOISET DE BALLAGNY. You ought to look forward to that name!
Why bother earning it when you're afraid
To hear it spoken? All your schemes are known:
A thousand men are ready to repress them.
But, hearing in my heart the voice of mercy,
I'd like to speak against the cries of vengeance,
Despite the Council's haste to punish you,
I simply want to talk to you today.
Don't think I'm acting out of fear or weakness . . .
Virtue is never overcome by terror.
To crime's dark evasions, it presents
An unruffled brow, and with a single blow,
Destroys the vile schemes.
MATTHEW LAISNÉ. This new approach surprises and
offends me.

My lord, I know the extent of your power,
And likewise, when you speak to me like that,
You ought to know that in Beauvais I still
Have some authority.
LOISET DE BALLAGNY. There's an unequal balance to our powers:
We will discuss them at another time.
Now, all you need to know is that by order
Of the king,
What happens here only depends on me:
When the trumpet sounds the call to battle,
The goddess of justice is at the mercy
Of the god of war;
In short, to stop your infamous intrigue,
With a word, I could put you in chains.
MATTHEW LAISNÉ. Until now, I thought a bit more prudence
Should be used with force and bravery
And that a person only deserved fame
When he added fairness to his virtues.
If you examined, with the self-same spirit,
The one who falsely betrayed me to you,
Perhaps, in *his* behavior you might find,
My lord, with better grounds, a reason to become
Suspicious.
LOISET DE BALLAGNY. I never stoop to trusting an informer;
Those odious methods signify weakness.
I only judge by deeds and not on gossip.
Do you plan to share in our endeavors?
For almost eight days now, an enemy
Has been concealed behind the walls of your house.
Have our walls seen you lend them your assistance?
MATTHEW LAISNÉ. They will see me, certainly. Perhaps
Today. Borrowing your enthusiasm
Of shining in the lists, I'll make you sorry
For accusing me so wrongfully.
LOISET DE BALLAGNY. Until then, I'll put off judging you,

And keep you, if I can, away from danger.

MATTHEW LAISNÉ. And so, who is the one accusing me?
Fame comes to those who follow in your footsteps,
And my heart doesn't fear them in the least,
Ballagny.

LOISET DE BALLAGNY. I'm not going to explain myself to you
On this issue. Only be assured
That these kinds of people do exist:
More worthy of scorn and disrepute
Than traitors, they too will be overburdened
By their crimes, and equally detested
By the side they choose as they are justly
Discredited by the side they betray.

MATTHEW LAISNÉ. (*Defeated, confused, lowering his eyes, and affecting an assurance which is very far from what he is really feeling; going out.*)
I never want to stray from this advice:
And soon you'll see if I know how to profit
By it.

LOISET DE BALLAGNY. (*Alone.*) False and scheming man,
I'm not your fool;
I can read what you're thinking in your eyes.
What should I do in this situation?
It's better to control the violence,
With which they wanted to get rid of him;
I will subdue the animosity
To better suit my plans, so that his cronies
In retaliation don't go digging
Holes from which he'll leap in fury, ready
To bring us to our knees. Yes, only threaten
Enough to bring him down. Here comes his daughter.

LOISET DE BALLAGNY. (*To JEANNE whom he sees enter with EMILY.*)
Oh, attractive woman!
May the Lord reward the fervent fire
Of patriotism burning within you,
By fending off the crimes that make us tremble.

JEANNE LAISNÉ. (*Quickly.*) My lord, explain yourself.
LOISET DE BALLAGNY. Ah, you should understand me. I wouldn't
Know how to go into greater detail.
I see tears falling from your tender eyes
And I don't intend to add to your troubles.
(*Going out.*) Goodbye.
May your valor in combat today
Wash away the crimes of such a father! (*He exits with his escort.*)
JEANNE LAISNÉ. (*In distress.*) It's all over, you see, and my misgivings
Have very certain and cruel foundations;
My father has been tricked. Oh, my beloved
Emily, to punish his weakness,
They've asked for his life. And guess, good God,
Who was chosen to avenge that so-called
Crime by killing him?
EMILY. Who then? You take me by surprise.
JEANNE LAISNÉ. Well, it was your brother!
EMILY. What a dreadful crime! Killing your father?
Can it be true?
JEANNE LAISNÉ. (*Continuing quickly.*) A blind delirium
Won him over to that dreadful murder.
But I averted that horrible act
When his love, his admirable frankness,
His heart, and his conscience, more than my
Advice, made him drop that inhuman sword
From his hand.
By focusing his spirit, I secured
His glory; I directed the virtues
That make his soul sparkle. Worthy of us,
At last, he's at the French camp, Emily,
A hostage,
Anxious to guarantee our success.
By fighting with the greatest fervor,
We will insure your brother's safe-conduct.
His triumph, finally combines with honor
The interest of his glory and that of my

Heart.
EMILY. Ah! I'm afraid for him.
JEANNE LAISNÉ. Don't be concerned.
He knows what prize is waiting for him after
His success. He's going to deserve it.
Well, have you stirred up all the women's hearts
With our enthusiasm?
EMILY. They're getting ready, my friend, and I think
They want to show their support for our cause.
Your unselfish example electrifies
Their hearts.
JEANNE LAISNÉ. Our sex, although weak, has its share of
valor,
Courage, and ambition, zeal, and pride,
Love of her country, like the other sex!
Who knows even . . . who knows if this secret
Inclination
To tenderness (established by her birth
As a woman) could not, all at once
Commingled with her fire, become
More ardent, more passionate, more tender,
Even more deserving, in a word,
Of the feeling which, with so much pleasure,
Is nourished deep within her for her king.
Thus, this emotion . . . always irresistible,
Would find itself in us much more invincible,
So much stronger since it would possess
Both the delicacy and the fire of love.
(*Breaking off.*) Tell the women to hurry. Chimai
Is coming and I want to shed light on
Whatever
In this affair could vindicate my father. (*EMILY exits.*)
(*JEANNE knows very well that her father has betrayed the city,
but she does not know that he has offered her to CHIMAI, or how
CHIMAI has tricked her father; and to vindicate the father she
adores, it is essential for her to solve this mystery. That is what moti-
vates this scene.*)
CHIMAI. Will you always find excuses (that

I can easily see through) to avoid
My company?
JEANNE LAISNÉ. Mine ought to have little interest for you,
My lord;
We are all here in a time of stress:
The blood which will be shed after your barbarous
Attack allows little communication
Between us from now on.
Besides, aren't you our master's enemy?
CHIMAI. What do you see in me that makes you say that?
Ah! The need to love what's tried and true
Extends to every heart here and unites them.
JEANNE LAISNÉ. I know of little use for all this talk,
My lord. Raised in these parts, I have a poor
Understanding of the language, which
Hiding beneath the ornaments of tricks
And evasions,
Cannot achieve its potential in our
Climate,
And only comes into its own at court.
CHIMAI. When the peace treaties tie us to France,
Those courts of which you have no understanding,
Will be expecting you to go and see them
Nonetheless;
You'll cultivate your taste for combat there;
There a thousand knights will fight for your
Attention, dressed in your colors and proud
To do your bidding. They'll receive the prizes
In a tournament from your own hands.
(*Smiling at her.*) I venture to predict you'll love the court!
JEANNE LAISNÉ. Oh, no, nothing could ever lead me there!
I should hope that my life would always be
Happy enough never to have to live
Within its dangerous surroundings. Content
With the oblivion of an obscure birth,
And looking at the heights with indifference,
If I survive the horror of my miseries,
My days will pass, your honor, in the shadows

And in peace.

CHIMAI. Are you ignoring enterprises full
Of charms whose sweetness supersedes these times
Of stress? Or are these worthy endeavors
(I fear) opposed by your cruel designs?

JEANNE LAISNÉ. (*Pretending interest.*) And what are these
endeavors?

CHIMAI. (*Surprised.*) What do you mean? Your father . . .

JEANNE LAISNÉ. Rarely revealed to me his business secrets.

CHIMAI. I think he wants to join the two of us
Together.

JEANNE LAISNÉ. (*With a disdain she cannot hide.*)
Me, my lord, with you? Could I agree
To it? (*Recomposing herself.*) Besides, aren't you forgetting who
you are?
Chimai, who's related to everyone
In France . . . who numbers kings among his ancestors,
Would condescend to my humble existence?

CHIMAI. To better deserve this great privilege,
I would place a jewel at your feet.
What I know of you does me even greater
Honor.
I've only got a name, you offer goodness.

JEANNE LAISNÉ. Your honor, it would hardly take the place
Of titles, of the honors which are due
Your family;
And this illusion that pleases you now,
Would overwhelm me with misfortune, when
It disappears. When my fragile attractions
Lose their dominion over you, they'd prove that
When love is nothing but a passing fancy,
It fills us with dishonor and regret.
Thus, for a few days of imperfect happiness,
Filled with guilt and hardly worth the trouble,
You would have wrought destruction in my life.

CHIMAI. Heavens! Now I see it all. I know
What you're doing and I understand
The reasons for your shameful arrogance.

Another has your love; another man
Knows how to please you. Give a name to him
Your heart prefers. Tell me his name, Madame,
So that I can send him to his death
Immediately!
JEANNE LAISNÉ. This is not the time for anger, Chimai,
And you're too impatient to decipher
My soul. Fears are not vehement refusals!
I'm going to confess my secret feelings,
Only if you answer a few questions.
(*Skillfully.*) What has my father said to you about
Your intentions concerning me?
CHIMAI. (*Gradually returning to his senses.*)
He undoubtedly approves of them.
JEANNE LAISNÉ. (*Purposefully.*)
Are they his desires, or does your love
Have to overcome his refusals?
CHIMAI. (*Without harshness.*)
What does this vulgar question have to do
With my passion for you?
JEANNE LAISNÉ. Everything. My father alone has
Control over my soul. Prove to me that he
Desires it, and everything is solved!
CHIMAI. There's no doubt about it: these bonds please him.
JEANNE LAISNÉ. (*With skill, grace, and sweetness.*)
You're not answering me and that evasion
Worries me; my goal is to find out
From you if he demands these ties between us,
Or if you only received his consent.
In the first case, I'd obey without
Hesitation.
CHIMAI. Will I only ever have you by force?
JEANNE LAISNÉ. (*Slightly ashamed, with her eyes lowered.*)
How badly you anticipate the outcome
Of your power over me.
Feelings can appear along with duty,
And their union in a tender soul
Makes the nuptial knot even more prone

To that delicate emotion, which your
Heart requires, and which you deserve,
By virtue of your many titles, my lord.
CHIMAI. Well, then ... will you love me?
JEANNE LAISNÉ. (*Very vague.*) That admission
Should only follow yours, undoubtedly.
Proceed to open up your heart to me,
And you'll see my indifference disappear.
CHIMAI. The fatal power of the female sex!
How it masters our hearts, how it begs,
How it urges. Our entire will
Submits to its voice...
The least of its desires makes up our laws.
(*With the greatest confidence; taking her aside.*)
You want the truth? Well, then, I'm going to tell you.
Your hand's the seal of victory to which
I aspire.
It fulfills my desires. Thus you see
In these secret schemes which unite us,
You put three people, all at once, in danger:
My master, your father, and myself,
Who is a thousand times more interested
In such sweet victories, since in succeeding,
They unite me to you.
JEANNE LAISNÉ. (*In half-voice, trembling, controlling her anxiety as best as she can.*)
So you claim that Beauvais is the security
That has to insure my father's consent?
CHIMAI. (*In a very low voice.*)
Yes, but be quiet about it. I want it.
It must happen. Yes, in our engagement,
The city is your dowry.
JEANNE LAISNÉ. (*In a shrill voice, with a very rapid delivery.*)
Good Lord, that's it, then. That's the wretched secret!
My father's innocent. He is incapable
Of such conspiracies without your help.
It's you, then, barbarian, liar, and cheat,
Who plunged him wantonly into the abyss!

Undoubtedly, in his eyes, you disguised
The crime and that appalling trap in which
You could ensnare him. You knew how to tempt him
With glory and grandeur. You encouraged
His bad habits.
Though his sweet good nature could take pride
In such a vile and vain association,
Should you have thought that, as weak as he is,
You would find support for your crime from me?
That my hand would reward this treachery,
And vindicate your hideous deceit?
Ah, you must better understand my heart:
It wasn't made for you. It wasn't made
For sale, and for abandoning its king.
Neither your pledge of faith, nor your affection,
Neither your noble name, nor your possessions
Would ever make me share in your villainy.
I am a woman, and I'm French. Listen,
You hypocrite, my country is my wealth;
Honor is my treasure.
If, for a moment, I could have neglected
The truth, which guides my steps, and marks my soul,
I would have figured out your worthless tricks.
What did we do to you to earn such punishment?
My father gave you refuge in his house;
In return, you happen to betray
His city!
And for your information, your repulsive
Schemes (for which you feel no guilt at all)
Are driving him to death!
You should have resisted the severity
Of our attack through bravery, not artifice . . .
Your laurels would have been pure; you just dirtied them.
(*The artillery from the city and the camp is heard making a tremen-*
dous racket.)
Ah! This is the moment that will make us
Equal! You still have a way to make up
For your crimes:

Go out and match your bravery with mine.
There, on our walls, prepare to make amends
For having ruined us by your deceit.
You owe it to me, cruel man. Alas,
Never would my father have become
A criminal without your cursed tricks.
Because of you, he's guilty; and our citizens
Are going to find out from me about
Your deadly talents.
(*The WOMEN OF BEAUVAIS are armed with pikes. EMILY carries two of them.*)
EMILY. (*With all the energy and speed possible; the delivery could not be too quick or energetic.*) Oh, Jeanne, have I embraced your plans of victory
To satisfy them? Come walk at our head.
It only took a word, the single name
Of their king, and everyone
Is ready to soar with you into battle.
JEANNE LAISNÉ. (*Taking a pike from EMILY.*)
Yes, I'm going to lead you. What a privilege!
I'll prove myself deserving of so great
An honor. Let us show how much our hearts
Are stirred today, and let them set a good example!
(*Several bombs damage the battlements surrounding the town square. The women become alarmed and angry. Violence and rage is painted in their eyes.*)
Let us all swear, here and now, to face
This thunder, not to leave our walls until
They're reduced to powder . . . to confront
Today, all danger without fear!
ALL THE WOMEN. (*Passionately, with the gesture of taking an oath.*)
Yes, we swear to conquer or die with you.
JEANNE LAISNÉ. (*Boldly to CHIMAI.*)
Ah! I'm triumphant at last. You, go
Tell your master, if he wants to judge
Our hearts, he ought to come and get to know them;
And describe to him, above all else,

When you unfold the tale of these events,
How Beauvais serves his enemy the king!
Let's move ahead!
(*Leading the women, JEANNE leaps up onto the battlements in the
midst of the most deafening gunfire and a new swarm of bombs, some
of which explode near the battalion. Many of the women are knocked
down; the others walk over their bodies. Nothing can stop their enthu-
siastic procession.*)
CHIMAI. (*Alone, going out.*) Holy act of patriotic love!
How great and how heroic is your example!
Fiery sex, proud sex, there's nothing you won't
Do, when love and glory walk with you.

END OF ACT FOUR

(*The artillery continues during the intermission. Many soldiers cross
the town square to reach the battlements. These activities continue
through the entire intermission. Battle music is played.*)

ACT FIVE

CHIMAI. Well, all is lost, since Charles is moving forward,
He must think that we're France's prisoners.
And neither Coucy, nor his followers,
Will have been able to alleviate
The crucial dangers that he's had to face.
MATTHEW LAISNÉ. Our friends have seen them, my lord, calm yourself,
All three have safely left the city.
CHIMAI. But once they're outside, there are other dangers . . .
MATTHEW LAISNÉ. (*Interrupting him.*)
That's just a trick; and while Charles draws our fire
On the battlements, you can be sure
He's marching zealously toward the Bresle
Gate. What were you saying, my lord, about
New reversals of fortune? My daughter,
Rushing down the road to honor (where my
Rank and duty should force me to follow
Her, with so much shame, alas, if I
Wanted to survive) . . . my daughter says:
"Chimai did it alone, my father's innocent.
My people, give him your love and respect.
My father is like you, incapable
Of committing a crime. You're about to see,
From my mighty deeds, if treachery
Is born in the blood from which I come!"
And leaping over the tops of the walls,
She hurls herself amidst the fighting. Her blows
Have their affect already on the trembling enemy,
Surprised by her enthusiastic zeal . . .
Her spirit forced them to control themselves.
They were only moving sluggishly
To the attack, anyway, since they thought
It was just a simulation.
CHIMAI. As your daughter shares your arrogance,
I thought she'd have some kind of an interest

At least, in the secret that unites us.
One trusts the object of his passion, willingly,
To join respect with the sweetness of love,
And I confessed everything to her,
Expecting her to return the favor.
The wretched result of pride, since in my weakness,
I saw clearly that someone else, alone,
Had possession of her tenderness!
I wanted to be wrong. I wanted to be
Enraptured . . .
Soon her cruelty made me regret it:
Her heart burst open and overran me
With her hatred.
(*The artillery which has been heard throughout the scene up to this
point suddenly stops. It is the moment for the attack to begin.*)
MATTHEW LAISNÉ. Wait for time to return her to you,
Your honor. Now that Charles is getting closer,
Her fervor will fade.
Then, you can be sure, she'll love you dearly.
Such personalities must feed on love:
Today, war is appealing with its martial
Allure . . .
After its idle pleasures, those of love
Will follow, and that god will easily
Know how to attract her in its own way.
Listen! Am I wrong? Those war machines
Which death invented to depopulate
The earth . . .
(Infernal, contemptible creations!)
It seems to me the air's no longer shaken
By their racket.
(*He listens again.*)
I'm not mistaken. They're certainly quiet.
All my hopes revive again, my fears
Subside.
There's no longer any risk of error:
Burgundy is going to come.
CHIMAI. Above all, we must make sure that a signal

Warns us immediately when he's in sight.

MATTHEW LAISNÉ. A reliable man has got the job.

(*Three dynamic and very loud drum rolls are heard. MATTHEW LAISNÉ changes his expression; his limbs start to tremble; he appears confused and bewildered.*)

MATTHEW LAISNÉ. You hear it, my lord?

(*He becomes weak and props himself up against the walls.*)

Heavens! I'm dying.

Here I am, then, covered with eternal

Disgrace! I really had foreseen

That at the moment of the crime,

The serpent of remorse would punish me.

(*In tears and in despair.*)

Go away, my lord, go away.

You got what you wanted. Leave me alone

To contemplate the horror of my crime!

Go, meet Charles, he's entering the city.

(*Indicating the Bresle side.*)

That gate is his, the access is easy.

Go offer him my homage and my faith.

(*With a choking voice.*)

The laurels are for him, the Cyprus trees

Belong to me!

CHIMAI. (*Leaving.*) Look forward to the laurels that will dignify

Your head. You've served us. The reward is ready.

Be more self-confident, my friend. You should

Be safe now. This is the moment of triumph,

Not of regret.

MATTHEW LAISNÉ. (*Alone.*)

It's all done. I yield to the weight of disgrace!

Was it to be, then, at the end of my life,

After spending so much time without

Regretting anything, that an eternal

Humiliation should overwhelm me?

My family will be filled with shame forever!

Oh, worthy daughter, you spoke rightly to me.

In your tenderness, you wanted to spare me

The sadness of the trouble that affects me
And devours my heart.
You, who in your folly dared to will
A crime, at least did not asphyxiate
Your conscience,
Whose voice resounds to the depths of your heart.
This instinct toward virtue still fights for you,
And desires to defend you, even though
You're afraid to listen to it . . .
It's one of Heaven's last attempts to save
You. When this voice is silenced, guilt begins . . .
Oh, days so fortunate! Oh, times of innocence!
(*Turning to the city, in tears.*)
Oh, beloved country, ever since
I was a child you gave me every gift
Imaginable to satisfy my needs.
You welcomed me within your walls, and there,
Made me a home.
Did I have the power to betray you?
And adding for good measure,
When my daughter offers her blood to set
You free, to take the same moment to dare
Enslave you,
Trampling on your laws, nature's restraints!
At least don't reward my impertinence.
Almighty God, crush me with all your vengeance,
Before a prize is bestowed on my crimes.
(*The Royalists enter the city. Soldiers fill the streets around the town
square. Some of the soldiers proceed to the battlements. As soon as
MATTHEW sees them he continues.*)
Am I mistaken? Oh, heavens!
What do I see? The French! I'll die happy.
Great God almighty, I appreciate
Your justice. Even in your goodness, You
Cannot allow a traitor to succeed.
(*Recoiling in terror, he is lost in the crowd. Enter CHABANNE,
LAVAL, MAILLÉ, YOUNG DE PILE, CHIMAI, COUCY,
CHAMPLET, DAUTREY—the last four in chains—a troop of*

*officers, squires, and soldiers of the French detachment which has just
seized the public square.)*

CHABANNE. (*Entering from the Bresle side with his troops, hold-
ing YOUNG DE PILE by the hand. At the back of the stage, to his
officers, while he looks around the square.*)
Here it is, my friends, this noble city,
Evermore renowned for its loyalty!
How I love to fill myself with the air
They breathe here! It elevates my soul,
It warms it, it inspires it;
Its sweet scent is that of the laurel tree.
It's the breath of Mars: it ought to please
A soldier.
(*To YOUNG DE PILE, coming downstage.*)
Of all the virtues, eagerness and courage
Are the ones which always pleased me most.
(*To one of his officers.*)
He should be decorated, what do you say,
Maillé? And I want it to be worthy
Of his endeavors.

MAILLÉ. Chabanne, he's satisfied, I promise you.
What else is necessary when a man
Serves his country? The most gratifying
Prize for a French soldier, and the only
One that interests him is victory!

CHABANNE. (*To some of the officers in his party, indicating those
of Burgundy.*)
Here, let their language be their only restraint.[40]
Unlock those shackles. Ah, those marks of hatred
Flaunted by our proud ancestors, wounds
Humanity much too deeply in our eyes.
(*The fetters are removed immediately.*)
Chimai,
These three soldiers, coming from your camp
This morning, fell upon one of our outposts.
Do you know them?

CHIMAI. As brave friends. (*He takes COUCY's hand.*)

---

[40] Burgundians spoke in a Langue d'oil dialect.

COUCY. (*Quickly.*) Whose troubles are relieved with you,
Chimai.
(*The BURGUNDIANS, filling a corner of the stage, remain close to
one another until the end of the play.*)
CHABANNE. (*To CHIMAI in a friendly tone.*)
Would you tell me, at least, what you intended?
CHIMAI. (*Proudly.*) You know, my lord, the fortunes of war. We
hoped
That, taking more time, being better prepared,
We might be close to victory.
We were mistaken ... and you are the victors.
CHABANNE. I don't condemn you. When you serve your
master,
Whatever the means, you're never a traitor.
Run to take the news to our camp, Laval,
To assure our soldiers that nothing
Was equal to the courage, to the fervor
Of the people of this city.
LAVAL. (*To CHABANNE.*) When you arrived, preceded by de
Pile,
Forming the rear-guard with a troop of soldiers
From the post entrusted to my care,
I could observe their miraculous feats
Even better than you.
Nothing can describe those deeds of valor.
Heroic women fighting side by side
With soldiers ... one, above the rest, combining
An icy calm with boldness, she alone
Could pride herself in having saved the day.
Exciting every heart, and with a steady
Arm, making the purple standard float
In the air, happy and glorified
Among the soldiers' ranks,
She raised her victorious hand to Burgundy.
I saw her overthrown, and without fear,
By turns, yielding and recovering her strength,
Break loose from a trap,
Push her adversary into it,

Ward off the murderous fury of a foe,
By sending yet another to his death;
And all, at last, surrendering beneath
Her noble efforts. If the conquered enemy
Happened to flee, my lord, it was her doing.
(*More slowly.*) But that boundless zeal has cost her dearly.
When I came in I saw her on a stretcher.
YOUNG DE PILE. (*Quickly, and in tears.*)
What do I hear? She's dying and I dare
To be away from her.
MATTHEW LAISNÉ. (*Going out quickly.*) What a terrible
blow!
YOUNG DE PILE. (*Likewise going out, to CHABANNE.*)
We owe everything
To her devotion, to her noble courage.
Oh, too wretched fate! Don't try to stop me . . .
(*He rushes to the back of the stage; he is driven back by what he sees.*)
They're carrying her into the square!
(*Enter OLD DE PILE, LOISET DE BALLAGNY, TORCIS,
a troop of officers and soldiers of the garrison, all the citizens of
Beauvais, all the women, EMILY, and JEANNE LAISNÉ.
JEANNE is on a stretcher filled with battle trophies and adorned
with palm branches and laurel wreaths. She is being carried by
the women who, a moment ago, had fought by her side. She is pale,
overcome, her hair in disarray. An arm sling extends from her left
shoulder across her body and hides some of the wounds with which she
is covered. Lying beside her is the banner with the Cross of Burgundy
which she managed to carry away from the enemy. EMILY and
MATTHEW LAISNÉ are standing beside her and are comforting
her. CHIMAI is close at hand as well.*)
YOUNG DE PILE. (*In tears, throwing himself upon the body of his
beloved.*)
Ah! Day of wrath! Day of torment! Ah! Let me
Inundate your laurels with my tears.
JEANNE LAISNÉ. This lovely day's not meant for sadness,
friend.
My prayers have been answered. I am dying
In the bed of honor!

CHABANNE. (*Approaching her, with a gesture of respect.*)
Admirable union of nobility and grace!
LOISET DE BALLAGNY. (*To CHABANNE.*)
You owe the safety of the square to her
Noble heart alone. Your honor, I was
In command here, and I entrust it to you.
CHABANNE. (*To BALLAGNY.*)
Your efforts and your glorious success
Cannot be praised enough.
OLD DE PILE. Her voice encouraged and guided the elderly.
TORCIS. (*Likewise indicating her.*)
Her brilliant achievements inflamed the young.
JEANNE LAISNÉ. (*With a weak voice.*)
Precious eulogies! How much I savor
Them! I've fulfilled my destiny in the
Flower of my youth; what happier fate,
Even if my life were twice as long,
Could have interested me, or pleased me
As well? I saved my city and my honor,
People hold me in esteem, and I'm
Dying for my king.
(*To YOUNG DE PILE.*) I reserved my hand
As a reward for your courage.
(*Showing him the trophies upon which she lies.*)
Here's the marriage bed, here is our altar!
Let's not adore the everlasting decree
Less. (*To the officers of the army, indicating her beloved.*)
Please take care that he'll learn even more,
In admiring all of you, whom he
Just convinced, by facing the enemy,
That he is capable of conquering him.
Protect his youth. He is worthy of you.
CHABANNE. (*To JEANNE LAISNÉ.*)
He will reach the greatest heights, if he
Can equal you and follow in your footsteps.
YOUNG DE PILE. (*Noticing the death agony on the altered face of his beloved, putting his head in his hands; in tears.*)
Ah! What do I see? She's dying.

(*He hurls himself into his father's arms.*)
Father, in this time of tribulation,
In the name of Heaven, tear out my heart,
Or in a moment, I'm going to . . .
OLD DE PILE. No! Respect your life. You're not its master;
It belongs to your country. Complete
Your duties first in working for your king.
Die if you like . . . (*Indicating JEANNE.*)
But die like her!
(*YOUNG DE PILE throws himself at the feet of his mistress. She takes his hand as soon as she sees him beside her.*)
JEANNE LAISNÉ. (*With the greatest tenderness, a weak voice.*)
Live to serve your prince; and if you want
My name to shine, with glory, in the shrine
Of memory,
In the midst of danger, always carry
In your heart, and keep before your eyes
Two things: my face and honor.
YOUNG DE PILE. (*Kneeling, his hands soaking wet with tears.*)
They alone will govern my successes;
They alone will be my laws and guides.
JEANNE LAISNÉ. (*Untying the flag and giving it to the general.*)
Oh, Chabanne, give this flag to Louis;
The only triumph to which I aspire
Is that he'll condescend to accept it.
Tell him that I've gone to Heaven, asking
At the feet of the King of kings, that his
Days be happy, that his reign be long,
And, above all, that he do great things!
OLD DE PILE. (*Placing his hand on the flag.*)
Placed in the temple where you're going to wait
For us, may it have the ability
Someday, by electrifying your ashes,
To reanimate them to fight on our side
Again. When we want to excel, it will
Soar above us.
JEANNE LAISNÉ. (*Seized with convulsions from the pain.*)
I can no longer endure the pain.

(*Turning toward her father.*)
Let my final moments correspond
To nature's laws ...
(*Throwing herself into her father's arms.*)
Father, hold me in your arms!
MATTHEW LAISNÉ. Model of virtue, you teach me my duty.
Your example thrusts itself upon me,
It forbids me to live. Embrace me, daughter,
It's time to follow you.
Oh, you who surround me, fearless Frenchmen,
I was a traitor and I betrayed you.
(*He tries to kill himself.*)
CHABANNE. (*Vigorously stopping him.*)
Good Lord! What new crime are you going to commit?
(*Indicating JEANNE.*)
Live, and respect the blood that gave her birth.
When you pay such tribute to her heart,
You can, one day, set the example
Of virtuous behavior.
JEANNE LAISNÉ. (*Taking CHIMAI's hand.*)
Chimai, so many regrets!
CHIMAI. I can't escape them.
SOUCY. (*Very quickly to CHIMAI.*)
Disguise them at least, if you can't keep them
Quiet. Ah! What a difference between you,
And who doesn't recognize it: you were
Doing your duty. Was he doing his?
JEANNE LAISNÉ. I'm dying ...
YOUNG DE PILE. Ah! Good Heavens!
(*After a moment of the most profound sadness, he addresses
CHABANNE with the fluency of a madman.*)
I hear her calling me!
She wants my blood. Ah! Right now, like her, let me
Go lose myself in the midst of battle:
That is the price of dying in her arms.
I'm still unworthy of it.
CHABANNE. (*To his officers.*) Friends, what heroism!
There's greatness and patriotism everywhere!

Let us carefully note these various
Examples, and one day, let them prove
To the eyes of the world,
How fidelity, glory, and bravery
Were at all times the virtues of France.

END OF THE FIFTH AND LAST ACT

JEANNE LAISNÉ

AFTERWORD

A SUMMARY OF THE EVENT
ACCORDING TO THE BETTER HISTORIANS OF THE DAY

Having been degraded, debased, under Charles VI, France had repaired its misfortunes under Charles VII, through a wise administration on the one hand, and an incredible valor on the other; and undoubtedly, more than anyone knew, by the incentive and heroic courage of that celebrated woman[41] who, obstinate in her pursuit to crown her king at Reims, dared to lead him there from combat to combat, from the depths of the Touraine where the most unforgivable indolence was sleeping in the breast of St. Agnes. This course of action is infinitely more extraordinary than anyone knows, because it supposes, first of all, a very great woman, and furthermore, that the forces were moved by the most able and vigorous hand. This course, I say, pitifully demeaned by the greatest minds in France, nevertheless brought back the throne to the king; and there we were when Louis XI, jealous of Charles's glory, jealous of his wisdom of government, and unfortunately gifted with a character that was deceitful, suspicious, and vindictive, had just taken the reins of the empire, at the border of the Duke of Burgundy's estates where he had taken shelter from the rightful resentment of his father. The changes that he introduced into the kingdom, his ingratitude toward some of generals to whom his father owed the crown, his apprehensions, his suspicions, his inconsistency, his excessive ambition, the effects of which only served to demean his vassals, and to return to him the portions of authority that he dreaded to see distributed to them. Every mind revolted, every spirit turned sour, and from the begin-

---

[41] Joan of Arc.

ning of his reign he had to endure a civil war, the cause of which was said to be the *public good*. However, the only reason causing the subjects to undertake it was revenge against the master's behavior.

Charles the Bold, still Count of Charolais, son of Philip the Good, Duke of Burgundy in whose house Louis XI had gone to take refuge, was one of the fiercest princes in that war. The King had just re-entered the towns of Picardy which had been annexed to him by the Treaty of Arras. Because that behavior upset Charles's ambitions, the Count of Charolais joined with the malcontents, incited, and swept away the duke of Brittany. Louis was undoubtedly about to become more unfortunate than his grandfather, if the treaties of Conflans and Saint-Maur had not stopped the blows that destiny seemed to have in store for him.

But in the treaties, Louis promised everything that everyone wanted; and because he hoped to hold on to nothing, and because he claimed to dodge everything, the war flared up again very quickly. The Duke of Guyenne, displeased with his privileges and who wisely restored to the King, his father, all that he [Louis] had made his own, was vehemently seeking to cause trouble on his part; and to strengthen himself against his sovereign, he was actively seeking the Duke of Burgundy to give him that celebrated Mary, his daughter, whose marriage to Maximilian[42] changed the face of Europe for all time. Likewise, the High Constable of Saint-Paul was plotting on behalf of his accounts; all the lords in general wanted to drag Louis into these discussions, by means of which he would leave them satisfied, which they knew was impossible as long as he was breathing. Thus the king began: pretending that he had complaints against his vassal, he confiscated his lands and withstood the judicial proceedings, taking possession of all Picardy.

To avenge himself, Charles marched in haste to the aid of the province. With the intention of repossessing it, he put everything to the torch and the sword, and burned the outskirts of Beauvais, when an unforeseen resistance stopped him at the walls of this ancient city.

Beauvais was not very strong by itself, but the valor of its inhabitants was well known. A city as old as it was commendable because of its extreme fidelity, Beauvais or *Bratuspautiun* from the commentaries of Caesar, the capital of the Belgian territories, had on

[42] Maximilian I (22 March 1459 – 12 January 1519), the Holy Roman Emperor.

occasion stopped the armies of that hero. It held the highest rank among the cities of Gaul, and always offered in the assemblies, more than twice the men and silver than the others. At the time of the general defection in the kingdom, during the imprisonment of King John, Beauvais, as much as it was able, remained faithful to France; and when the English were masters of the kingdom completely, this city was in some way exempt from the necessity of eluding its lawful sovereigns, since those proud conquerors never lay siege to the city. As soon as Charles VII was crowned, that city was the first to render obedience, which drove the English to such despair that they tried to become its masters once again; and from that moment, the inhabitants, defending themselves with the greatest vigor, demonstrated what they were capable of, and what they were soon about to begin again.

Such was the town that the Duke of Burgundy was hoping to subdue, and that protected the French army camped nearby, commanded by Lord Dammartin, Count de Chabanne.

Charles undoubtedly suspected that it was going to be a waste of time: the negotiations seemed very sound. He pursued them. He secretly wrote some very strong letters to the Burgundians to ask them to open the doors to him; but these brave people despised such appeals and wrote to Charles saying that they were going to answer him with their blood. The angered Duke promised to make it flow beyond doubt, and twenty-six days later, this unfortunate city was fired on by all of Burgundy's artillery.

Several bordering landowners had recently rushed into the fortress. Among them were Méru, Torcis, Loiset de Ballagny, commander of the city, Joachim de Rohault, and several others. The resistance was incredible; and on 9 July 1472, the men were about to be finally overcome in an assault, when all the women under the leadership of Jeanne Laisné (according to Fourquet, the daughter of Matthew Laisné, Burgess of Beauvais), flew impetuously on to the ramparts where they performed incredible acts of bravery. Jeanne Laisné, their leader, pulled a flag out of the hands of a port ensign with which she fought a long while, in hand-to-hand combat. And finally all the men armed with slings, the others with Greek fire, repelled the assailants so successfully that the next day, 10 July, the Duke of Burgundy lifted the siege.

The act of bravery of those generous citizens was quite note-worthy: the lifting of the siege that resulted was so important, that Louis XI wrote on that subject, from the field, in the following letter to the general controller:

> Mr. du Plessis, my friend, I am writing to tell you that I've vowed to eat no meat until the vow I made to send 1,200 *écus* for 200 marks of silver which I ordered to build a city at Beauvais (in remonstrance of which God had given me this city), is accomplished. And for that I pray you, as much as I am able, to deliver immediately by Brisonnet the agreed 1,200 *écus*, and have them build a city and send a very good man there, above all one without a single fault, for if he had difficulties, my vow would never be realized. And seeing that I'm so close to the Duke of Brittany, I should doubt that my Besoignes would not be well inclined to it." Signed Louis.[43]

The King didn't stop there, and wishing to give those illustrious women some token of recognition, at the celebration of the holy mysteries on the feast day of Saint Agadresme, patron saint of the town, he granted them the right to precede the men to the offertory, dressed in their bridal gowns, and in addition, to wear as long as they wished, the fabric, the sashes, and all the various adjustments that characterized the nobility at the time, which pleased them immensely. And yet, he rewarded them not as they deserved, for they behaved like men and Louis treated them like women.

He married Collin Pilon to Jeanne Laisné whom that young man loved, and granted them both total exemptions from poll-tax and income tax, be it at Beauvais or wherever in the kingdom they chose to settle. The flag that Jeanne had raised against the enemy was buried with great solemnity at the Church of the Jacobins in the city, and the portrait of this famous woman was placed in the town hall.

Sometime after this event, the Duke of Burgundy showed his arsenal to a foreign minister, and said to him pompously: "Well, lo and behold! Mr. Ambassador, there are the keys to all the cities of Europe." Immediately after this conversation, the duke's jester began to prowl and search in every corner of the arsenal. "What

---

[43] In the manuscript, Sade added, "How well this letter displays the superstitious character of that prince."

are you doing there?" says Charles to him. "Nothing, sir," replied the jester, "but since you said the keys of all the cities of Europe are there, I'm looking for those to Beauvais without being able to find them." Undoubtedly the joke was infinitely valued more than the boast.

That's all that history provided me. It's a mere trifle, obviously; there's hardly a single scene there and yet I've created from this basic idea, five acts and more than 1500 lines of verse. It was, of course, necessary to invent, to contrive, as the provincial poets used to say. I believed that nothing could be better than the creation of Matthew Laisné, father of our heroine. In his being the mayor of the city and doing what he does to yield to the Duke of Burgundy's innuendos, I'll be able to find one fine scene and brilliant conflicts.

Instead of the bribery by letters which will never have been provided me, I thought a negotiator, falling in love with Jeanne, would give me the opportunity to portray all the arrogance of his manly and courageous virtues. I've chosen for this character a man named Chimai who was, at that time, very much in favor in his master's house. I had been fluctuating somewhat between him and Philippe de Commines, but the latter having changed sides, the same year, did not appear suitable to me.

The Chimai I use here is the same Chimai that Philippe the Good had sent to Louis XI on the occasion of that monarch's desire to create a salt tax in the Duke's States, and to whom he gave the response that you are about to read.

The king who knew that Chimai was coming himself to oppose his wishes, did not see him at all. The annoyed ambassador chose to lay siege to the door to his majesty's chamber. Angered, Louis asked him why he was acting so, and what his master had that was greater than the other princes of the kingdom. "A very big title, sire," answered Chimai haughtily. "He's given you a hospitality that no one else has dared," and the king lowered his eyes.

Dunois[44] asked Chimai how he'd been able to speak in such a way to the monarch. "His ingratitude revolted me," replied the negotiator, "and I would have returned from a distance of 100 leagues to give him that reply if it hadn't come to me immediately."

---

[44] John of Orléans, Count of Dunois, also known as Bastard of Orléans (23 November 1402 – 24 November 1468).

I thought that the same lord employed by Philippe in 1462 was most certainly able to exist ten years after Charles.

Except for the mayor's role which I have reworked as Matthew, Jeanne's father, whose treachery never had effect, everything that happens: Charles's negotiations through Chimai (even though they only took place through letters), the love of Chimai for Jeanne, the father's plan to let the enemy into the fortress, the daughter's plan for the arrival of the French [Royalists], and everything through the same door, because that was the one that was guarded the least—except for what happens at the end of the play, I say, the rest belongs to history. It has given me the brave defenders of Beauvais, their names, the love of Jeanne for Collin Pilon, and the flag, etc., etc.

But the death of our heroine and her father's intense repentance are still my own invention. Was it possible to finish the work without that? The events led there: what is simpler than Jeanne who *really* fights to be wounded to death *spectacularly*! What is more natural than a would-be traitor crushed by his own remorse!

This is my subject. It's now for the public to pronounce judgment on the situation I've created from it. Would that this play give them as much pleasure as I had in writing it. Would that this piece were able to make flow those sweet and delicious tears, which so often come to bathe my eyelids and that necessarily tear out of a French heart those sublime features of patriotism that has been, for all times, his natural virtue.

The Bedroom
or
Certified Folly

Introduction

In the *Descriptive Catalogue of 1788* Sade indicates that his one-act, free-verse comedy, *The Bedroom* was written to be performed after his tragedy, *Jeanne Laisné*. Originally entitled *The Gullible Husband, or The Foolish Test*, Sade changed the name to *The School for Jealousy, or The Foolish Test* and *Jealousy Set Straight, or School for Coquettes* before finally deciding on *The Bedroom* in 1793. On 17 August 1790, Sade gave a reading of the play at the Comédie Française. Only one member of the play selection committee voted in its favor and Sade received a rejection notice a week later.[45] Though the committee was unwilling to reconsider *The Gullible Husband* without substantial changes, Sade was invited to submit any other play he had for the theatre's perusal.

We next hear about the play in a letter to Reinaud on 6 March 1791 when Sade reports to his lawyer that *Jealousy Set Straight* is accepted for production by the Théâtre Italien. Perhaps because of the reception that greeted Sade's *The Briber* at that theatre on 5 March 1792, *Jealousy Set Straight* was never performed. Because *The Briber* had been written by an ex-member of the nobility, a Jacobin

---

[45] On 18 August 1790, Sade wrote to Julien-Marie Naudet (1743-1830), a sociétaire at the Comédie-Française, inquiring about the reading and begging for a quick decision. Sade ends his letter with another of his emphatic proclamations about his interest in the theatre: "For twenty-five years, sir, I have made it my business to openly serve and defend the Comédie-Française. Mr. Molé, your superior, can verify that fact. I have in my portfolio, thirty or so acts of every genre to suggest to you. Yesterday morning, people treated me coldly, I'm not hiding the fact. Whatever happens, I'll sow in another field and write like Scipio: 'Ungrateful country, you won't even have my ashes.'" On 25 August, Naudet notified Sade that the play had been officially refused.

cabal, all wearing red pointed bonnets, stopped the performance during the fourth scene. The 10 March 1792 edition of *Journal des Théâtres* gives a full account of the altercation:

> On Monday March 5th this theatre put on a one-act verse comedy called *The Briber*. There was a hubbub during the first scene. We could not tell why, for nobody had listened, with talking going on in the stalls as if the curtain never gone up. With the second scene the din grew greater; at the third, it reached its height, and with the fourth the actors gave up. What was the purpose of this? We had no idea and could not even hear the explanation. But during the interlude we saw patriots donning the red bonnet with the tip turned forward, like the Phrygian *corno*. One of those dressed in such a fashion said in a loud voice that from now on this red bonnet in public places was going to be the signal for rallying all patriots, especially in theatres.

Undaunted, de Sade wrote Delaporte, the secretary of the Comédie-Française (now performing at the Théâtre de la Nation), on 1 March 1793 and invited the theatre to peruse the newly revised script of his *The Bedroom, or The Gullible Husband*. He notes that although the Comédie-Française had rejected the play previously, he has completed the changes the committee requested before and would happily renounce all rights and royalties should they find the play acceptable for presentation. Two weeks later, having received no reply, Sade penned a litigious note to Delaporte asking for the return of his play if there was no interest in it. On 19 March, Sade received his answer:

> Citizen:
> The Comédie-Française has given me the honor of responding to the letter you sent me. Here it is: despite its regulation that a rejected play cannot receive a second reading, the Comédie-Française, out of regard for Citizen Saint-Fal, has consented to hear the little play by Mr. de Sade, although it falls into that category. The day had been decided. Another reading having lasted longer than expected prevented the Comédie from keeping its promise to Citizen Saint-Fal. It was never the intention of the committee to take advantage of Mr. Sade's gracious offer. Accept the work if it is good. Refuse it if there's no hope for success.

Those were the decisions of the Comédie-Française. As they are particularly busy at the end of the year, the sociétaires of the Comédie are unable to respond as quickly as Mr. Sade might wish. The Comédie-Française, therefore, has the honor of returning his manuscript with best wishes.

Sade humbly responded that he had been too hasty, that he bore no ill-feeling toward the Comédie-Française and never had. What followed was somewhat of an anomaly for Sade, a desperate plea to have the play performed:

> I wanted to have my little play read. I still want it to be read. I know it can succeed. I'm simply asking for the soonest possible production. I'm begging the Comédie to do it as a favor for me. I have very strong reasons for asking it, and since I want no one to think that self-interest has anything to do with it, I will take no royalties from this play. Whatever this trifle will make I'll donate to the war effort. But I beg you to produce it.

Evidently, Sade's approach was successful for a note written to the Marquis by Delaporte, on 12 April 1793, indicates that the play would indeed be read, though not on 13 April as planned. The following day, Sade received yet another message promising to inform him of the new date for the reading. *The Bedroom* never received a second chance at the Comédie-Française.

The play surfaced once again on 10 June 1795 when Miramond, the director of the Théâtre Feydeau, rejected the play. Four years later, after Sade reversed a premature obituary notice in the newspaper, *Ami des Lois*, with the rejoinder, "No, I am not dead, and I would like to imprint proof of my non-equivocal existence on your shoulders with a very large stick," he resubmitted *The Bedroom* to Miramond. This time, on 16 October 1799, the administration of the Théâtre Feydeau refused the play on moral grounds. In their opinion, the plot of the play did not conform to the rules of propriety; the characters in it would disturb the moral members of the audience. They suggested that the work was too serious to be a comedy and would perhaps be better served by the Comédie-Française. The rejection notice ended with the advice that Sade put his talents to better use.

Though refusing the play on moral grounds may appear unwarranted (Sade had published the infamous *Justine, or The Misfortunes of Virtue* in 1791 and *The Bedroom* hardly approaches its libertinism), Miramond was not alone in his position. The Marquis submitted a copy of the play to Julie Candeille, a famous beauty and above-average actress who found the character of Mrs. Dolcour too risky to perform. While admitting that the play was well written, she suggested that its subject matter was too dangerous to put before an audience, and that the playwright should make use of his talent on some other subject.

We last hear of *The Bedroom* in April 1808 when Sade, now in charge of the theatrical presentations at the Charenton Asylum completes a final draft of the play, which he labels "clean copy, edited and corrected for the last time."

There is no record of a performance of the play at the asylum. The first known production of *The Bedroom* occurred in 1992 at The Lab Theatre in Tallahassee, Florida, in an English translation by this author. Critics and audiences alike found the work to be amusing, but conspicuously tame, and most left the theatre scratching their heads in disbelief that the comedy had been refused production on the grounds of moral turpitude.

THE BEDROOM

or

CERTIFIED FOLLY

Verse Comedy in One Act

CHARACTERS

Mr. Dolcour, *a man of means*
Mrs. Dolcour, *his wife*
Sérigny , *a young relative of Mrs. Dolcour*
Lucile, *Mrs. Dolcour's maid*

(The play takes place in Paris in Mrs. Dolcour's bedroom. The room is furnished expensively and in good taste. To the right is a love-seat close to the curtain line. Facing it is a good-looking chest of drawers, perhaps a little large for the room. Between the chest and the wings is an arm-chair coincidentally set up in such a way that whoever sits in it finds himself on stage but hidden from the characters who are in the bedroom although he is able to get a glimpse of them and hear them perfectly. It is eight o'clock at night.)

LUCILE. (*As if in the middle of a conversation.*)
Give Mrs. Dolcour a break.
To think that she's in love with Sérigny!
No. No. You ought know my mistress better than that, sir;
And you can be sure that no one interests her
But the man to whom she pledged her hand and her heart.
DOLCOUR. What? You're telling me that she loves me alone?
LUCILE. I swear it!
DOLCOUR. And on what evidence?
LUCILE. A thousand proofs, and a thousand sighs
Of love most tender heaved for you;
Which you'd see for yourself if you'd open your eyes!
Yesterday, you invited the whole world to your house;
And despite the fact that she had the vapors, in an effort to
please you,
She acted the gracious hostess.
In the middle of the party, someone remarked that you were
unwell,
And all she could think of was going to your side;
And she became so sulky and pensive
That she began to bore everyone to death.
Florival teased her and she didn't even notice.
Alceste tried to amuse her, but she was stubborn.
Not even Célimène who dotes on her these days
Was able to get a single smile out of her.
She was unhappy. Relentlessly unhappy.
A dozen games were suggested to change her mood
But she refused them all, and with a sharp tongue.
"No. I am going to keep him company," she said;
And everyone laughed at her bizarre behavior.
Sounding like a judge, that good-looking Saint-Fond said
That she was going to bring back
The old days of Philemon and Baucis[46]
And that there ought to be a law against it.
But no matter what anyone said, her mind was made up.
And she rose above the chatter

---

[46] In Greek and Roman mythology, Philemon and Baucis were a generous, old married couple who, according to Ovid's *Metamorphoses*, gave refuge to Zeus and Hermes after everyone else in town denied them.

And flew to your side, listening to nothing but her heart.
DOLCOUR. (*Tenderly.*) It's just that I love her so much.
LUCILE. Oh, I believe you. No one is more beautiful ...
Such delicate features: voluptuousness adorned with wisdom,
And obedience tempered by love.
DOLCOUR. Yes, but she flirts too much.
LUCILE. With her eyes?
DOLCOUR. The way she behaves.
LUCILE. Good God, what stupidity.
Look at it under a different light,
And what you call flirting
Should make you proud, not angry.
I'll bet you, it's one of the ways,
That love makes a person more attractive.
You wrong my mistress
If you think she's attracted to young people.
DOLCOUR. After all what can a young and foolish lover
Offer her, when he's still wet behind the ears?
LUCILLE. Pain, torment, horrible cares,
Lots of sighs to get his attention,
Lots of worries trying to hold on to it.
Will he escape? She starts to sulk;
She's afraid that he will slander her viciously.
So, terrified as well as attracted,
Having felt only an illicit passion,
Nourished at the breast of torment,
A woman gets a scandalous reputation,
The scar of misbehavior,
Without ever finding happiness ...
But in the arms of an older and wiser husband,
Love becomes a sweet entrapment ...
Ah! Don't talk to me about such a pleasing bond
Or tomorrow I'd go marry a man as old as you are.
DOLCOUR. (*Nervously.*) But after all, Sérigny ...
LUCILLE. (*Reassuring him.*) What a strange thing to be afraid
of!
If all married men could have a friend like him around,
The world would be a better place.

DOLCOUR. He's very . . . energetic . . .
I'm afraid he'll make a mess of things . . .
That he'll seduce the heart and soul of Mrs. Dolcour;
Yes, that's what I'm afraid of.
They were supposed to be married;
A few regrets, yearnings perhaps,
Sooner or later might rekindle the spark.
So you see the horror of my fate!
LUCILLE. Yearnings? Not on your life, sir. They will never
appear.
Far from it, on my honor.
DOLCOUR. But why every day in the same room,
Which she made me decorate so carefully,
And which she calls her bedroom,
Why . . . solve this problem for me . . .
Does she entertain him there with such enthusiasm?
LUCILE. (*Softly, almost mysteriously.*)
It's the only quiet place in the house.
It's the only place where they can apply themselves . . .
Without getting too exhausted . . .
To their studies.
DOLCOUR. What do you mean by exhausted?
You're not making any sense.
Lucile, speak to me a little more clearly.
LUCILE. That would be betraying a secret they've entrusted to
me.
They'll punish me.
DOLCOUR. They wouldn't dare. Go on.
LUCILE. (*To herself.*) Heavens! How am I going to get out of
this damn maze?
(*To DOLCOUR.*) First of all, set your mind at rest, completely,
Nobody's taking a swipe at your marriage vows.
The thoughts which sprawl about this room
Never distressed a husband;
But promise not to say a word,
Because I'm afraid I've said too much already.
DOLCOUR. (*Impatiently.*) Very well.
LUCILE. Very well, sir, without the least hint of scandal,

Behaving themselves, directed by virtue,
(*Taking him aside, and speaking mysteriously.*)
The two of them are writing a treatise on morality.
DOLCOUR. Writing a treatise on morality? You've got to be
kidding.
She'd never . . . But tell me,
Otherwise my mind will never rest on this subject,
Why do they have to lock themselves in
If all they're doing is writing?
LUCILE. (*In charge of the situation.*)
They need absolute silence, sir.
The least little thing will interrupt their concentration.
Their commingled souls are unable to soar to heaven
With beatific ardor
If someone should disturb them for even an instant.
DOLCOUR. And you have proof of these holy activities?
LUCILE. Proof? Who? Me? Now and then,
But I can't make heads nor tails of it.
These are unique doctrines,
Strenuous dissertations . . . and sacred mysteries,
And my poor spirit can't rise to the occasion.
DOLCOUR. (*After consideration.*)
My child, you know that I hold you in high regard. I like you.
Hundreds of times have I passed over your mistakes
In the service of your mistress;
Promise, immediately,
To do me an important favor.
LUCILE. Whatever you want, sir, I'm yours to command.
Whatever you want me to do,
I'll obey without the least delay.
DOLCOUR. I want to see the effects of everything you say . . .
(*Hesitating.*) Not that I doubt my wife for a moment,
When you know her like I do, there's little to fear . . .
But by watching that Sérigny I'm going to prove,
Or dismiss my suspicions, once and for all.
Will they see one another tonight?
LUCILE. Yes. What are you planning to do?

DOLCOUR. First of all, we must be very quiet, then, with great care,
I'll cleverly hide myself in the room.
(*Looking around.*) Yes. . . There. In that corner, where, thanks to your cleverness,
I'll be able to hear easily what your mistress says
Without anything getting in the way.
LUCILE. (*Distraught, but containing herself.*)
Sir, I want the best for you, but be reasonable.
To spy on the moment when the heart gives way to the spirit!
I don't see what good can come of this unseemly project.
DOLCOUR. Even if it shows me your mistress is completely innocent?
LUCILE. Since at the moment she is innocent in your eyes,
You cannot esteem or love her more.
And if by chance, your expectations
Don't work out as you planned . . .
(Everything is bound to sound like a love affair.)[47]
Then you'll transform the most innocent deception
Into the most shocking truths.
DOLCOUR. Your pretty logic doesn't satisfy me.
I'm going to see for myself.
LUCILE. (*As if struck by an idea.*) Well, this chest of drawers
Will come in handy.
DOLCOUR. (*Going to sit in the armchair hidden by the chest of drawers; sarcastically.*)
It certainly will.
I can see everything in the closet at least from here.
LUCILE. And will you be able to hear?
DOLCOUR. Wait, that's the purpose of all of this.
Where do they usually sit?
LUCILE. (*Throwing herself on the love-seat.*) Here.
DOLCOUR. Both of them?
LUCILE. Often.
DOLCOUR. Ahem! Imitate their voices.
LUCILE. (*Muttering with her lips closed; aloud.*) Can you hear me?
DOLCOUR. Oh! Good Lord, no!

---

[47] Sade's parentheses.

Do they talk so quietly?

LUCILE. (*Getting up and leaning on the chest behind which her master is sitting.*)

Sir, that depends on the enthusiasm affecting their spirit.

At first when they begin, the conversation is very quiet.

By degrees, it gets louder and often it erupts

At the conclusion of their discussion

To such a point that they are making noises you couldn't imagine.

DOLCOUR. (*Getting up and coming back on stage.*)

I imagine, then, that I'll be able to hear them.

I'll hide here.

LUCILE. (*Hearing a noise; very quickly.*) Someone's coming.

Get out of here. It's that time. It's your wife.

DOLCOUR. I'll come back. She has eyes at the back of her head.

I don't want her to see anything

Or have the least suspicion

Of the plot I'm hatching.

You're sure she'll return later?

LUCILE. Yes.

DOLCOUR. (*Quickly.*) You'll come to get me

Before she arrives and before

A single word passes

Between the little lovebirds.

LUCILE. Oh! Sir!

DOLCOUR. (*Very quickly; taking her hand.*). No, not a word.

LUCILE. You can count on my eagerness to please you.

DOLCOUR. And you can count on my gratitude!

(*Enter MRS. DOLCOUR.*)

MRS. DOLCOUR. (*She is scantily dressed like an elegant coquette, with a sort of carelessness in her demeanor and a weariness in her delivery.*)

What? Are you here, sir? It's indecent!

Ah! If anyone knew that you were going to visit my bedroom

Without the least bit of warning,

They'd think you had something to be jealous about.

DOLCOUR. I'm sorry. I'm wrong, I know it.

I was looking for you, and the surest way

To ease the pain caused by your absence
Is to visit the rooms that give you so much pleasure.
MRS. DOLCOUR. Always the sweet-talker. All right, you appease me.
I was going to become angry with you
But you're forcing me to remain quiet.
DOLCOUR. That's not the effect I was looking for.
MRS. DOLCOUR. Are you contradicting me?
DOLCOUR. No, but I would have liked to please you;
That would have been my goal.
MRS. DOLCOUR. (*Coldly, but pretending beautifully.*)
Well then, you have succeeded.
(*MR. DOLCOUR places a jewel box on one of the corners of the desk, as if by chance, not wanting to be seen.*)
LUCILE. (*Observing him and drawing the attention of her mistress.*)
Look, Madame. Another present, I'll bet on it.
MRS. DOLCOUR. What have you got there?
DOLCOUR. No. No. Don't look.
MRS. DOLCOUR. (*Going to take the jewel box.*)
Ah, let me, I beg of you.
(*She opens the box and takes out a beautiful set of diamonds; then without interest.*)
You were wrong. It's nothing.
LUCILE. (*Looking at the diamonds.*)
How beautiful. Look how they shine!
MRS. DOLCOUR. (*Putting them back into the box; sarcastically.*)
Your generosity shines.
Was that necessary to win my heart?
(*She gives the box back to LUCILE.*)
DOLCOUR. Do not take away from my generosity
That which could double its enjoyment.
MRS. DOLCOUR. Ah, you're not very smart.
DOLCOUR. Will this mood pass with the night?
MRS. DOLCOUR. Oh, I'm always consumed by it;
It's my nerves, and I'm sick to death of them.
DOLCOUR. Then you ought to move around a bit,
Work up a sweat, get a little exercise.

Sitting around all day you're bound to get depressed.
MRS. DOLCOUR. Where do you want me to go when everything
Bores me to death? I am so tired of life,
Its tedium depresses me so much
That, one of these days, I won't be able to stop myself
From falling into the depths of despair.
DOLCOUR. When you are so well provided for all the pleasures of life?
MRS. DOLCOUR. No. They don't mean anything to me. I'm tired of them.
DOLCOUR. Your mood disturbs me, and I feel sorry for you,
But what can you do about it?
Aren't we supposed to dine at Célimène's tonight?
MRS. DOLCOUR. You want me to eat out, feeling the way I do?
Inflicting my migraine on everybody else?
Don't do this to me.
Honestly, I'll die. I'll be a cold fish.
You have no idea how my mind becomes obsessed
With building castles in Spain.
DOLCOUR. (*Peevishly.*) By yourself?
MRS. DOLCOUR. Of course! Why are you looking at me?
It's the only pleasant way . . . there, without a single care,
In complete relaxation, one can think about
The ridiculous monotony offered by the world to us today.
One can enjoy the bizarre comparison
Between an idiot and a genius:
Should the one amuse you through his lumpish ignorance,
The learned attitude of the second, behaving
As if good sense exists for him alone,
Would inspire your silent respect.
One laughs at the horrid role of those low-class whores
Who, having just flattered whoever is useful to them,
Get down on their knees to burn the incense
That sweetens their fragile and stupid god.
If some happy illusion carries us off one moment,
The heart undeceived promptly brings us back;

Very little remains of what is enticing,
One can hardly see it; one can barely feel it.
This flash of happiness is like lightning,
Which, in preparation for its deafening thunder,
Lets the illusion dissolve and disappear
In the torrents of rain that no one saw coming.
Your world, in a word, seems to me pitiful;
It is false and deceitful . . . and unbearable.
The wise man doesn't know how to take a step without trembling;
Even the sweet appearance of wisdom has been frightfully abused
Ever since vice and its shamelessness
Assumed the mask of virtue in our eyes.
Ah! You will agree, this heap of injustice
Of wickedness, of abnormality,
Causes, in fact, the suffering
Of those who can see, without rose-colored glasses,
So many fools vegetating on this miserable planet.
DOLCOUR. Look, all of that is ridiculous.
It's better to go and have fun
Than to try to be philosophical.
Leave the moralizing to old fogies with their stuffed-shirts
And come with me to dinner over your friend's house.
MRS. DOLCOUR. Don't push it, I'm warning you,
It would depress me.
I'd be lousy company anyway,
So why waste a perfectly good evening.
Besides, absence makes the heart grow fonder.
The less they see of me, the more they like me.
My mind is made up!
DOLCOUR. Since it's impossible to persuade you,
I'll give in.
But Célimène and d'Olbreuse
Are going to tease me something awful
When I show up without you.
MRS. DOLCOUR. (*Smiling.*) Be insolent and face the music.
DOLCOUR. (*Teasing her.*) All right, I'm going, you little tart,
Just so there won't be any disagreement between us.

MRS. DOLCOUR. See how a little artifice and a little foolishness
Win out while being on the defensive!
LUCILE. Oh, Madame, he's deceiving you,
And it makes me tremble even now.
If you only knew the plot he's hatching at this very moment.
MRS. DOLCOUR. You're making me nervous. Tell me about it, quickly.
LUCILE. Sérigny worries him, and your husband cannot contain
His ravenous pangs of jealousy;
He pulled out of me . . . with great difficulty . . .
The reason why he comes to your house so often.
MRS. DOLCOUR. What did you tell him?
LUCILE. Madame, in the face of his wrath,
I could think of only one lie to appease him;
And so I told him that the two of you were in the bedroom
Writing a treatise on morality.
MRS. DOLCOUR. (*Laughing hysterically.*) What a great lie!
LUCILE. But that's not all.
MRS. DOLCOUR. What's the rest of it?
LUCILE. Listen. I wasn't sure if he bought the story.
His eyes showed he needing convincing. . .
(*Trembling.*) So he forced me . . . .
MRS. DOLCOUR. What? Forced you to do what? Speak.
You're sending a chill down my spine.
LUCILE. He intends to hide behind the chest
During your conversation tonight
With Sérigny.
MRS. DOLCOUR. You agreed to that?
LUCILE. What else could I have done?
Must a mystery be left
Where it really doesn't exist?
MRS. DOLCOUR. All right then, but to prevent any embarrassment,
Go tell Sérigny that I've changed my mind about staying at home,
That I'm dining out tonight.
LUCILE. Is that necessary?

Will this ordinary lie change your husband's mind?
What he can't accomplish tonight
He'll do tomorrow. I thought it would be to your advantage
To find yourself in the position of showing him
That nothing happens between you and Sérigny
That would make decency blush.
(*Pointing to the chest.*)
Let the master quietly enlighten himself there.
MRS. DOLCOUR. You're right, but it worries me;
I don't approve of the means,
And what are we going to talk about?
LUCILE. The dangers of love and the pain it causes
When someone foolishly exposes himself to its arrows.
MRS. DOLCOUR. I can steer the conversation in that direction;
It's a very promising text.
LUCILE. You're pleased?
MRS. DOLCOUR. (*Sighing.*) Yes, indeed.
At least I can take revenge on Cupid
For throwing me into this mess.
LUCILE. Don't judge him too harshly;
Come what may, Sérigny will make an appearance.
Above all, tell him to try to be master . . .
MRS. DOLCOUR. (*Dryly.*) Of what, young lady?
LUCILE. Why, of the feeling you don't feel
But nevertheless he does . . .
MRS. DOLCOUR. Him? Love?
LUCILE. That's not what he really wants, I know that well-enough;
But, if he doesn't change his attitude,
He'll never fool the one on whom
Your peace of mind depends.
MRS. DOLCOUR. Go, calm down. I hate jealousy.
When a husband is jealous without cause,
He should be treated like he expects;
In similar situations, Cupid takes revenge
With arrows straight to the heart.
Truly the way he does things is strange!

LUCILE. Without a doubt . . . Someone's coming.
It must be Sérigny. Come on!
Try, if you can, to make a giddy youth
Who takes nothing seriously into a prude!
(*Enter SÉRIGNY.*)
SÉRIGNY. (*Light and jovial.*) What's up, cuz?
Your old man spending the evening at Célimène's?
I discovered the fact not without a great deal of trouble,
So, I've come to dine alone with you.
LUCILE. (*Aside.*) A great start for a lesson in morality.
MRS. DOLCOUR. (*Smiling.*) What a joker.
I doubt that there's anything that'll make you serious.
SÉRIGNY. Yes indeed! I'm beginning to appear intelligent,
Everybody sees it; you're the only ones
Who are naughty and won't admit it.
Everyone else thinks that I'm making fun of
That dull common sense so dear to our grandmothers,
Those old prudes, who, already too dead
To give love the credit it deserves,
Imagine they can save themselves only by the use of logic.
LUCILE. (*Quickly to SÉRIGNY.*)
Don't indulge in such awful gibberish.
You're hateful for even having such a terrible notion.
Happiness always lies in common sense;
In short, a woman with a pleasant mind,
A beautiful personality, and a big heart
Can grow old without fear;
She will always appear young, as long as she's good natured.
SÉRIGNY. She's become a philosopher!
MRS. DOLCOUR. But she's right!
Cousin, give up this foolishness.
I can't abide the sound of it.
SÉRIGNY. Ah! Pity me. Every day I plan on
Approaching you with the stoic behavior of a Cato,[48]
But then I see you, and your eyes turn my head.
MRS. DOLCOUR. Then you have to steer clear of their looks,
And above all suppress these outbursts.

---

[48] Marcus Porcius Cato (234 BC – 149 BC), Roman statesman, soldier, historian, and epigrammatic writer.

SÉRIGNY. Isn't it allowed to worship at the shrine of the god
you adore?
Unhappy is he who, looking for ways to please her,
Can only serve her by words.
LUCILE. Madame, if we don't hurry up,
I'm afraid we'll have to give up our plan.
SÉRIGNY. Why are you rushing us? The old man is far away;
There's no fear of being caught.
MRS. DOLCOUR. (*Seriously.*)
He is here, young man, and I'm not afraid of anything.
Listen, nevertheless, to what I am forced to do
Having been too often exposed to the innocent pleasure
Of entertaining you in this room.
I will not be able to do it anymore. My husband is jealous of you.
His head is filled with a thousand foolish ideas,
And I must undoubtedly relieve his fears.
A prude, in public, would have dismissed you from her sight,
And without the slightest hesitation,
Would continue to meet you somewhere in secret.
But I'm going to behave differently
And not deprive myself of a good time
Because of some foolish mistake.
So we have to be smart, and above all, very careful.
I'm warning you, he plans on surprising us;
He'll be sitting over there to overhear us;
So control your tongue and give him the reassurance he needs.
If you behave yourself, I will reply in kind;
If not, take care, a single word, a single gesture,
Will separate us forever.
SÉRIGNY. What a terrible dilemma.
And how could we have guarded against it?
The wild old man! In your place.
I would do nothing to remove his foolish fears;
In an instant, I'd verify his suspicions.
How dare he dine at home when he's supposed to be in the city!
MRS. DOLCOUR. (*Interrupting quickly with a smile.*)
Now run, little cousin, go hide in Lucile's room.
And don't come out until someone comes and gets you.

SÉRIGNY. All right. I'll be quiet.

I hope I'll be lucky enough to overcome

The terrible ache in my heart. (*He leaves briskly with LUCILE.*)

MRS. DOLCOUR. So no matter what you do or don't do,

There's no way to reverse a husband's suspicions.

Oh! I'm going to punish him for this. I hate jealous people

For not trying to change

When the opportunity is staring them right in the face.

(*Re-enter LUCILE.*)

LUCILE. All right, I've calmed Sérigny down.

I was afraid that I wasn't going to be able to convince him,

Since he was dead set against our plan;

But in the end, I won out.

He swore to me that he would be the master

Of his sighs, the ones you'll condemn in him tonight.

MRS. DOLCOUR. Tonight, as always.

LUCILE. Oh yes, Madame, yes. I agree with you.

MRS. DOLCOUR. But not entirely, it seems to me.

LUCILE. Oh! Heavens, to break apart what love puts together is cruel.

(*Pause.*) It's not that important.

MRS. DOLCOUR. Love is wrong when logic forbids it.

You can't compromise your conscience;

Remember that.

LUCILE. All right, but why don't you go speak to him,

Calm his suspicions. Our success could depend on it.

MRS. DOLCOUR. You're right. I'll go.

When everything's ready, let me know. (*She exits.*)

LUCILE. Yes, yes, without making an issue of it,

If I were mistress of these circumstances,

I would immediately set my husband straight

With a lot less consideration.

Ah, a jealous husband is an imbecile!

It must delight him to go so far

To stretch the boundaries of decency,

Simply to uncover our secrets;

And to correct this madness,

Quite frankly, you have to be brazen

And expose him to a few more qualms than he already has.
Here he comes. Not another word.
LUCILE. (*Tentatively and sadly to MR. DOLCOUR as he enters.*)
Ah! I've been expecting you.
You see how I keep my word in spite
Of whatever may happen to me.
DOLCOUR. (*Giving her a purse.*)
First of all, here's payment in full.
LUCILE. (*Taking the purse.*)
You're too kind. If you're going to hear
Some things which may unfortunately make you angry,
You might blame me
For my cooperation in this dreadful business.
(*Trying to give it back to him.*)
Here, take it. Don't pay in advance,
Wait until you know what will come of it.
DOLCOUR. No, keep it. But what are you trying to say?
You're chilling me to the bone; tell me more.
If the fact is proven, why should I be afraid of it any longer?
LUCILE. Sir, in these cases, supreme knowledge, I think,
Consists in convincing ourselves.
No one is ever satisfied
Until he's seen it all with his own two eyes.
Then of its own free will, our conscience finally rests.
Worries can no longer bother us;
We say to ourselves: I've seen it all, I don't doubt a thing.
DOLCOUR. Suddenly, for no reason, you're making me nervous
. . .
I must stay calm . . .
LUCILE. Me? I've told you what I think.
And you responded with this elaborate plot.
To be better informed, must you deny
Whatever might advise you to the contrary?
DOLCOUR. Why are you keeping me in suspense?
What am I supposed to do?
LUCILE. Ah! If I were in your place,
I know what I would do.
DOLCOUR. Tell me for God's sake.

LUCILE. (*Touching his forehead.*)
First, I would come to this conclusion.
DOLCOUR. Which is?
LUCILE. That nothing can contain a woman
Who wants to escape her bonds;
The more pains you take to penetrate her passion,
The more she uses to mislead you.
That's what we do, sir, like it or not;
Thank heavens for glances which cover up our methods
While hiding our plots . . .
You use them to conquer us; we use them to deceive you.
Not to trouble myself any further with this established fact,
I would go immediately to Mrs. Dolcour,
And her virtue, her goodness, her truthfulness,
Would give me such a good report of her heart
That I wouldn't need a visible proof
To satisfy me.
DOLCOUR. But without seeing anything, I continue to be alarmed
By this burdensome fear.
LUCILE. But in seeing too much, you may not be consoled
By your "honest mistake."
DOLCOUR. What an awkward position I'm in.
I want more than anything to settle this.
LUCILE. I understand what you're going through.
DOLCOUR. In spite of myself, I'm staggering between these two tortures
And I don't know how to stop.
You make up my mind, then.
LUCILE. All right! I'll try.
Let's take a look at the worse that could happen: she's unfaithful!
In this sort of thing, whoever is the most afflicted
Looks upon himself as the victim.
But, I tell you, the unhappiness he experiences
Isn't all that extremely important.
Think about it, sir.
You know, sir, in the age in which we're living,
That is the role of all men.

Much less foolish than in earlier times,
They know the torment that invariably results
When they rely on a woman's virtue.
Today, they get over it in their hearts and their souls
And build monuments to war heroes;
So, bite the bullet, and don't be afraid.
DOLCOUR. If you say so, I agree; I'll risk the unexpected.
LUCILE. Good luck then.
Ah! Once you've seen everything. . .
What supreme tranquility!
Hurry. It's your wife.
Come on, sir, come on. Calm down.
What's making you so nervous?
DOLCOUR. (*Quickly placing himself behind the desk.*)
Wait a minute; look around,
Nobody can see anything?
LUCILE. Nothing shows. But be careful not to make a noise.
(*It goes without saying that everything that DOLCOUR says until
the last scene is aside and in a low voice; but as he is seen by the audi-
ence, his bearing and his movements must always betray what he is
thinking. When MRS. DOLCOUR enters, LUCILE whispers in her
ear that all is ready.*)
MRS. DOLCOUR. Lucile, are you certain
That Mr. Dolcour has left?
LUCILE. Yes, Madame, he's gone.
MRS. DOLCOUR. Very well. Can you believe it?
I was just saying to myself
That I made up my mind too soon;
My headache is gone and I feel a lot better;
And if it weren't too late,
I'd go over to Célimène's anyway.
I'm afraid that my quarrelsome behavior
Might have offended my husband's good nature.
You should have scolded your mistress
And not let her get away with
Antagonizing the best of all husbands.
DOLCOUR. (*In hiding.*) How I love her!
LUCILE. He forgives you.

He knows how you are.

MRS. DOLCOUR. No, really. I've taken advantage of his noble
and sensitive nature;
The moment after, I was mortified,
For behaving with such ingratitude.
He must think that I'm in great demand,
That I enjoy myself to excess,
When he sees this outrageous behavior.
This is not the usual flim-flam
I invent in similar circumstances.
He can think me false, but when my heart confesses,
I face remorse and terrible apprehension.

LUCILE. Banish them, or calm them, Madame,
Mr. Dolcour can see to the bottom of your soul . . .

DOLCOUR. Oh! God, yes, I'm not hiding from it.

LUCILE. (*Continuing.*)
You make up for it with so many other allurements,
That he easily attributes those few faults to your youth.
Those minor failings make the gifts heaven gave you,
With so much magnificence, burn even brighter.

MRS. DOLCOUR. Right now I want to hold him in my arms.
(*DOLCOUR moves suddenly as if to go to her but quickly contains
himself.*)
I'm always afraid that he isn't aware of it
But, in truth, I adore him
As a charming husband and a worthy friend!

DOLCOUR. I've got a good feeling about this.

MRS. DOLCOUR. How am I going to spend this sad evening?

LUCILE. Entertaining Mr. Sérigny.

MRS. DOLCOUR. (*Interested.*) Is he here?
Then I'm going to be a little less devoured by boredom,
And sheltered from the vapors at least.
So much the better; we'll chat. Tell the doorman
That I'm not at home for anyone today,
And, absolutely, to let no one in but him.

DOLCOUR. Shit! That's going too far.
All right, fatal star, enlighten me. I'm ready!

LUCILE. I'll go give everyone the orders for the evening.

MRS. DOLCOUR. (*Pretending to be alone.*)
A woman is betrayed by so much idle gossip
That, when I entertain this cousin of mine,
I ought to be very careful to stay non-committal
So that the rumor going around constantly
Won't make him out to be my lover.
Him, my lover? I know that people think it . . .
And what can be done about it after all?
To worry would be useless . . .
At most, the suspicion could wound my husband,
But in the end, there's nothing that would offend him.
I can acknowledge Sérigny without shame.
DOLCOUR. Ah!
MRS. DOLCOUR. (*Continuing quickly.*)
So my virtue ought to be greatly praised
Since I've made nothing of him but my friend.
Ah. Here he comes.
DOLCOUR. God bless me, I'm numb all over.
(*Enter SÉRIGNY.*)
SÉRIGNY. (*Controlled, serious, embarrassed almost throughout the
scene, in which he is very far removed from his own personality.*)
How grateful I should be, madam,
Every moment your heart surpasses itself, in the goodness . . .
MRS. DOLCOUR. (*Interrupting him.*) I do what I ought.
Your argument is solid, I am your cousin,
By right, without fear,
I can receive you in my bedroom.
(*She sits on the love-seat.*) Come sit beside me.
(*He takes a seat.*) Alone here just now, I was saying to myself
That a person would have a hard time
Convincing the women of today
That we were not in love.
"She shuts her door and gives a private interview!
Aha! The folly is complete!"
Our benign beauties would say smirking!
"Surely she's lost her head;
We've got to tell all of Paris about it."

DOLCOUR. It's certain that, in watching them take liberties
like these,
More than one husband could be put on the rack.
SÉRIGNY. You're not stopping this horrible injustice at all.
People think that shortcomings can be hidden
In pretense and trickery;
People think that you cannot be seen except as an accomplice
To the crimes you yourself find fault with at every turn;
What's more, it's no sacrifice to vanity
To suspect vices everywhere,
Since people take a great deal of trouble establishing the need
For virtues which they themselves cannot practice.
MRS. DOLCOUR. Virtue isn't the word, and I cannot
acknowledge it
Used in terms of such useless desires.
DOLCOUR. This calms me down and reassures me a little.
SÉRIGNY. (*Continuing quickly.*) Allow me a moment.
It depends on how great or small a fire
Love can burn in our hearts.
MRS. DOLCOUR. But I do not embrace these fantastic flames
And he who lights them is in need of common sense,
Which is easily mastered.
SÉRIGNY. (*Stuttering.*) I understand that these impulses
Which I renounce and scorn here, following your example,
Are more cruel than attractive.
MRS. DOLCOUR. (*Continuing quickly.*)
To persuade you in a way that is undeniable,
I ask you to cast your eyes
On the dangerous desire within you
Which, every day, happens to embrace these fires.
Take a look at the reprehensible sentiment
You force to conspire against us;
In cold blood your guilty heart
Almost always seeks to mislead us;
And when your arrows are shot at us, your defenseless victims,
When seduction forces us on our knees,
Without the faintest sympathy
For those feeble and sweet inclinations,

Which you yourself have skillfully nourished within us,
Your god of love, or your foolishness
Comes out the winner and chains us to you!
Does this tender pretense, at least, please you?
Do you value a flirt
Who costs you so many sighs?
No. You forget her when your passion wanes,
You abandon her to the care of her fears
And her useless regrets,
So that her dishonor, her sadness, and her tears
Happen to create an even greater triumph for you!
And you do not want us to conquer or defy
That corruptible feeling. No! You throw your fatal mistakes
Right under our feet and smile as we fall.
And that's the epitome of misfortune!

DOLCOUR. (*Still aside.*) Ah, I adore her, and make no secret
Of the feelings burning inside me today.

SÉRIGNY. (*Answering MRS. DOLCOUR.*)
What you've just said is nothing but stupid nonsense;
In spite of the pains we take to suppress it,
The cause of our greatest calamities is love.

MRS. DOLCOUR. (*Continuing very quickly.*)
The ravage of years, the troubles of war,
Have never so destroyed people;
Love has broken more restraints
Than all of the crimes in the world.

DOLCOUR. Ah. How I'd love to show them the truth in that.
(*From here to the end of the scene, both are caught up in outdoing each other, observing, nevertheless, an artistic build that lasts until the sudden burst in the last speech of MRS. DOLCOUR.*)

SÉRIGNY. (*Animated, with little restraint.*)
Let its mysteries, absorbed by our hands,
Be annihilated never to appear.

MRS. DOLCOUR. Ah! To prevent this folly from being reborn,
Let us firmly oppose the charming bond of friendship.
(*They begin to get into position for the end of the scene.*)

SÉRIGNY. Sweet feeling, honest and tender,
Which almost always knows how to make us

More compatible, and happier!

MRS. DOLCOUR. O saint and virtuous desire!

Marvelous and divine ecstasy!

Does he, who, in himself, knows how to receive you,

Need any more immediate pleasure?

(*They are in one another's arms.*)

DOLCOUR. (*Still hiding but aloud.*)

Oh! I've won. She's faithful!

(*Getting up suddenly.*) I'll go show her my passion;

I'll go fall at her feet. (*He goes to them.*)

Happiness of my heart, how this moment is sweet!

(*Here MRS. DOLCOUR, who was playing dismay during the first of her husband's lines, nearly faints. She is held by SÉRIGNY who looks firmly at DOLCOUR, who remains on his knees in front of them.*)

MRS. DOLCOUR. (*Terrified.*) Oh, good Lord, I'm going mad!

Very well, sir, what have you heard?

DOLCOUR. Nothing that doesn't add to your virtue

But then weren't you saying ...

MRS. DOLCOUR. (*Quickly.*)

Then why, sir, this bizarre behavior?

DOLCOUR. (*Still on his knees; to his wife.*)

Alas, I was wrong! Come punish me,

I suspected you; take revenge on a barbarian!

You ought to arm your arm against him!

MRS. DOLCOUR. (*Back to normal, and firmly to her husband.*)

Such behavior should alarm me,

Sir, I ought to fear everything involved in such a scene,

And the role that it forces me to take

Is to go to my mother's house immediately and lock myself in.

(*She acts as if she's leaving.*)

DOLCOUR. (*Getting up in despair and running after her.*)

What did you say? Heavens! What did I just hear?

You want to abandon me?

Me who only wanted to render

Due worship to your virtues!

(*From this point the scene should play as quickly as possible.*)

MRS. DOLCOUR. (*Continuing to appear as if she's leaving.*)

Oh, yes. Don't speak any more about it.
DOLCOUR. (*To SÉRIGNY, who is also trying to leave, but who returns.*)
Sir, by the grace of God, I beg you . . .
SÉRIGNY. (*Stopping, as if in spite of himself.*)
But will you always be so jealous?
DOLCOUR. (*Leaving SÉRIGNY to follow his wife who looks as if she's going.*)
Ah. Don't treat me like that!
Only blame the love in my heart!
MRS. DOLCOUR. (*Allowing herself to return.*)
Very well, to avoid rumors and scenes,
I will stay here under the weight of my chains.
(*Firmly to SÉRIGNY.*) But, Sir, you cannot visit me anymore.
SÉRIGNY. (*Pretending the greatest sadness.*)
What a crushing blow!
DOLCOUR. (*Very agitated.*) Never to receive him!
I urge the contrary, and, not to displease you,
I want him to visit you here every day at his convenience.
SÉRIGNY. (*Faking an exit.*) No, sir, it's over. The command is sacred.
DOLCOUR. (*Rushing after him to bring him back to his wife.*)
Sir, I beg you. Stop him, Madame.
MRS. DOLCOUR. My heart is too wounded by your behavior.
SÉRIGNY. (*Brought back and held by DOLCOUR, but fighting back.*)
No, I'm not going back, I tell you.
DOLCOUR. (*Very quickly to MRS. DOLCOUR and not letting go of SÉRIGNY.*)
If it is true that a husband has rights concerning his wife,
In the name of our marriage bonds, I want Sérigny,
Always and forever, to be free and clear with you.
MRS. DOLCOUR. (*Going quickly.*) In that case, I'm leaving.
DOLCOUR. (*Letting go of SÉRIGNY to follow MRS. DOLCOUR.*)
You're breaking my heart!
(*He brings her back but SÉRIGNY exits.*)

SÉRIGNY. (*Leaving*.) I'm like you, sir, confused by everything here!

DOLCOUR. (*Quickly to LUCILE who has just entered, and giving her his wife so he can run after SÉRIGNY*.)
Lucile, hold on to your mistress for a minute,
She's driving me crazy. (*He runs after SÉRIGNY*.)

LUCILE. (*Holding on to MRS. DOLCOUR*.)
Ah! Let's talk some more about the eloquent language of your tenderness!

DOLCOUR. (*Returning with SÉRIGNY; to his wife, still held by LUCILE, and to SÉRIGNY*.) Oh! Hell, this time you ran out for nothing.
(*Standing between his wife and SÉRIGNY, he takes their hands and joins them*.)
Yes, I want friendship to unite you forever;
Forgive me, both of you, for my insufferable behavior,
Forgive the effects of a too passionate affection.
Being a stranger to love, I had to learn
That, if you want the niceties of love,
The first thing you have to do is trust.
For a long time, in ways I now find reprehensible,
I wanted to debase my wife's good reputation
Every time I heard an idle remark.
I was wrong. This is proof that my happy fate
Intended your soul for me!

SÉRIGNY. (*To DOLCOUR*.)
Could you know her and want to hurt her?

LUCILE. (*Quickly to MRS. DOLCOUR*.)
Madame, enough is enough. Give up the game;
For the happiness of both of them, make the sacrifice.

MRS. DOLCOUR. (*To LUCILE who is at her right*.)
All right, I'm willing. Let's forget his foolishness.
Since he's sorry for what he's done, he's punished enough.
(*Letting fall one of her hands, more with grace than coquettishness, into the hands of her husband, who is to the left of her; and sending him the most tender and artful looks*.)
Let us experience the delight of mercy;
We always have it when we forgive.

(*DOLCOUR bends to her hand and kisses it passionately. The Curtain falls.*)

COUPLETS

MRS. DOLCOUR. Without honor being shocked or offended,
Without turning aside the boundaries of duty,
All of the activity in the bedroom
Can be accomplished prudently.
SÉRIGNY. In the lessons addressed to you here,
Oh, young men crowd around to see
That, more often than not, chastity
Carries its weight in the bedroom.
DOLCOUR. Tyrannical husbands, in your rabid jealousy,
In your attacks of despair,
Don't always think that your tender spouses
Are behaving badly in the bedroom.
LUCILE. Charming sex who laugh at our games,
Realize when you see them again,
That one can often improve on love
When Minerva[49] is in the bedroom.

THE END

---

[49] Minerva was the virgin Roman goddess of wisdom, magic, and poetry.

Introduction

Tancrède must have been completed in the early months of 1784 since, in a letter dated April 1784, Sade replies to the Abbé Amblet's criticisms of the play. An earlier letter from Madame de Sade dated 14 February 1784 also makes reference to the play:

> I've received, my tender friend, your manuscript. I've read it, and re-read it as soon as d'Amblet dropped it off. It did not please me as much in the reading as the piece you read to me, which, I confess, in your voice, gave me the greatest pleasure, and struck me as first-class, which is how you want it to be perceived.

Sade replied on 16 February that he was disappointed that his play failed to please his wife but added, "Undoubtedly it would benefit from being read aloud, or performed."

According to the French editors of Sade's plays, the manuscript of *Tancrède* is in the hand of a copyist, with marginal corrections in the author's own handwriting and dates from the period of Sade's incarceration at the asylum at Charenton after Napoleon's expedition into Egypt. It is possible that the allusion to the "star of the universe . . . reigning over land and sea," an obvious reference to Napoleon, was added at this time.

A "lyric" scene in hexameter verse based on Tasso's *Jerusalem Delivered* (1580),[50] *Tancrède* was clearly following Jean-Jacques

---

[50] In her unpublished dissertation, "The Place of Theatre and Drama in the Life of the Marquis de Sade, *homme de lettres extraordinaire*," Annetta Foster briefly discusses a significant difference between Sade's play and its model: "In the death scene Tasso has Clorinda forgive Tancrède and receive baptism from him. Sade's death scene is expressed in pantomime with no baptism and no verbal forgiveness." The atheism expressed in Sade's 1782 *Dialogue Between a Priest and a Dying Man* explains, perhaps, why Sade portrayed Tancrède as a character moved more by love and honor than by faith at the siege of Jerusalem during the First Crusade.

Rousseau's recent experiments in music drama. A "lyric scene" in one act, with a libretto based on Book X of Ovid's *Metamorphoses*, Rousseau's *Pygmalion* was a spoken drama with musical interludes. When this work premiered in Lyons in May 1770, Rousseau believed he had created a new musical dramatic form in which music depicts action or thought before spoken dialogue expresses it. In his April 1784 reply to the Abbé Amblet, Sade argues on behalf of his innovation:

> Undoubtedly all operas are composed of several lyric scenes creating the acts: it is no less appropriate to give that name to a short drama, be it in prose or verse, with one or two characters, in which the dialogue—recited and not sung—is interrupted by musical interludes. They also call them melodramas, which, (you know better than I) by translating the first word in Greek, means drama in music . . . I know that *Esther* and *Athalie* are performed without music, but I know also that Rousseau's lyric scene, *Pygmalion* is done with very beautiful and very good music, and this little work ought to be in that genre, and I hope one day it will be.

There is no indication that music was ever composed for Sade's play or that the work was ever produced.

TANCRÈDE

Lyric Scene

CHARACTERS

Tancrède
Peter the Recluse, *called the Hermit*
Raimbaud, *Tancrède's squire*
A company of squires
A crowd of Christians

The action takes place at Godfrey de Bouillon's camp close to the walls of Jerusalem. Military music is heard; the curtain rises and reveals an immense expanse. In the distance, to the spectator's left, is seen the city of Jerusalem, surrounded by high walls trimmed with battlements and guard-towers. It is situated on two adjacent hills of different heights; a valley (the Valley of Josephat) separates them and divides the city. This valley lies across the entire background and ends in a dark forest that fills the right side of the stage. On this side of the valley, that is to say, coming downstage, is the Mount of Olives, between the forest and the city. At the foot of this mountain, a river breaks loose which, after having wandered momentarily through the plain, hurls itself noisily into the valley. Between the Mount of Olives and the right side of the stage, the ground is raised a little. A block of raw marble is leaning on this elevation on which are found two laurel trees and a pine, the top branches of which crown the rock. All of the left side of the stage, from the proscenium up to a certain distance from the wall of the city, is taken up by Godfrey de Bouillon's camp. TANCRÈDE's tent is nearest the footlights. Opposite the tent, and likewise at the edge of the proscenium, is a bed of grass. The area, of which we have just spoken and which exists between the city and the camp, is a small open plain, now filled with a lot of war machinery in disarray. Among other pieces of equipment, the audience sees a large lathe overturned. This machinery is what had been used in the "unfortunate assault" on the city, and has recently been burned by an enemy detachment. It is burning when the curtain rises. The horizon is illuminated only by the rays of the moon and the fire from this blaze. There is a great deal of activity everywhere on stage.

In the city, people are repairing the walls that appear to have taken a great beating. At the camp, people are trying to put out the fires and a troop of Crusaders commanded by TANCRÈDE pursues the enemy detachment which, a short time ago, set the fires. A number of Saracens are fortunate enough to re-enter Jerusalem, but the doors are locked once again, and CLORINDA, a young Parisian girl fighting for Mohammed, unable to enter the city, encounters the enemy who are pursuing her. Both those who re-entered the city and those who are following them vanish in the distance. In this way, a single combat ensues between CLORINDA and TANCRÈDE, but he is very far from suspecting that the object of his most tender affections is under the armor of the young Saracen whom he is about to fight. The warrior is dressed in a black overcoat, her helmet is without plumes and without a crest.

The two warriors begin to fight and the music, which has not stopped playing since the beginning of the play, expresses their conflict that takes place beneath the city walls, between the walls and the river. The fighting is violent, equally unremitting on both sides. Suddenly, the sun rises and its first rays draw attention to the River Jordan and the Mediterranean Sea, neither of which had yet been seen, and which take up the entire backdrop. Meanwhile, the fighting continues intensely. TANCRÈDE is wounded; he wounds CLORINDA. The loss of blood weakens her; her knees give way and she falls. A doleful music replaces what we have been hearing up to this point. As soon as TANCRÈDE sees his enemy fall, he runs to the river, draws water with his helmet and removes that of his adversary to administer the spiritual relief he seeks to bring to her. What happens to him when he discovers the features that captivate his soul? Suddenly, the music changes and depicts the turmoil that must exist in the heart of a lover at the sight of his mistress, dying from the wounds he has just caused. TANCRÈDE recoils in terror. Nothing can express the feeling of horror with which he is seized; his blood begins to run cold, and his deaf cries mingle with the somber melody that musically depicts this situation. He imagines that he catches a trace of life in the throbbing body of his beloved; he throws himself upon her, he weeps, he embraces her. She lifts her head toward him for a moment, extends her hand to him and tries to speak. The words die on her lips and she sinks back forever into the arms of death. Completely engrossed at the sight of this, TANCRÈDE hurls himself at the foot of a tree, lost in sorrow.

    Meanwhile, a band of Crusaders enter from behind the mountain. The leader pauses; at the same moment, RAIMBAUD, TANCRÈDE's principal squire, arrives from camp at the head of a number of squires attached to his master. The two groups sadly gaze upon the sight. The leader of the knights orders his soldiers to take away CLORINDA's body. TANCRÈDE's squires surround their master, dress his wounds, and lift him up. Both groups silently proceed toward camp. CLORINDA's body is placed on a white satin bed, near the entrance to TANCRÈDE 's tent, and covered with a purple veil. The body is turned in such a way so that the audience can see it in its entirety. Brought back by his men, TANCRÈDE is put down on the bed of grass opposite the tent. Since CLORINDA's body is to his right, and somewhat behind him, he does not see her at first. His squires disarm him entirely; he is unconscious. His senses revive only gradually and the music must accompany all the nuances of the situation with the greatest skill. The orchestra stops playing.

TANCRÈDE. (*In a weak and mournful voice.*)
Fond, unhappy witnesses of my
Disastrous error, don't trouble yourselves
Prolonging my relief; but to repay
Him for the day Tancrède has won for you,
My friends, employ no longer useless remedies
And let me die.
(*He falls, prostrate. He gets back on his feet again, with rage.*)
Oh, may a flash of lightning
Unite my passing with Clorinda's death!
Heaven, come destroy this deadly hand
Or I'll accuse your kindness of injustice.

No. Let me live . . . a too swift termination
Halting the course of my horrid fate
Would be a joy that I cannot expect.
Alas! I am too guilty to aspire it.
Oh, heaven, let me live! Yes . . . let me prolong
My shame and misery, disgracing myself,
Disgracing the earth. For, in lengthening
My life beneath the sharp sting of the serpent
Of self-reproach, this terrible decree
Of your severity, undoubtedly,
Will better suit my savagery.
Each natural emotion coming from my
Broken heart will reopen the wound;
I'll blame the night for causing my mistake,
And when the star that comforts humankind
Comes from the oceans' depths to light the air,
I'll curse a hundred times the dazzling light,
Whose inopportune rays view the madness
Exposed to my eyes, my crime and misfortune.
(*He relapses into the deepest despondency; his squires surround him.*
Heart-rending music is heard. To his squires.)
Take those futile concerns you have for me
And share them with Clorinda. Gather up
Her ashes . . .
Should I not be allowed to see them? Friends,
What's become of them? What place is blessed
With her dignified remains? Don't let
A greedy monster, in the height of rage,
Engulf God's most extraordinary work.
Alas! Much less than you, ill-fated Tancrède,
That monster would cause terror in the world , , ,
Nature's horror would come from your hand:
With your hand would it seize its bloody food.
(*He rises impetuously; his squires restrain him.*)
Knights, let me go! Don't intercept my steps;
Let me revisit the fields of our battles.
Fear me. Flee me. Despair is leading me . . .
Perhaps she's still there, lying on the sand;

Maybe she's breathing. Would a raging tiger
Have eaten those invaluable remains?
I'll go expose myself to its cruel fangs,
And ready to conclude my wretched life,
I'll thank the Lord that such a dismal fate
Will join me with Clorinda, in the self-same
Grave. Where, then, is she, friends?
(*Experiencing an emotion that causes him pain, he catches sight of her
and hurls himself toward her image, uttering a soulful cry.*)
Adored heroine!
Oh, charm of my life . . . idolized mistress!
Ah! May a just decree of vengeful fate
Come animate your hand to take revenge
Upon my crime.
Behold that hand, by which she pledged her troth.
(*He takes it.*) It was the token of her sweet devotion.
She could have loved me, and I destroyed her.
May I become again, for just a moment,
Intoxicated by her features?
(*Trembling, he lifts the veil.*)
What somber and unsullied stillness reigns
Upon her face! Like a sky without clouds
On a dark night.
My God, it's the tranquility of virtue,
A simple heart's serenity, without guile.
Nothing can change my exquisite mistress!
The manly pride of that volcanic soul
On that radiant brow where valor reigns,
Blends, once more, with the features of a tender
Weariness.
In withering a loveliness so pure,
Death should be frightened of offending nature's
Laws. I seem to see her under this dense
Foliage,
Where, for the first time, I witnessed her charms,
Weighing the developments of fame
With the scales of love, and plucking from her
Hand, the fruits of my success. Oh, death,

Cruel death! Be just for once. If there must be
A victim to your savage laws, then end
The life of wretched Tancrède. He alone
Deserves to feel your wrath. If you can, let her
Live at the expense of my existence.
Oh, death, if you can, grant that I may live
In her;
Let my soul sparkle in those bloody ashes.
A terrible mistake has stolen life
From her; grant that it be returned to her
And through the hands of love.
(*He pauses in ecstasy before her.*)
I think she's moving . . . and her mouth is breathing.
On her blooming lips love puts a smile.
Ah! Fateful fantasy, you're just deceiving me
To punish me the more by your impression:
To torture me more viciously, you seem
To render her to my idolization.
And then you disappear the moment joy
Might be created from your dark delusion.
You are not Clorinda any longer.
(*He is prostrate at the feet of his mistress, entirely contained in his grief.*)
Ah! When that coward was about to slay you
Beneath his deadly steel, and so intensely
Did I ward off the contemptible blow,
I only robbed his passion of its victim
To execute the crime one day myself!
Clorinda, for a moment, open up
Those lovely eyes again. Those eyes which have
Created so much passion in my soul.
My Clorinda, at your feet your lover
Implores you. With his tears of blood he washes
Your wounds. He seeks to expiate his crime
With his life. I look for your forgiveness.
(*He rises, in a rage.*) Ah! Great God in heaven, it's all over!
Her features are engulfed in boundless space:
I will never see their like again.

Ah! Stop your tears, then, wretched man. Is that
The way to pay off all your debts? No, no!
The way to pay your debts is through your blood!
(*He rips the dressings from his wounds; his blood flows over
CLORINDA's body.*)
RAIMBAUD. (*Slowly drawing near him.*)
If you please, my lord, depart this doleful
Scene. Glory invites you to subdue
The sorrow that this spectacle provokes.
(*Hurrying, as soon as he sees the condition TANCRÈDE is in.*)
What do I see, here? Ah! His blood is flowing!
(*He stops the bleeding and carries TANCRÈDE, nearly unconscious,
on to the grassy bank.*)
Lover, too unfortunate, how far
Did destiny betray your joyless vows!
(*He sets TANCRÈDE down; fatigue overcomes the knight, and he
falls asleep. The squires withdraw upstage. A sweet and melodious
music is heard—the sound of angels at the foot of God's throne. The
agitation of a nightmare is seen on his face; gradually this restlessness
stirs him to the point of making him move and speak as if awake. The
music continues. During each pause in the monologue, he gets up and
wanders randomly.*)
TANCRÈDE. God, what is then the voice that strikes my ears?
Clorinda, is it you who wakens me?
Breaking the bonds that make me pine away,
Do you come to share with me the blessings
You enjoy?
(*He listens with astonishment.*)
Whence can these enchanting sounds have come?
What causes me to hear that which I cannot
Understand?
(*Brighter.*) Ah! It is God's celestial chorus. He
Welcomes you, Clorinda; and a thousand
Of his most lovely melodies salutes
Your memory. I hear you. I see you.
Amidst your glory, you delight in casting
Your glances here below.
(*He thinks he sees her in the walls.*)

Good God! Extend your arms to me, Clorinda.
(*He shades his eyes with his hand.*)
Subdue the glow around you for a moment.
I don't dare gaze upon your sparkling halo;
Ah! I'm still nothing but a wretched mortal,
Only imperfectly can I see Heaven's
Majesty and its useless attempts
To beautify you.
Its purest treasures are not worthy of you:
Amidst the rays of this majestic luster,
It is your loveliness alone, Clorinda,
That dazzles my eyes.
(*He enjoys a silent ecstasy; the music becomes still sweeter.*)
I'm resting on your breast: our intermingled
Souls have just returned to God almighty,
And my chains are broken.
(*Compulsively, he approaches the corpse. He touches it, and that terrible sensation restores his senses.*)
Horrid dream!
My eyes are opened just to see this!
(*He goes mad; as RAIMBAUD approaches, TANCRÈDE seizes his sword and tries to stab himself. RAIMBAUD stops him. The other squires also circle around him.*)
No longer stop the violence to which
My madness yields, you, who force me to live
In spite of myself. Are you stained, like me,
With such a crime?
Have you slaughtered the most sacred being
That nature ever placed upon the earth?
Are you bloodthirsty monsters just like me?
By what right, and for whom, do you preserve
My life, when I cut short the course of hers!
(*The HERMIT appears and comes forward slowly, looking at TANCRÈDE from time to time.*)
RAIMBAUD. My Lord, if it is possible, try not
To think about it. For a moment, try
To console yourself with Peter. I think
I see that smooth-tongued hermit, blessed master

Of the Christians, whose fervent devotion,
Which nothing dampens ... which nothing restrains,
Knew how to lead the world to the assistance
Of the Holy Land.
TANCRÈDE. (*Still mad.*) What do I care about the Christian
victory?
I'm no longer tied to its concerns.
The Supreme Being that created me
To execute such an atrocity
Should no longer count upon the service
Of my arm.
And it's here, henceforth ...
(*Indicating his heart.*) Yes, here, that it's going
To strike the only blows that still remain
For it to govern.
HERMIT. (*Coldly.*) To what shameful perversion are you
yielding,
Tancrède?
What deadly demon haunts and troubles you,
The champion of the Crusades in this
Sad state!
TANCRÈDE. (*Overwrought.*) I don't know you anymore.
(*Indicating the body.*) Look, look at
My atrocity, what your cruel God
Capriciously made me commit.
Look where his hatred led me ... or his anger ...
(*Hurling himself into the HERMIT's arms.*)
Oh, pious hermit, oh, revered old man!
Forgive the outbursts of a desperate heart!
My misery drives me mad; and in my madness,
In this terror that seizes my soul,
Feeling guilty towards love, resisting
Friendship,
I am only worthy of your pity.
HERMIT. (*Holding him affectionately.*)
You are my concern; that sterile pity,
Companion of contempt, that quiet virtue
That man offers his fellow man in humbling

Him, belongs to pride more than affection.
I love and hug a brother in misfortune
Who warns me of the ills which heaven might
Inflict on me. And since I'm frightened myself
By his appearance, my heart only flies
To him with a holy reverence.
Could I be numb to your ordeals, my son?
I know they're awful and that it's impossible
To make up for what happened at that cruel
Battle.
But maybe this misfortune is a judgment
From heaven. Perhaps God is testing you.
Ah! Don't resist his almighty command;
And feeling reprehensible emotions,
Do not forget the duties of a Christian.
TANCRÈDE. What are they?
HERMIT. To follow me.
TANCRÈDE. Ah! Never!
HERMIT. How far he's wandered. He's delirious!
TANCRÈDE. (*Angrily.*) Eh! You just said
You were affected by my wretched fate.
Have you ever seen a destiny
More frightening crush a man with so much cruelty?
HERMIT. I say to you again, no one's concerned
With the troubles of his fellow creatures
More devotedly than I, my son.
But if, without making any effort
On his part, sleeping underneath the yoke
Of the weight that's crushing him,
The wretched man resists a helping hand
That comes to break the bonds with which he's tied,
Then what does he deserve?
TANCRÈDE. (*Passionately.*) Equal affection!
Why forsake him when he's lost the means
Of listening to good advice? When someone
Cannot break away from suffering, Father,
He ought to be pitied and not punished.
HERMIT. What a lame excuse, my son! Mankind

Is free, and if the soul, that sacred light
Which drives him and inflames him, fluctuates,
For a moment, from virtue to vice,
It's so the triumph over it might be
More remarkable. Besides, the source
Of your love is dead; you've nothing more
Than a wretched corpse, offering your eyes
The horrible sight of so short a road
Leading to oblivion. My son,
Tear yourself away from that destructive
Thing and follow me.
TANCRÈDE. I cannot.
HERMIT. (*In a loud voice.*) I swear, if you refuse to leave this
place,
You'll answer to God for the misfortunes
Of the Christians.
TANCRÈDE. Father, pity me.
HERMIT. (*Sharply.*) I'd pity you
For living
If you could still refuse to follow me,
And, not renouncing those romantic feelings,
You still withstood the voice of honor. Spend
A moment with me and I swear to you,
Your eyes will pierce the darkest night for centuries
To come.
A creature without ancestry or fame
Can have no right to immortality.
But he who drew a name covered in glory
Must engrave it, without blemish, in the
Temple of memory.
He owes an explanation to the state
About that name which is respected. If he
Lives without honoring it, he taints it.
Following this reasonable law,
Which governs everything, determine if
You want people to tell an astonished
Universe, it was for love that Tancrède
Took up arms . . .

It was to nourish his unlawful passion
That he made an appearance for a moment
At Sulaiman's stockades.
And when our soldiers, mounted on those ramparts,
Are about to claim their victory,
Do you want it to be said that Tancrède
Tearfully, next to a woman, was
Surrendering his soul to base regrets?
(*Taking his hand.*) You want more holy, more precious concerns?
Everything, everything here, my son,
Enables you to see them.
(*Carried away with ecstasy.*) Divine Redeemer of human
misfortunes,
You, whose burning love inflames my veins,
Who, in this place converted with your blood,
Rescuing us from the debt of hell,
Deigned on that holy mountain, by a cruel
Death,
To show us the way to immortal glory.
Come, lend to these words that battle sign,
Some flashes of the fire with which my heart
Is burning.
May I arouse in him the recognition
That when it is a matter of destroying
The power of the loathsome infidels
Who defile the holy sanctuaries,
At that very moment, the blade sparkles
In his hands. Since never does the ingrate
Escape justice, let him tremble, let him
Shudder at the consequences of his
Actions. Tancrède, it is a time when weakness
Can wear out the benevolence of God
Almighty.
What am I saying? Oh, what am I saying?
Perhaps the time is past. Your callousness
Has just provoked your master.
A terrifying precipice is present
All around you.

Endless pits are opening before
Your eyes,
If you want to throw yourself inside.
(*Trumpets sound.*)
Listen to the clamoring of war.
(*With the greatest passion.*)
Come, make amends for last evening's disgrace.
Roger and Baudoin, Guelfe, Guy, Garnier,
Even Bouillon and Renaud, have named you
The first to lead our soldiers to the breach
This morning. Will I tell Godfrey the reason
You cannot go with them to confront
The dangers of the day?
That your arms are bound by the chains
Of love?
Do you even think, do you believe
The object of your tears would offer thanks
To you for putting down your arms? No! no.
I don't think so. Bear in mind her courage.
To join her, you must imitate her spirit,
In purifying her with wholesome tears.
That heaven where you sent her through your worthy
Efforts ...
That heaven, which you'd like to see her enjoy
Here and now, is only at the price
Of the laurels which you'll earn today.
If you want to celebrate her memory,
Fly, like her, into the heart of victory.
TANCRÈDE. (*In tears, throwing himself into the HERMIT's arms.*)
Father, you win. How can I oppose
The vehement and holy zeal that just
Came over you? Like you, her passion stirs me
And moves through me.
I surrender to the consequences
Engendered by her zeal. To let you see
How dear they are to me, I am prepared
To follow you to the end of the world.

Still, don't expect my courage to destroy
Her exquisite image in my heart.
It would be a useless pledge.
But that holy love will make more zealous,
Will make more reverent the deep sensations
Of the duties that enchain me.
When they are pure, those bonds lead us to virtue
And at the bottom of my heart, you'll always
See the words imprinted by her hand:
God—Love—and Honor.

HERMIT. (*In tears, squeezing TANCRÈDE in his arms.*)
Glorious soldier, flower of chivalry!
If, for a moment, your life was unsettled
By misjudgment, you're only the stronger
For it, hero, worthy of respect!
Your resolution terminates our troubles.
Tremble, proud Saladin, Tancrède will fight you.
The Crescent is going to fall beneath
The sign of the Cross.
Collapse, you ramparts. Vulgar infidels
Flee. The tomb where lay the one true God,
Liberated by his youthful courage,
Is going to open itself to the rapture
Of our earnest homage.
As soon as he advances, he should conquer.
He's fighting on the side of heaven!

TANCRÈDE. Ah, may your heavenly words be carried out!
They are the symbols of my present victories.
Following the hope with which you flatter me,
Can there be a danger that I dare not
Confront?
(*To Raimbaud.*) Let's go, it's time. Bring me my arms.

HERMIT. You want, I feel it, oh, great God of Israel,
To grant me, for a moment, the great gift
Of prophecy,
To give him some pledge of his future happiness.
(*Highly enthusiastic.*) Through the depths of centuries, I read
In fiery flashes that one day there'll come

A hero like you, guided by success,
Who, offering the French his glorious laurels,
Having disposed of their misfortunes, will be
Chosen by them to redeem the world.
His precious blood will give birth to the star
Of the universe.
I see him reigning over land and sea,
Placed by God upon the throne of Titus,
Whose name and virtue he will overshadow.
Beloved Tancrède, yes, you can believe me,
He will overshadow for all time
The long remembrances of history.
With God himself placing him in the Temple
Of Memory, the ages to come will see
Only his accomplishments.
TANCRÈDE. Ah, may your heavenly prophecy come true . . .
That he may reap the fruit of every danger
I encounter.
And if he has brought happiness from one pole
To the other,
I yield to him the honor of our holy
Deeds. Let's go. It's time. Bring me my arms.
(*To his squires.*) Be sure to treat respectfully the object
Which caused my tears to flow.
(*Indicating the marble stone.*)
Beneath the noble silhouettes of twenty
Skillful chisels,
May this curved mass, as soon as possible,
Form a tasteful resting place for her
Beloved ashes. And as simple emblems
On the marble you'll engrave: my love
On one side, her virtue on the other.
Let's go defeat them, father.
(*He leaves, arm-in-arm with the HERMIT.*)

The sculptors appear and immediately go to work; a serious and highly rhythmical music marks their labors. In an instant, the stone is transformed into the shape of two allegorical deities—Strength and

Victory—sustaining a sarcophagus under which there is a statue of Cupid breaking his arrow. The three trees that crowned the stone now find themselves shading the tomb. Someone hangs the shield and sword of the fighting woman on the pine tree (the one in the middle). When everything is ready, a doleful march is heard. TANCRÈDE 's squires carry the body on their shields (traveling by the path at the back that forms the hill on which the stone is supported) and arrange themselves even with the sarcophagus. They lay the body in the tomb (which they had opened beforehand, and which they close up again afterwards). Immediately, the entire army of Crusaders file past to the music of a sad, though military, march, and pay their respects to the heroine in the military fashion of days gone by.

During all of this, a young soldier escapes from the crowd of knights lining the back of the stage. It is TANCRÈDE. He scales the hill as swift as an arrow, appears between the trees, and hurls himself upon the tomb. Everything is in suspense. The knights surround the tomb and the music stops.

TANCRÈDE. Oh, sad tomb
You contain within you everything
That nature made most touching; everything
That nature made most perfectly for love.
I swear to you, one day, I'll reunite
My mortal remains with these beloved
Relics.
(*To the leaders.*) Knights, swear to unite me with her.
It's the only recompense I want
From my military service. In the
Name of God Almighty, swear it, friends.
(*All make the gesture of taking an oath.*)
Oh, marble, while waiting for that day
I long for,
The only happy day my eyes will see,
Marble, which will make known my misfortunes
From age to age, convey to her these kisses,
Moistened with my tears.

(*He remains, overwhelmed, at the tomb until the end of the funeral. The ceremonies continue: the military march is heard once again. The troops finish filing in front of the monument, and gradually, as they march off again toward the back of the stage, they disappear into tents and the curtain falls.*)

THE END

Count Oxtiern

or

The Dangers of Debauchery

Introduction

The first mention of the three-act drama *Count Oxtiern* exists in a letter from Miramond to the Marquis de Sade dated 25 July 1791. Representing the play selection committee of the Théâtre Feydeau, Miramond refuses the play on the grounds that "a work based on such hideous atrocity" should not be performed. He goes on to praise the third act for its ability to inspire "great terror" in the audience, and raises several dramaturgical questions concerning the verisimilitude of the play. His first major objection concerns innkeeper Fabrice's ability to secure Herman's release, given the disparity in power base between a hotelier and a count, not to mention the twenty-four hour time limit. Miramond's second major problem deals with the heroine Ernestine's ability to defend herself against a swordsman of her father's caliber. Miramond admits that though the Colonel's age might be a factor in Ernestine's favor, her unfamiliarity with weaponry would certainly work to her disadvantage. Not surprisingly, the one comment in Miramond's letter that drew an immediate response from de Sade was simply that "the style of the writing leaves a great deal to be desired." At that point, de Sade scrawled in the margin, "That's not true."

Sade's reaction is not unexpected for a writer who, since his release from the Asylum at Charenton on 2 April 1790, had a novel, *Justine or the Misfortunes of Virtue*, published and seven plays accepted for production, or public readings at a variety of theatres in Paris. Writing to Reinaud, his lawyer, on 6 March 1791, Sade boasts that his *Sophie and Desfrancs* was accepted by the Théâtre de la Nation, *The Immoral Man* (previously known as *The Briber*) and *The Bedroom* (then entitled *Jealousy Corrected; or, The School for Coquettes*) at the Théâtre-Italienne, *The Virtuous Criminal* (*The Madness of Misfortune*) at the Palais Royal, and *Azélis* at the Théâtre Rue de Bondy. Even during his imprisonment, first in the Bastille and later at Charenton, Sade was not accustomed to disappointment. In his study of the French Revolution, *Citizens*, Simon Schama writes that, after complaining about the cruel condition at the Bastille, Sade had his room furnished with a desk, a wardrobe full of shirts, silk breeches, coats and dressing gowns, tapestries, velvet cushions and mattresses, and a library consisting of about 600 volumes including the complete works of Fénelon, the novels of Fielding and Smollett, the *Iliad*, the plays of Marmontel, and travel literature about the South Seas.

The Marquis de Sade's disappointment was short lived for, on 6 September 1791, he received a letter from Jean-Francois Boursault accepting the play on behalf of the Théâtre Molière, a theatre which specialized in patriotic plays. Evidently, Sade was anxious about the production and distrusted Boursault's ability to direct the play, for the executive secretary of the Théâtre Molière wrote to invite the playwright to a run through, apologizing that "it had never been our intention to keep you away from rehearsals. . . . Come, if you like, tomorrow, and you can be in charge." Finally on Saturday, 22 October 1791, *Count Oxtiern, or the Dangers of Debauchery* was performed with modest success. It was due to receive a second performance on 29 October but because the playwright's revisions were so extensive, especially in the recasting of certain roles, it had to be postponed until 4 November.

The nature of these revisions is suggested by a communication from Boursault to Sade on 23 October, the day after the premiere. The director argues that it is difficult to take roles away from actors, especially when he has to deal with them for the rest of the season and that providing new costumes for a play that might not be a success would be very difficult. A further communication on 29

October details the inability of the actors to learn Sade's revised text since "these little changes often are more trouble to learn than a long role." The only substantive matter discussed was one of Oxtiern's lines at the end of Act Two, Scene Five. The original line, "Surrender, you wretched creature. Your lot is to suffer and ours is to dominate!" was greeted with cries from the audience and as Oxtiern continued to speak the audience shouted, "Enough! Enough!" The line was subsequently changed to "I was expecting less animosity from you ... more of an absolute surrender."

Following the 4 November performance, *Le Moniteur* wrote:

Count Oxtiern or the Dangers of Debauchery, a three-act prose play, was successfully performed at this theatre.

Oxtiern, a great Swedish nobleman, is an inveterate rake. He has seduced and abducted Ernestine, Colonel Falkenheim's daughter, and secured the imprisonment of her beloved on a false charge. He takes the unfortunate young woman to a place a mile from Stockholm, but the proprietor of the inn is an honest man. Ernestine's father finds her. Then to take revenge on the monster who has dishonored her, Ernestine challenges him to a duel with swords in the garden at eleven o'clock at night. The letter is written as if by Ernestine's brother. Her father also challenges Oxtiern who, aware of Ernestine's plan, conceives the horrible device of getting father and daughter to fight one another. The two arrive at the garden and fight fiercely, but Fabrice, the innkeeper, has managed to get Ernestine's beloved out of prison and the young man separates father and daughter. He then fights Oxtiern and kills him and, having thus avenged the honor of his beloved, marries her.

This play is interesting for its spirit, but the character of Oxtiern is a revolting atrocity. He is a worse, viler rascal than Lovelace,[51] with none of his more likeable qualities.

A small incident threatened to disturb the second performance of the play. A dissatisfied or malicious member of the audience cried out: "Lower the curtain".... The stage hand made the mistake of doing so more than halfway when many other members of the audience had it raised again and cried "Turn him out!" ... This

[51] Lovelace is the charismatic villain in Samuel Richardson's novel *Clarissa*.

resulted in some measures of dissension in the audience. A very weak minority hissed while the author was well-rewarded by the considerable applause of the majority. He was called for after the performance: it was the Marquis de Sade.

On the second page of the same issue, Boursault wrote a piece called "Article of the Moniteur, the day after the second performance of this play at the Théâtre Molière," where he praised the changes in casting, the vigorous style, and the well-drawn characters in the play, but criticized the abrupt denouement as leaving "something to be desired." Boursault went on to express the hope that more plays by Sade will be performed so that the public will be able to better appreciate the talents of the writer. The Marquis de Sade, on the other hand, was less than pleased by the events of the second night. In an undated letter to Charles Gaufridy, his lawyer, he complains that the disturbance forced him to cancel performances of the play until the winter even though Boursault had, in fact, committed to further productions of the play in a document dated 11 November 1791.

Oxtiern was never again performed in Paris. On 13 December 1799, the play was revived with the conspicuous omission of the word "Count" in the title, on the stage of the Dramatic Society of Versailles with the playwright in the role of Fabrice, the innkeeper. (Two years earlier, Sade had learned that his name had been placed on a list of émigrés and that he was liable to be arrested again and his property confiscated. A period of hand-to-mouth existence followed during which Sade lived in an unheated attic and worked as a prompter for the Dramatic Society at forty sous[52] a day.) According to a letter dated 30 January 1800, the revival of *Oxtiern* met with great success, and Sade acquitted himself well in the role of the innkeeper. What is even more important is the fact that the author began negotiations for further productions of the play in Chartres where he offered to appear once again as an actor. There is no evidence that these negotiations came to fruition.

After the revival at Versailles, *Oxtiern* was published by Blaisot from a manuscript copy which almost certainly dates from Charenton. The manuscript suggests that the play was based on *Ernestine, a Swedish Novel*, one of the eleven serious novels Sade

---

[52] In French currency, forty sous was worth two livres, or two pounds of silver.

wrote in the Bastille and published in 1800 as the *Crimes of Love*. While the basic plot of both works remains the same, there is a sufficient disparity in detail to merit a comparison between them. Some of the alterations are essentially cosmetic. In the novel, Ernestine wears red to the duel; in the play she wears white. As Graham Rodmell suggests, this is a sensible change since the whole point is that she should be readily seen in the dark. The character of Falkenheim appears in the novel as the narrator, not Ernestine's father who turns out to be a character called Colonel Sanders. Fabrice and the hotel play no part in the novel as Sade was not restricted by the neoclassical dramatic rules of unity of time and place in his narrative prose.

The book is somewhat more "sadistic" than the play. In the Swedish novel, Oxtiern not only has Ernestine's lover, Herman, imprisoned, he arranges that he be executed directly beneath the window of the room where he is keeping Ernestine. He throws open the window and offers to spare Herman in return for her sexual favors. Heroically, Ernestine faints, Oxtiern rapes her and Herman dies. The denouement of the novel is also much more complex than that of the play. Due to Oxtiern's machinations, Ernestine is killed by her father in the duel. The count, however, is subsequently brought to justice and sentenced to hard labor for life. Colonel Sanders begs for Oxtiern's release and then challenges him to a duel. Oxtiern refuses to defend himself and gives his sword to Sanders who is unable to stab an unarmed man. In the name of justice, Oxtiern runs on his own sword but is not mortally wounded. Colonel Sanders forgives him and Oxtiern sets out on the path of righteousness. This "happy ending" is both ironic and blasphemous and not, as Maurice Heine has observed, necessarily "more somber and richer in content" than that of the play. Sade transformed his novel into a stage-worthy vehicle following eighteenth-century dramatic rules and conventions. The unities of time, place, and action are observed; both verisimilitude and decorum are served by off-stage deaths; Oxtiern and Ernestine each have confidants; and a *raisonneur* sums up the evening with a fine moral lesson. Though there are defects in the plot and structure of the play, they were of little concern to French audiences in the Revolutionary period who, more often than not, delighted in action and sensation in the theatre, no matter how improbable.

COUNT OXTIERN
or
The Dangers of Debauchery

Prose drama in three acts

Produced at the Théâtre de Molière in Paris, 22 October 1791, and at Versailles under the auspices of the Dramatic Society, on 22 Frimaire, the 8ᵗʰ year of the Republic (13 December 1799)

Woe to the villains unchecked by remorse.

Oxtiern, III, 3.

CHARACTERS

Count Oxtiern, *a Swiss nobleman*
Derbac, *friend and confidant of the Count*
Colonel Falkenheim
Ernestine, *the Colonel's daughter*
Amélie, *Ernestine's maid*
Casimir, *the Count's valet*
Mr. Fabrice, *keeper of the Inn, where the action takes place*
Herman, *Ernestine's lover*
Charles, *bellman at the Inn*

(*The action takes place at Mr. Fabrice's Inn, not far from Stockholm, on the Nordkoping Highway.*)

ACT ONE

(*The setting for the first two acts is a sitting room of the inn which opens into several adjoining rooms. A writing table is on one side of the room; an armchair is close to the table.*)

FABRICE. (*Showing him one of the adjoining rooms.*) Mr. Casimir, do you think this room will be suitable for the young lady your master is bringing here today?

CASIMIR. (*Looking it over.*) I think so, Mr. Fabrice. Is there an adjoining room for Amélie, her maid, and another room where Miss Ernestine might lie down?

FABRICE. Yes, there are two rooms adjoining this one; one key locks all three. I can assure you they'll be very comfortable here. It's a quiet wing . . . facing the garden. They won't hear even the slightest noise from the other travelers.

CASIMIR. Perfect. (*Taking FABRICE aside, and mysteriously.*) Mr. Fabrice?

FABRICE. Yes?

CASIMIR. My master's a most remarkable man. Admit it, you've known him since he was a boy . . .

FABRICE. I've known Count Oxtiern for a long time, and for that reason, I would venture to say that in all of Sweden, there's no man as dangerous as he.

CASIMIR. Yes, but he pays well.

FABRICE. And that's what makes him all the more terrifying; there's nothing more deadly than money in the hands of vile men. Who can resist the man who possesses the surest means of corruption? My friend, I wish that no one but honest men had any money. But, tell me, if you will, about this latest adventure.

CASIMIR. A lovely girl. Oh! Mr. Fabrice, what a pity! (*Looking heavenward.*) Good Lord! You permitted this to happen! For such a creature to be the pawn of deceit and debauchery.

FABRICE. (*Very surprised.*) What? Has the crime already been committed?

CASIMIR. It has, Mr. Fabrice, it has. Meanwhile she's the daughter of Colonel Falkenheim, the great nephew of Charles

XII's favorite. He abducted her . . . raped her. I tell you, Mr. Fabrice, she's ruined!

FABRICE. (*As above.*) He hasn't even married her! He's bringing here a virtuous girl he's seduced, deceived and raped. Casimir, run to your master; tell him there's no room at the inn. Tell him that I cannot see him. I've already had more than my share of the liberties he thinks he can take under my roof. I want nothing to do with a great lord's protection if it only results in my abetting his licentiousness. (*He exits.*)

CASIMIR. (*Running after him to stop him.*) Wait a minute . . . wait a minute. You'd lose everything and nothing would be gained. Continue your hospitality towards him; and should the occasion present itself, secretly try to be of some service to the young lady. (*Stressing what follows.*) Stockholm is only three miles away. It's not late; they'll be going to bed. You have friends in the capital. Do you understand me, Mr. Fabrice?

FABRICE. (*After thinking a minute.*) Friends! Yes, I do have them; but there are other ways . . . surer ways which I hope will prove successful. Now explain to me . . . (*The sound of the COUNT's carriage is heard.*)

CASIMIR. Shhh. A carriage is coming. We'll meet again later in your room; then I'll explain in greater detail. What a racket! No doubt about it, it's the count. It's a shame that vice has to flaunt itself so boldly!

FABRICE. I'd rather your count would go live with his devils and leave me alone. It's a terrible business, running an inn when you have to open your doors to all kinds of people. It's the only part of the job I hate.

(*Enter CHARLES.*)

CHARLES. (*To FABRICE.*) Sir, two women from Count Oxtiern have come asking for rooms here. The count himself will arrive shortly. He and his friend, Mr. Derbac have stopped off a short distance from here and he wants you to put the ladies in your very best rooms until he arrives. There are more than twenty guards escorting the carriage . . . really.

FABRICE. (*Peevishly.*) All right, Charles, leave it to me. I'll take care of them. Here's where they'll stay. Not a word, Casimir; and we'll try to help the unfortunate girl when the opportunity arises. It feels so sweet to do a good deed, my friend, that we should never waste the opportunity when we're so lucky to find it. Charles, follow me.

CASIMIR. (*Alone.*) What a good man! There's where you find virtue . . . in an anonymous fellow . . . without any background or breeding. While those born in the midst of a magnificent fortune often have nothing to offer but corruption and vice. But why is the count not coming with Miss Ernestine? Ah! Undoubtedly he's hatching some plot with Derbac, that illustrious aide to his debauchery; but since he's somewhat more virtuous than the Count, I hope he'll voice an objection to this latest adventure.

(*Enter FABRICE, ERNESTINE, and AMÉLIE.*)

FABRICE. (*To ERNESTINE.*) I hope, miss, that this room will suit you. I have prepared it for you, with all the care you deserve, in careful obedience to the Count's instructions.

ERNESTINE. (*In the deepest despair.*) It's very nice, sir, it's very nice, much too good for me. The deepest solitude is the only thing that would really suit me.

FABRICE. Since the lady would like to be alone, I will look after other matters to make my lodgings more bearable for her. (*He exits.*)

CASIMIR. (*To ERNESTINE.*) Will the Count be coming to your room, miss, when he arrives at the inn?

ERNESTINE. (*Sadly.*) Isn't he the master . . . the master of my whole existence! Go away, sir, go away. We want to be alone.

AMÉLIE. Your melancholy state worries me, miss. How pleased I'd be to see you get a little rest!

ERNESTINE. Rest . . . I rest? Good Lord! Oh! No, no, there can be no more rest upon this earth for poor Ernestine!

AMÉLIE. What! Can the inhuman author of your misfortunes do nothing to make amends?

ERNESTINE. There can never be amends, Amélie, for such cruel injuries. By means of the most arrogant deception, this man abducted me from my family, from my fiancée, from everything I hold dear in this world. And did you know that he had the man I love, that fine upstanding Herman, cast into irons? The poor man was humiliated by false accusations, slander, informants, and traitors! Gold and Oxtiern's crimes have done him in. Herman is a prisoner . . . perhaps already condemned. And it's upon the chains of this man I love that the cowardly Oxtiern comes to sacrifice me, his unfortunate victim!

AMÉLIE. Ah! You're making me tremble!

ERNESTINE. (*In despair.*) Is there any hope . . . anything to look forward to? Good Lord! What can I do?

AMÉLIE. But what about your father?

ERNESTINE. You know that my father had been away from Stockholm for some time when Oxtiern, having cruelly lied to me, took me to his home, under the pretense that I would be helping my fiancée obtain his release . . . and perhaps even his hand in marriage with the help of Oxtiern's brother, the senator, who was supposed to be there. Undoubtedly it was a venture as reproachable as it was foolish. How could I think of an engagement without my father's consent? Heaven has punished me dearly. Do you know who I discovered there instead of the patron I expected? Oxtiern, ruthless Oxtiern, a dagger in his hand, offering me the choice of death or dishonor without even giving me the opportunity of making my own decision. Had I had the opportunity, Amélie, I never would have hesitated. The most frightening tortures would have been sweeter to me than the obscenities that vile man had prepared for me. Repulsive chains prevented me from defending myself. The bastard! And to make matters worse, heaven allowed me to survive; the sun casts its rays upon me and I am ruined! (*Consumed by misery, she slumps into a chair close to the table.*)

AMÉLIE. (*In tears, taking her mistress's hands.*) O most unfortunate of women! Ah! please do not despair! Your father knows all about your departure. Do you think he'll waste a moment in flying to your defense?

ERNESTINE. He's not the one I expect to punish my executioner; he's not the one who should avenge me.

AMÉLIE. What if the Count were to keep his word? It seems to me he spoke of cherished ties, eternal bonds...

ERNESTINE. Should Oxtiern even want them, could I ever consent to spend the rest of my life in the arms of a man I despise? A man who has committed the worse possible offence against me? Can a woman marry a man who has abused her?

Can she ever love anyone beneath her contempt? Ah! I am lost, Amélie, I am ruined! All that remain for me are sorrow and tears. My only hope is in death, and I will find it, I hope, in avenging myself.

AMÉLIE. (*Looking around her.*) Miss, we're all alone. What's stopping us from running away? From going to Court and begging for the protection which is your right and duty to claim.

ERNESTINE. (*Proudly.*) Were Oxtiern a thousand miles away, I would shorten the distance between us rather than flee. The bastard has dishonored me. I must avenge myself. I will never go to some corrupt court to ask for a protection that would be denied me. You don't know to what extent wealth and influence debase the souls of the men who dwell there. Monsters! I would be just another morsel for their obscene appetites! (*Enter FABRICE.*)

FABRICE. (*With a tone of interest and sadness.*) The Count has sent word that an important affair has detained him not far from here. He will arrive shortly. Miss, is there anything you need?

ERNESTINE. (*Pointing to the door of the room she believes is hers.*) Isn't that my room, sir?

FABRICE. (*As before.*) Yes, Miss.

ERNESTINE. Then I'd like to go there. Come, Amélie, let us consider the important plans that occupy my brain, plans which alone can offer some relief to your poor mistress.

FABRICE. (*Alone.*) Casimir was quite right. This girl is beautiful; she's lovely. Oh! Count Oxtiern, damn you for destroying this innocent young lady. Why should she, who so well deserves your affection, become the victim of your wickedness and brutality? But here he comes. Not another word. Villains cannot bear the truth. No other men in the world like flattery as much as they do. The thought of crime is repulsive even to them who, in numbing themselves to the evils that possess them, want to be thought of and constantly pictured as paragons of virtue.
(*Enter OXTIERN.*)

OXTIERN. (*In a light tone.*) How can I ever thank you, my dear Fabrice. Your friendship, your longtime affection for me, keeps proving itself over and over. I can't find the words to express my gratitude.

FABRICE. (*With a straightforward and affectionate tone.*) I would appreciate a little more candor, sir, and a lot less gratitude. Spare me the thanks purchased at the cost of an immoral act. That would degrade me. Tell the truth. Who is the young lady you have brought to my inn, and what do you intend to do with her?

OXTIERN. (*Quickly interrupting him.*) My intentions are honorable, sir. Ernestine is respectable, and I'm not keeping her here against her will. An excess of love has perhaps hastened a bit the usual steps involved in uniting us forever, but she must be my wife, and she will be, my friend. Would I dare to consider her otherwise, and would I bring her *here* if it was any other way?

FABRICE. That's not what people are saying, sir. Still, I have to believe you. Should you be lying to me, I'd have to evict you.

OXTIERN. I forgive your suspicions, Fabrice, since they are born of virtuous motives. But set your mind at ease, my friend. Let me repeat: my plans are as pure as she who inspires them.

FABRICE. (*Firmly.*) Count Oxtiern, you are a noble lord, I know. But please convince yourself of this: the moment your conduct makes you appear evil in my eyes, I will see nothing in you but a man all the more contemptible because he was born to be honest. And having been blessed, more than other men, with titles which ought to merit esteem and respect, such a man is all the more guilty for not having taken advantage of them.

OXTIERN. But why all this concern, Fabrice? What have I done to make you suspicious?

FABRICE. Nothing yet, so I want to believe. But . . . where do you plan to take this girl?

OXTIERN. To my estate near Norrkopinh, where I shall marry her as soon as we arrive.

FABRICE. Why didn't her father come with her?

OXTIERN. He wasn't in Stockholm when she left; and the force of my love has no room for formalities . . . which I thought I could easily dispense with. You're overly hypercritical, my friend. I've never seen you so strict before.

FABRICE. It's not about being strict, sir, it's about justice. If you were a father, would you like to see your daughter abducted?

OXTIERN. I wouldn't like to see her disgraced. Will Ernestine be disgraced when I marry her?

(*Enter AMÉLIE.*)

AMÉLIE. Gentlemen, the lady requests that you move to another room; she's resting at the moment, and would like . . .

OXTIERN. (*Spiritedly.*) Assure her, my dear Amélie, that we will obey her request. Is there anything in the world I should want more than the peace and happiness of your mistress?

AMÉLIE. Ah! Sir, and how far she is from either one.

OXTIERN. (*To FABRICE, without paying any attention to what AMÉLIE has just said.*) Come, Fabrice, I want to finish convincing you that those disturbing ideas have never entered my mind. Amélie, please ask Ernestine to let me know when she wants to see me. (*AMÉLIE exits. To FABRICE.*) Let's go, my friend.

FABRICE. (*Alone.*) I'll be along in a moment. His friend? Me, that man's friend! Oh, no, no, never. Even if he gave me his entire fortune, I wouldn't be his friend. Instructed by Casimir, I can now be of some use to Ernestine. I'll hurry to Stockholm. They're not leaving until tomorrow, I still have time. I must save this poor girl or lose my life in the attempt. Honor and integrity make it my duty. They are the most sacred laws of my heart.

END OF ACT ONE

ACT TWO

OXTIERN. That creature is so sensitive.

DERBAC. Most enticing, isn't it? Women are really charming when tears add the excitement of sorrow to their features. You, my poor Count, are what people call a libertine.

OXTIERN. What do you expect, my friend? It was in the company of women that I learned every vice I use to ravage them today.

DERBAC. Aren't you at least going to marry her?

OXTIERN. Can you suspect me of acting so foolishly, even for a moment?

DERBAC. But once you're in your mansion, what excuse can you offer Ernestine to justify your behavior? She'll never let you live with her as a lover and his mistress.

OXTIERN. Oh! Her intentions, her desires, her wishes are the least of my worries. My happiness, my satisfaction! That's the objective in all of this, and the objective has been reached, Derbac. In adventures like these, if I can be happy, so should everybody else.

DERBAC. Ah! My friend, my dear Count, let me take a moment to question these very dangerous principles!

OXTIERN. No, you'd only upset me without convincing me. I have the misfortune of being set in my opinions. Never forget that your fortune depends on me. What I'm looking for in you is a partner in crime, not a father confessor.

DERBAC. Since you consider me nothing but a friend, I was hoping that you would want my advice. What you're planning to do is terrible.

OXTIERN. In your eyes, I can understand that, because you are an inferior being, full of gothic superstitions, upon which the torch of clear thinking has yet to shine its light. A few more years under my instruction, Derbac, and you'll no longer pity a woman for such a minor offence.

DERBAC. Acting more for our happiness than for her own, the sweet and sensitive creature who so tenderly considers her virtue her only pride and joy, has very clear claims on our love and protection, when libertines seek to insult it.

OXTIERN. (*Bored.*) Ah! You're moralizing, Derbac!

DERBAC. What if I am? Come on, let's just discuss your own vulnerability. Don't you see that you're in danger here? The Colonel, the Colonel's son . . . or young Herman, who's so dearly loved by this admirable girl. Aren't you afraid of any of them?

OXTIERN. The colonel is old, he won't put up much of a fight. In fact he won't fight at all. His son will never get to me. I'm having him followed. (*In a low voice.*) If he ventures close to my estate, my friend, he's a dead man. (*Aloud.*) As for Herman, the chains binding him aren't the kind that can be broken. I had the foresight to implicate him in an important matter, from which he'll never disentangle himself without a lot of money, which is well beyond his reach. It was all rather expensive: perjured witnesses, corrupt magistrates . . . I dare him to get out of that.

DERBAC. And the law, my friend, what about the law?

OXTIERN. It's only made by men . . . interpreted by men. I've never known it to resist the power of gold.

DERBAC. And what about the interior voice always defending the rights of virtue? What about your conscience?

OXTIERN. Perfectly clear. Completely at rest.

DERBAC. But the court, my dear Count, the court which views you as a delightful ornament. What if the court should hear of your behavior?

OXTIERN. That's the only thing that worries me about this rabid girl. She threatened me. That's why I have to keep her under lock and key. Don't forget to give the orders for everything to be ready tomorrow at the crack of dawn. I want to get away from Stockholm as quickly as possible. Fabrice is becoming ethical all of a sudden, and we're too close to the capital for me not to worry about that idiot's guilty conscience. I can think of nothing more horrible, or more humiliating, than having to treat those sons of bitches nicely when you need them. It's one of the responsibilities of crime. But damn it all, my friend, it's hard on your pride. I've thrown my valet at Fabrice to convert him. Who would believe it? Even Casimir isn't as solid as I had imagined.

You have no idea, my friend, how a girl's tears can affect all these faint-hearted, lily-livered souls.

DERBAC. Fortunately for the world, there are only a few souls as perverse as yours.

OXTIERN. That's because I've worked at it, my friend. I've seen a lot, done a lot. If you only knew where too much experience leads you . . . if I could just prove to you that excessive compassion leads to vice . . .

DERBAC. Someone's stirring in Ernestine's room. It's Amélie. I'll bet somebody wants to see you. Lucky bastard!

OXTIERN. (*With an evil laugh.*) I've already told you, the only way to get a woman's love is to torture her. I know of no surer way, nor any other that delights me as much! (*Enter AMÉLIE.*)

AMÉLIE. Miss Ernestine wants to see you in this room, sir, to speak to you for a few minutes, if your schedule permits.

OXTIERN. Is there anything more sacred . . . what am I saying, anything dearer to me than talking to your lovely mistress? Amélie, tell her I await her with a lover's affection. And a lover's impatience.

AMÉLIE. (*Surprise mingled with anger.*) You, sir?

OXTIERN. Yes, me. Do my feelings surprise you?

AMÉLIE. Oh, no, no, sir. Nowadays, nothing surprises me about you. The lady will be coming shortly; I'll tell her you're expecting her.

DERBAC. That girl has got you pegged, my friend, and I can read expressions on her face which teach me the turmoil in her mistress's soul.

OXTIERN. How can anybody tremble over the turmoil in a woman's soul? We can be entertained but not frightened by it! Poor Derbac, your fears make me laugh. Go on and prepare for our departure. Remember we're not out of the water yet. We must get to port and get there safely.

DERBAC. I dread the reefs more than you do, and I'm afraid the end of this business is nowhere in sight.

OXTIERN. Go on, don't be afraid. (*Touching his forehead.*) In here, there are more tricks than we'll need to set all of Europe on fire. Judge for yourself if I ought to be concerned over one little liaison.

DERBAC. (*Vehemently.*) Ah! My dear Count, goodbye. Since you want neither admonition nor advice from me, perhaps you won't see me as a friend for long. (*He exits.*)

OXTIERN. (*Alone.*) I feel sorry for all these people; a trifle upsets them and chills them to the bone. I don't see my soul in any of them. I'll continue to lie to Ernestine. What an angel! There are times when the feelings you stir inside me almost weaken my determination . . . times when I should be betraying you, I can think only of loving you. Ah! This is no time to be sentimental. Ernestine is too offended not to be feared, and if I spare her, I'm lost.

(*Enter ERNESTINE.*)

ERNESTINE. However painful it is to appear before you, sir, whatever humiliation I feel, it is however necessary that I inquire, following the horrible crime you committed against me, what reparation your integrity can offer me.

OXTIERN. Is it my integrity that should be questioned, Ernestine, when it is my heart that you have captured . . . when it belongs to you entirely?

ERNESTINE. You don't think, do you, that this gift can make me happy? Why do you even suggest it? After stooping so low, how can you think your cruel heart is worthy of me?

OXTIERN. Your harsh words overwhelm me, all the more so since I deserve them. Ah! Don't punish the errors of love so cruelly.

ERNESTINE. Of love? You? Oh God! If this is what love inspires, may my heart never experience a feeling so capable of disgracing mankind! No, sir, this has nothing to do with love; this is not life's consoling emotion, the basis for all good deeds. Could love possibly excite you to commit a crime?

OXTIERN. My behavior was abominable, I admit; but I loved you and I had a rival.

ERNESTINE. (*Firmly.*) And what has become of this rival?

OXTIERN. I didn't have anything to do with it.

ERNESTINE. (*As above.*) You're the one who stole him from me. You're the one who has to bring him back.

OXTIERN. My hand did not take him away from you, Ernestine. Herman was tried, sentenced, and sent to prison according to the letter of the law. I can only use my influence to lighten the severity of his sentence.

ERNESTINE. How could I humble myself to the point of asking you to break his chains when you're the one who forged them? Get out. I don't want anything from you. My offering you the chance to perform a generous act . . . the way to make me forget all of your obscenities? You see, Oxtiern, I'm losing my mind. All right, what are you planning to do with your victim? Tell me, where are you taking her?

OXTIERN. Ernestine, I offer you my hand as well as my heart.

ERNESTINE. Tie myself to my executioner? Never. Never!

OXTIERN. Is there any other choice?

ERNESTINE. Yes, indeed, there is. Don't you even suspect it, sir? Are you unaware that I still have a father . . . a brother. (*With the greatest pride.*) Haven't you noticed that I'm still alive?

OXTIERN. All these miserable alternatives would serve no purpose. They'd cause a great deal of bloodshed and would in no way restore your honor. Only the one you accuse of having taken it can restore it to you. Become his wife and all is forgotten.

ERNESTINE. (*As emphatically as possible.*) You bastard! What alliance can you conceive of with me after having disgraced me? Forever between shame and humiliation, grief and tears, trying to interest my husband in ties he would have formed only out of duty. Tell me, Oxtiern, what moments of peace and happiness can I look forward to on earth? Hatred and despair on the one side, duress and remorse on the other. Our nuptial torch would be lighted with fire from the Furies; snakes would create the bonds between us, and death would be our only hope.

OXTIERN. (*Falling to his knees in front of ERNESTINE, but still lying to her.*) Very well! Since I alone deserve it, strike me. Ernestine, here's my heart. Spill this guilty blood with your own hands. It no longer deserves to keep alive a creature so inhuman to have misjudged you so cruelly!

ERNESTINE. (*Pushing him away even more forcefully.*) Let it be spilled without watering the ground. It would sprout even more crimes.

OXTIERN. (*Getting up.*) What is it you want, Ernestine? And how can I prove to you my love and regret?

ERNESTINE. (*With scorn, strength, and anger.*) Your love, never. Your regret I'll believe when you break the bonds that bind the man I love, imprisoned through your villainy. Go confess your conspiracies to the magistrates. Go accept the death sentence your crimes deserve. Burden the earth no longer with a weight that wearies it. Even the sun is less chaste for shining its rays upon you.

OXTIERN. (*With controlled pride.*) It seems to me that Ernestine isn't aware of the situation she's in.

ERNESTINE. (*Nobly and emphatically.*) You're right, Oxtiern. If I were thinking about it, either I would cease to live, or you would die.

OXTIERN. When a woman considers herself unhappy, she ought to deal a little more tactfully with the person who controls her destiny.

ERNESTINE. (*Proudly.*) This woman depends only on herself. She is responsible only to herself. She alone will determine her fate.

OXTIERN. Let's continue in this direction, Ernestine. Tomorrow we'll reach one of my estates. Maybe there I shall succeed in calming you down and sweetening your disposition.

ERNESTINE. (*As before.*) No, I'm not going any farther. You led me here against my will. Here I must avenge myself or die.

OXTIERN. These frantic outbursts are fatiguing and solve nothing, Ernestine. I was expecting from you a little less hate . . . and a little more acceptance.

(*Enter CASIMIR and AMÉLIE. This scene must play very quickly. Each new character takes his/her master/mistress aside to one corner of the stage.*)

CASIMIR. (*To OXTIERN.*) Sir?

OXTIERN. What do you want, Casimir?

AMÉLIE. (*Entering a little after CASIMIR.*) Miss?

ERNESTINE. Have you come to give me more bad news?

CASIMIR. (*To OXTIERN.*) An officer's arriving at the inn.

AMÉLIE. (*To ERNESTINE.*) A soldier I haven't been able to see yet is eagerly asking to speak to you.

OXTIERN. (*To CASIMIR.*) Try to find out who he is.

ERNESTINE. (*To AMÉLIE , with an expression of joy.*) It's my father! He must have received my letter. He's here!

CASIMIR. (*To OXTIERN.*) Sir, don't come out. It is very important you don't encounter this man.

OXTIERN. (*To ERNESTINE.*) Excuse me, urgent matters are calling me. May I expect to find you somewhat calmer when I return?

ERNESTINE. (*Nobly and firm.*) Yes, yes, you can count on me, Sir. You will never again see me as you think I am. You undoubtedly considered me contemptible; your behavior proved that much to me. Soon you will admit that I was worthy of your respect.

OXTIERN. (*Going out.*) Ah! You will always be worthy of my heart.

ERNESTINE. (*Very quickly.*) Amélie, run and find out who this stranger is. Heavens! Let it be my father!

AMÉLIE. (*Leaving in haste.*) May he come to end all of our woes!

ERNESTINE. (*Alone.*) Oh, height of misfortune and shamelessness! Between myself and Oxtiern, we present the picture of the one and the other! I defy the hand of fate to put on earth, at the same time, a creature more to be pitied than I, and one more indecent than he. He offers me his hand to compensate for the wrongs committed against me by his treachery; in accepting, I would complete my own destruction. No, no, Oxtiern, I don't want your hand, I want your head. Only your death can appease the wretched state into which your inhumanity has ground me.
(*Enter COLONEL FALKENHEIM.*)

ERNESTINE. (*Rushing toward him, then immediately backing away in fright.*) Father. Ah, father! I am no longer worthy of you.

THE COLONEL. What's this I hear?

ERNESTINE. (*Sadly.*) Father, why did you ever leave me alone? Disastrous journey . . . wretched circumstances. The cruel man, he picked the time when you were away. He deceived me. He filled me with hope for the happiness you were hesitant to give me, and taking advantage of my weakness, he made me unworthy of being alive and of being your daughter.

THE COLONEL. Unjust heaven! Did you prolong my life only to have me witness such an abomination? The villain must die.
(*He begins to leave.*)

ERNESTINE. (*Stopping him.*) No, no, vengeance belongs to me alone. I'll take care of it myself.

THE COLONEL. Your thoughts frighten me!

ERNESTINE. (*Quickly.*) Don't try to unravel them, they're justified. Proud like the soul I inherited from you. I'll let you in on them when the time is right. Have you seen him, father? Has he dared to present himself to you?

THE COLONEL. He's very carefully avoiding it. A look from me would cut him down to size.

ERNESTINE. You learned of my plight through my letter?

THE COLONEL. It's what sped me here.

ERNESTINE. (*Quickly.*) Ah! Father, have you ever doubted me for a moment?

THE COLONEL. Never. But you didn't take anyone along to defend you.

ERNESTINE. Do the unfortunate have any defenders? Oxtiern is rich, he's influential. We were virtuous and poor. Oh, yes, father. Oh yes, he had to be right. And poor Herman, have you heard anything about him?

THE COLONEL. There was talk of a bankruptcy he was involved in. I'm told this dreadful affair will cost a lot of money to settle and we have none.

ERNESTINE. (*Aside.*) Oxtiern! Oxtiern, this is how you get rid of a rival!

THE COLONEL. Ah! If only I had agreed to your marriage with Herman! My misguided refusal was the cause of all of this!

ERNESTINE. You thought you were doing the right thing. Isn't that all I need to make me forget all the trouble it's caused? Who better than the creator of my life can judge what's best for me? Excuse me, father, I need to ask you to leave me for a moment. I have no time to lose. At the crack of dawn we're leaving for the Count's estate. Tomorrow I may be in chains forever if I don't free myself today. Stay away from Oxtiern. Don't have anything at all to do with him. Fabrice, the innkeeper, seems trustworthy to me. Ask him to hide you and leave the rest to me.

THE COLONEL. (*Disturbed.*) Fabrice wasn't here when I arrived. They told me he went to Stockholm on important business but was expected back sometime before morning.

ERNESTINE. (*Worried.*) Fabrice gone. Could I have been wrong? Gone to Stockholm. What's he doing there? Could he be under orders from the Count? He's known him for a long time! Another link in the chain that surrounds me? Everything takes me by surprise! Everything terrifies me!

THE COLONEL. (*With nobility and strength.*) Don't worry, Ernestine, your father will not desert you again. Dear unhappy child, either we'll succeed together, or we'll be destroyed in one another's arms. Goodbye, let Amélie come and tell me when you need me. And remember that I, the godson of Charles XII's favorite, lives only to maintain the honor and glory of his family.

ERNESTINE. (*Alone.*) No, there's only one way to satisfy me, Oxtiern. You must spill my blood, or I must shed yours to the last drop. I'll write him a letter. (*She sits at the table and reads aloud as she writes.*) "A decent man does not violate a virtuous girl without suffering the consequences. You know the codes of honor, abide by them. The opponent I offer you is worthy of challenging you to a duel. The garden of the inn will serve as the field. Your swords will be the weapons. Come to the appointed spot at eleven o'clock tonight. A young man dressed in white will appear before you. Strike him courageously and he will reply in kind. Bear in mind that one of you must die, Oxtiern. Be as brave as you have been base. Only on this condition will Ernestine forgive you. Goodbye." (*She seals her letter then rings for her maid.*)

AMÉLIE. (*Hurrying.*) I'm at your service, miss.

ERNESTINE. (*Quickly.*) Go take this letter to the Count. Take care that he doesn't encounter my father. Wait. I'm going into the other room. Bring the colonel here and have him wait while you're delivering my letter. Amélie, this errand is as important as it is secret. Give it your complete attention. (*She exits.*)

AMÉLIE. (*Alone.*) This letter worries me. Her expression when she gave it to me, the few times she's spoken about her brother in the past . . . I bet she's asking him to come here and challenge the Count to a duel. I must warn the Colonel. They're his children after all. I would never forgive myself for hiding my suspicions from him. Good Lord! What misfortunes the hateful schemes of a villain can cause. (*She starts to exit and runs into the COLONEL.*)

AMÉLIE. Ah! Sir, the lady your daughter asks that you stay in this room for a short time while I deliver this letter to the Count.

THE COLONEL. What does it say?

AMÉLIE. I don't know; but it must be something very important since the lady told me to give it my complete attention.

THE COLONEL. And you've no idea what's in it?

AMÉLIE. Excuse me, I think it has to do with a duel . . . the gentleman, your son . . . the lady, your daughter . . . Count Oxtiern . . .

THE COLONEL. My son? Explain yourself. I don't understand.

AMÉLIE. (*Eagerly.*) Sir, I'll bet that the lady, your daughter, is calling your son to seek revenge . . . that by this letter she's setting him up as Count Oxtiern's opponent in a duel . . . that these two men are going to fight. Oh! Sir, isn't there some other way to punish a crime like this without risking your son's life?

THE COLONEL. Undoubtedly there are other ways. There are other ways certainly. No matter. Go deliver that letter. Do as your mistress told you, and leave the rest to me. (*Calling her back impatiently.*) Amélie, if my son should arrive . . . if he comes anywhere near this house, make sure he doesn't speak to anyone. Have him brought to me immediately. Remember to do exactly as I told you.

AMÉLIE. (*Going out.*) Yes, yes. Sir, calm down. I understand the full importance of your instructions.

THE COLONEL. (*Alone.*) My son will not fight a duel. It's up to me alone to clear up this mess. Oh, daughter, daughter, your defense is my responsibility alone. I will test my courage with that hateful man, and we'll see if this hand, trained in combat . . . governed by the most justifiable revenge, will be guided by God, the patron of honor! I'll go tell all of this to that bastard the Count but keep it a secret from my daughter. I want her to find out about the duel only when she hears of my victory. Yes, my victory is certain. I'm going to destroy a monster. And providence is too wise to allow virtue to be crushed beneath the vile attacks of vice and villainy.

END OF ACT TWO

ACT THREE

(*The action takes place in the garden of the inn. The sun is setting slowly so that by the final curtain, the stage is in total darkness. The scene begins with a tone of mystery.*)

DERBAC. My dear Count, I asked you to come down into the garden so that we could converse more privately. There's a lot of commotion here, in this house. Since Colonel Falkenheim arrived, Ernestine has locked herself in her room and refuses to see anyone. Amélie is everywhere, and Casimir, who doesn't miss a trick, is telling me the most extraordinary things.

OXTIERN. What is it you suspect then?

DERBAC. I suspect nothing, my friend. I know everything. Begin by reading this letter, if the little bit of daylight left permits it. Amélie was supposed to deliver it to you. Not finding you, she left it with Casimir to give to you in the greatest possible haste. I snatched it out of the hands of your valet, and read it.

OXTIERN. (*Skimming over the letter, not stopping until the following words.*) "The opponent I offer you is worthy of challenging you to a duel." Do you know who this opponent is?

DERBAC. I think I can guess.

OXTIERN. Who then?

DERBAC. Ernestine herself.

OXTIERN. Ernestine?

DERBAC. I'm certain of it.

OXTIERN. What proof do you have of this nonsense?

DERBAC. I saw the bellman of the inn carrying the white clothes the letter describes. He was taking them to Amélie who's supposed to give them to Ernestine. And it's in this disguise that she's planning to assault you herself.

OXTIERN. It's unbelievable. That's what comes of her rabid behavior . . . and despair. Well, we'll have to retaliate, and nothing could be easier.

DERBAC. But now that the Colonel's here . . .

OXTIERN. Even if there were ten colonels, this creature is trying to kill me, and I have to stop her. I will not fight a duel with her. I'd kill her, and I want her to live. To live in perpetual regret. If she should escape me, I'm a ruined man. She'll cast herself at the feet of the King and disgrace me. My property, my possessions, my position, my prestige . . . all destroyed, everything. So I have no other choice than to . . . Derbac, see who's walking toward us under those trees.

DERBAC. It's Casimir. (*The daylight is gradually fading.*) (*Enter CASIMIR.*)

CASIMIR. My lord, Colonel Falkenheim has just asked me to deliver this message to you without delay.

OXTIERN. Give it to me. (*He reads it over quickly, then making a gesture to CASIMIR to leave them, he goes over to DERBAC and says mysteriously.*) My friend, it's a challenge from Ernestine's father. Knowing that his daughter is arming her brother against me, he doesn't want to yield the honor of so necessary a revenge to anyone else. He's coming down to the garden and wants me to wait here to engage him in a duel. You see, you were mistaken. Ernestine's brother must have slipped into the inn without our knowing. He's the opponent she had picked for me, and the white clothes were supposed to act as his disguise.

CASIMIR. (*Returning.*) Sir, if I might say a word.

DERBAC. Speak, my friend, tell us what you know.

CASIMIR. The white clothes aren't for Ernestine's brother, sir. The brother hasn't come into the house, I'm certain of it. I've kept a close watch on every new arrival and I swear to you that this young man, who I know perfectly well, has yet to make an appearance. These clothes are for Ernestine, you can be sure of that. The bellman, won over by your generosity, told me he was sent to fetch them somewhere in the neighborhood . . . and that he's supposed to give them to Ernestine in person.

DERBAC. (*Very emphatically.*) That clears up everything. You see what's happening, Oxtiern. To hide her plans from her father, Ernestine tells the Colonel that she's counting on her brother to avenge her. The Colonel believes her and not wanting his son to fight a duel, he's coming in his place.

OXTIERN. (*Very eagerly.*) And will Ernestine be coming too?

DERBAC. Undoubtedly.

OXTIERN. Will she come dressed in white?

CASIMIR. That much is certain, sir.

OXTIERN. (*With the most wild and vigorous rapture.*) Embrace me, my friend. We were looking for a way to get rid of this girl, and now fate offers us the perfect opportunity. (*More coldly.*) Casimir, go tell the Colonel that I'm expecting him. Soon it'll be dark. Tell him I'll be dressed in white. Tell him to attack, without hesitation, whoever he sees in the shadows wearing white.

DERBAC. (*With a cry of horror.*) Ah! You intend to have that girl killed by her own father!

OXTIERN. Quiet! Don't you see that fate is giving me the means of retaliation. And you oppose my taking advantage of it?

DERBAC. The crime is repulsive. I find it revolting!

OXTIERN. It's important for my peace of mind.

CASIMIR. (*Trying to calm down his master.*) My lord, my lord.

OXTIERN. Shut up, you idiot! If you can't take the heat, get the hell out of the kitchen.

CASIMIR. As you will, sir. The Colonel will be informed that his opponent will appear all in white, at the appointed time and place. (*Aside, as he goes out.*) Ah! I hope Fabrice will return before this obscenity is committed. (*He exits.*)

OXTIERN. That valet makes me crazy. He's lily-livered. These stupid idiots don't have any backbone. Anything that's different from the ordinary, run-of-the-mill vice or villainy amazes them. The concept of remorse terrifies them.

DERBAC. Woe to the villains unchecked by remorse. Woe to you if you prevail. A crime more vile was never conceived, even in hell.

OXTIERN. I admit it, but it's necessary. Didn't that arrogant creature plot my destruction?

DERBAC. She challenged you to a duel. She was risking her own life.

OXTIERN. Playing the heroine. I can't stand pride in a woman.

DERBAC. (*With much feeling.*) Ah! Isn't the creature who most deserves our respect entitled to a little pride?

OXTIERN. Right! There you go moralizing again. I leave you alone for a moment and I can hardly recognize you. Come on, Derbac, get a backbone. In case Casimir doesn't carry out my orders successfully, you take charge of them as well. The Colonel is coming here. Tell him to knock down the adversary approaching him dressed in a white. It'll be his daughter. We understand each other, Derbac? And I'll have settled the score. (*He exits.*)

DERBAC. (*Alone.*) No, I can't bring myself to attend to such an atrocity. Let Casimir take care of it, and I won't get involved. I want to rid myself of this man's company. I'll become poor again, the way I was before his influence retrieved me. That's really too bad. But it's better than becoming even more corrupt under his degenerate patronage. Misfortune frightens me less than crime. However much an honest man suffers, he finds peace in his heart. (*He exits as soon as he sees someone coming.*)

THE COLONEL. (*Alone. Groping his way through the shadows.*) Here's the field of combat. I thought he'd be here already. Certainly he won't keep me waiting long. Oh! Unfortunate man, what are you going to do? Cruel codes of honor, you're really unjust! Why must the victim risk life and limb, when it's the aggressor who's guilty? Ah! Let him kill me, slice me to ribbons. I can't survive in disgrace! (*He trembles.*) I think I hear him coming ... yet how is it that this opponent's arrival gives rise to feelings I can't control! Up to now, I have never known fear. The desire for retribution disturbs me and prevents me from finding the real source of the feelings that stir inside my soul. The night is growing so dark that it will be difficult to recognize the color of the clothes he said he'd be wearing. (*What follows is said very softly and, above all, so that ERNESTINE cannot hear it.*) Here he is. I'll attack him quietly and not advertise the duel.

(*He draws his sword and falls upon ERNESTINE dressed as a man in clothes of the color referred to above. Scarcely has the duel begun when two pistol shots are heard offstage, one of which is HERMAN's and the other the COUNT's. HERMAN rushes in having just killed OXTIERN. FABRICE runs in a moment later. This scene should play very quickly.*)

HERMAN. (*Still offstage.*) Die, villain! Ernestine is avenged. (*Running to separate the duelists.*) Merciful Heaven, stop. Can't you see whose blood you were about to spill? Wretched father! Acknowledge your daughter.

ERNESTINE. (*Throwing down her sword.*) Oh, God! (*She throws herself into her father's arms.*)

THE COLONEL. Dear, unhappy child!

FABRICE. (*Eagerly upon entering.*) Your troubles are over, Colonel. No sooner was I informed of the Count's atrocities than I flew to Stockholm and liberated your young friend from Oxtiern's bondage. You see the first fruits of his freedom.

HERMAN. The coward! His defeat took very little out of me. It's so easy to triumph over a villain. Victorious, I ran here, sir, to clear up the improprieties in which you had become unknowing participants, and to ask you for the hand of this lovely girl, whom I still desire, and dare to consider myself worthy of possessing. (*THE COLONEL makes a gesture of agreement and of sorrow.*)

ERNESTINE. (*To HERMAN.*) Can I still hope for such happiness?

HERMAN. (*Tenderly to ERNESTINE.*) Ah! Could the crimes of a devil like Oxtiern tarnish Nature's most beautiful creation?

THE COLONEL. Oh! Fabrice, I owe you a great deal. How can I ever repay you?

FABRICE. By your friendship, my friends. That's my reward. I made the best use of my money to punish crime and reward virtue. Let someone tell me if it's possible to invest it at a higher rate of interest!

END OF THE THIRD AND FINAL ACT

A Select Bibliography

Bloch, Dr. Iwan. *Marquis de Sade: His Life and Work.* Translated by James Bruce. N.p.: Brittany Press, 1948.

Bremmer, Jan, ed. *From Sappho to De Sade: Moments in the History of Sexuality.* London and New York: Routledge, 1991.

Cleugh, James. *The Marquis and The Chevalier.* New York: Duell, Sloan and Pearce; Boston: Little, Brown and Company, 1952.

Dawes, C.R. *The Marquis de Sade: His Biography and Writings.* New York: The Macauly Co., 1927.

Dictionnaire Dramatique, Contenant L'Histoire des Théâtres, les Règles du genre Dramatique, les Observations des Maîtres les plus célèbres, et des Réflexions nouvelles sur les Spectacles, sur le génie et la conduite de tous les genres, avec les Notices des meilleures Pièces, le Catalogue de tous les Drames, et celui des Auteurs Dramatiques. Three volumes. Paris, 1776; reprint, Geneva: Slatkine Reprints, 1967.

Du Plessix Gray, Francine. *At Home with the Marquis de Sade: A Life.* New York: Simon and Schuster, 1998.

Endore, Guy. *Satan's Saint.* London: W.H. Allen and Company, 1966.

Foster, Annetta. "The Place of Theatre and Drama in the Life of the Marquis de Sade, *homme de lettres extraordinaire.*" Ph.D. diss., University of California, 1975.

Gorer, Geoffrey. *The Devil's Disciple: The Revolutionary Theories of the Marquis de Sade.* Paris: Collection "Le Ballet Des Muses," 1933.

_____. *The Life and Ideas of the Marquis de Sade.* New York: W.W. Norton and Company, 1963.

Hartman, Janine Cey. "The Politics of Decadence: The Political and Social Ideas of Sade, Gautier, Baudelaire, and Flaubert." Ph.D. diss., University of Illinois at Chicago, 1986.

Hayes, Julia Candler. "The Representation of the Self in the Theater of La Chausée, Diderot, and Sade." Ph.D. diss., Northwestern University, 1982.

Horace. *Satires, Epistles, Ars Poetica.* Translated by H.R. Fairclough. Cambridge, Massachusetts and London: Harvard University Press, 1991.

Howarth, William D., ed. *French Theatre in the Neoclassical Era, 1550-1789.* Cambridge: Cambridge University Press, 1997.

Kennedy, Emmet. *A Cultural History of the French Revolution.* New Haven and London: Yale University Press, 1989.

Laborde, Alice M. *Correspondances du Marquis de Sade et de ses proches enrichies de documents, notes et commentaries.* 27 vols. Geneva: Editions Slatkine, 1997.

Le Brun, Annie. *Sade: A Sudden Abyss.* Translated by Camile Naish. San Francisco: City Light Books, 1990.

Lély, Gilbert. *Vie du marquis de Sade.* Paris: Mercure de France, 1989.

Lernig, Walter. *Portrait of de Sade: An illustrated Biography.* Translated by Sarah Twohig. New York: Herder and Herder, 1971.

Lever, Maurice. *Donatien Alphonse François, marquis de Sade.* Paris: Fayard, 1991.

Manceron, Claude. *Age of the French Revolution.* 5 vols. Translated by Patricia Wolf. New York: Simon and Schuster, A Touchstone Book, 1989.

Marchand, Henry L. *The French Pornographers: Including a History of French Erotic Literature.* New York: Book Awards, 1965.

Pauvert, Jean-Jacques. *Sade Vivant.* 3 vols. Paris: Editions Robert Laffont, 1986.

Rodmell, Graham F. *French Drama of the Revolutionary Years.* London: Routledge, 1990.

Sade, Donatien Alphonse François, Marquis de. *Lettres inédites et documents retrouvé par Jean-Louis Debauve.* With a preface by Annie Le Brun. Paris: Editions Ramsey, Jean-Jacques Pauvert, 1990.

_____. *Oeuvres complètes.* 16 vols. in 8. Paris: Cerde du livre précieux, 1966–1967.

_____. *Oeuvres complètes.* Vols. 32-35 Théâtre. With a Preface by Jean-Jacques Brochier. Paris: Jean-Jacques Pauvert, 1970.

_____. *Selected Letters.* With a preface by Gilbert Lély. Translated by W.J. Strachan. Edited and with a new introduction by Margaret Crosland and with an afterward by Jeremy Reed. London: Peter Owen, 1965.

Schaeffer, Neil. *The Marquis de Sade.* New York: Alfred A, Knopf, 1999.

Schama, Simon. *Citizens: A Chronicle of the French Revolution.* New York: Alfred A. Knopf, 1989.

Smith, Daniel T. Jr. "Libertine dramaturgy: Reading obscene closet drama in eighteenth-century France. Ph.D. diss., Northwestern University, 2010.

Thomas, Donald. *The Marquis de Sade.* New York: Citadel Press, 1992.

Toepfer, Karl. *Theatre, Aristocracy, and Pornocracy* New York: PAJ Publications, 1991.

Wilson, Colin. *The Misfits: A Study of Sexual Outsiders.* New York: Carroll and Graf Publishers, Inc., 1988.

CPSIA information can be obtained at www.ICGtesting.com
Printed in the USA
LVOW07s0710220713

343957LV00002B/58/P